Crime and Power
A History of Criminal Justice 1688–1998

Philip Rawlings

LONGMAN
London and New York

Addison Wesley Longman Limited
Edinburgh Gate,
Harlow,
Essex CM20 2JE,
United Kingdom
and Associated Companies throughout the world

First published 1999

ISBN 0-582-30401-6   Ppr

Visit Addison Wesley Longman on the world wide web at http://www.awl-he.com

British Library Cataloguing-in-Publication Data

A catalogue record for this book is available from the British Library

\

\ : \ . .

Set by 35 in 10/12pt New Baskerville
Printed in Malaysia VVP

Contents

Series Editor's Preface

Our society appears to be increasingly preoccupied with crime and with criminal justice. Despite increasing general affluence in the post-war period, crime has continued to rise – often at an alarming rate. Moreover, the pace of general social change at the end of the twentieth century is extraordinary, leaving many feeling insecure. High rates of crime, high levels of fear of crime, and no simple solutions in sight, have helped to keep criminal justice high on the political agenda.

Partly reflecting this state of affairs, the study of crime and criminal justice is burgeoning. There are now a large number of well-established postgraduate courses, new ones starting all the time, and undergraduate criminology and criminal justice degrees are also now appearing regularly. Though increasing numbers of individual textbooks are being written and published, the breadth of criminology makes the subject difficult to encompass in a satisfactory manner within a single text.

The aim of this series is, as a whole, to provide a broad and thorough introduction to criminology. Each book covers a particular area of the subject, takes the reader through the key debates, considers both policy and politics and, where appropriate, also looks to likely future developments in the area. The aim is that each text should be theoretically-informed, accessibly written, attractively produced, competitively priced, with a full guide to further reading for students wishing to pursue the subject further. Whilst each book in the series is designed to be read as an introduction to one particular area, the Longman Criminology Series has also been designed with overall coherence in mind.

This, the third book in the series, examines some of the origins of what we now understand as the criminal justice system. All too often our views of current issues are characterised by an unhelpful historical myopia. Philip Rawlings challenges this by taking us back to the early modern period in British history when criminal justice was highly localised. From this period on, socio-economic and demographic changes began to undermine, at least in part, the previously existing emphasis on individual responsibility and locality. By the mid-eighteenth century new policing strategies were emerging and the use of punishment – particularly in relation to transportation and the public spectacle of capital punishment – was changing markedly.

Rawlings shows how during the course of the nineteenth century central government became increasingly involved in penal policy, and yet tensions between the role of the central state and local authorities shaped the emerging new police in some surprising ways. The final quarter of that century was characterised by the increasing bureaucratization, centralization and de-politicisation of policy-making – so much so that Rawlings refers to it as the 'triumph of the Home Office'. The bulk of the period since has seen the continuation and consolidation of such processes, despite increasing evidence that appeared to suggest that, at least as far as crime rates were concerned, nothing much was 'working'.

As Philip Rawlings suggests in this book, the history of criminal justice policy often makes fairly depressing reading with the failures of the past being forgotten, only later to be disinterred and repeated. The only effective guard we have against such ignorance is an understanding of our own history. As he says in the introduction, 'history informs our understanding of the present and our expectations of the future'. All students wishing to understand the reasons why our criminal justice system is the way it is, and seeking a reliable guide to future possibilities, should read this book.

Tim Newburn
London
November 1998

This book is dedicated to the memory of
Emma Bray and to Sam Brewis

Introduction

It is not the activity of the present moment but wise reflexions from the past that help us to safeguard the future[1]

History informs our understanding of the present and our expectations about the future. We are all born into a history (family, neighbourhood, race, gender, country), some of which we reject, some we celebrate, most of which we are unaware. Like our skin, the past is part of our makeup, it is both unique and similar, and it is just there. What is certain is that, whether we like it or not and no matter how insignificant our lives may seem, we do not stand aside from history, we are all part of it – even historians. To understand ourselves we need to make sense of our past and the same is true of nations and institutions: to understand them and to plan for the future we must recover their past. This is not because of some desire to avoid repeating the mistakes of previous ages: after all, what are 'mistakes'? and, even if we could identify them, similar behaviour repeated today or tomorrow is unlikely to lead to similar consequences because circumstances will have changed. Nevertheless, apart from astrology and crystal balls, the past is all we have to go on. The study of history is, therefore, not just an amusing or dull introduction to the real stuff of criminal justice studies – the present day. Current debates are constructed on assumptions about the past, and the channels down which such debates run are often marked out by 'tradition', a sense that this is how things have always been and radical change would be too much of a risk. So, for example, many people (but, as will be seen later in the book, not all) argue that the prisons have signally failed to do anything about reducing crime and, indeed, that by both stigmatizing people and bringing together offenders, they encourage reoffending: so why do we continue to send people to prison? The answer may be that we feel that people who commit crime should lose their liberty, even if this merely increases the likelihood that they will reoffend, or we may believe that there is no satisfactory alternative. These answers beg lots of questions and rely on a tradition of imprisoning offenders: to an important extent, we still have prisons because we have always had prisons. If we started afresh would our answer to crime still be to create prisons?

This book is an attempt to elucidate one view of the history of criminal justice policy in England from the late seventeenth to the late twentieth century. Slicing history into bite-sized chunks is a task fraught with difficulties. Start writing from one date and you give the impression that nothing of importance happened before then, and also that history can be written in terms of a number of key moments. On closer examination the chosen starting date is likely to seem less clearly different from other, earlier dates, continuities are all too evident and key moments difficult to isolate. The historian's task is to be somewhat bolder (in a circumspect way, of course). I did once know a man who was able to shove a large chocolate cake into his mouth in one breathless movement: wondrous to behold and a harmless hobby, but for most people it would be a curious thing to attempt and a certain route to indigestion. People with smaller mouths and historians have to cut their cake up. This is the historian's job: to come to a view as to what was important in the past and then organize the narrative around that view. This book focuses on the period from the late seventeenth century because it was then that the criminal justice system which we have today really began to emerge. Among the most striking of the differences between the seventeenth and the late twentieth centuries is the shift from a system which relies on decisions taken locally by volunteers (victims, witnesses, jurors, constables and so forth) to one in which central government plays a key role and many of the decisions are in the hands of professionals, such as police officers, probation officers, prison officers, Home Office civil servants and criminologists. By the 1990s the emphasis was most definitely on seeing solutions to crime in terms of what Christie (1993) has called 'the crime industry' (more prisons, more police, more private security, more research).

Aside from the problem of the outer time limits of the book, there was the question of what should be included in a history of criminal justice policy: the organization of the courts, lawyers, the police, prisons, non-custodial penalties, bail, the private security industry and so forth all have a place. Although I have tried to give some indication of what was going on across this range, inevitably in a book this size it is impossible to be comprehensive, so I have focused on the issues which seemed to be regarded as important at the time in the sense that they occupied the centre stage in the discourse on policy. For the most part this meant issues which involved the expenditure of large amounts of money: local authorities, when most of the money in the criminal justice system was raised and spent locally, and, more recently, central government have been reluctant to experiment if to do so would involve more spending. Since the nineteenth century, the prisons and the police have dominated policy and debates on criminal justice because they swallow enormous amounts of cash; whereas non-custodial sentences and the private security industry have attracted less attention because they have tended to be seen as ways in which money can be saved rather than as innovatory methods of working.

Another difficulty in writing about the history of criminal justice policy is trying to see it within a context. Understanding why it developed as it did means looking outside narrow arguments about crime and considering the relationships with contemporary politics, economics, religion and so forth. Once again, space means that this important aspect is at best only crudely sketched in. What I have tried to indicate is the diversity of influences which have had an impact on policy. Policy never appears ready formed and is never translated straightforwardly into action. It is not simply a process of identifying problems and then devising solutions which are implemented. Each age sees different problems and different solutions: for instance, broadly speaking, the prison and the police were not much considered as solutions to crime until well into the eighteenth century, and yet a hundred years or so later it was impossible not to consider them. Policy initiatives are also the result of negotiation and compromise: there may be people who favour reform but cannot agree on its detail, and ranged against them are people who reject the need for any reform. Even when a policy initiative is formulated by government and whistled through Parliament, it may well be rearticulated by those who are meant to implement it and those on whom it is meant to have an impact, and both of these may cause policy makers to reconsider. Careful plans may be drawn up for a prison system to reduce reoffending among prisoners, but their implementation depends on the commitment of prison staff and on the cooperation of prisoners. Both of these groups are likely to have their own agenda: does it affect their lives in ways of which they do not approve, and, if it does, how can they reduce its impact? Some flavour of these processes of explicit and tacit negotiation are discussed in the book.

This book does not purport to deal with the stage at which 'crimes' are being defined by the courts or by Parliament. This obviously skips over some difficulties, not least of which is the problem of discussing what the term 'crime' means: at the beginning of the period covered by the book the word was recognized, but the subject which we now call 'criminal law' did not exist and its equivalent covered a broader field in which the distinction between what we would see as crimes and civil disputes (tort, contract) was not always as clear as it is today (and it can be pretty muddy even now). The book also largely ignores the whole question of why some actions are defined as crimes and render those who commit them liable to punishment, while other actions are either ignored by the law, even though they seem to be reprehensible, or treated as mere torts which, generally, leave action to be taken by the individuals affected and result in compensation. None of these issues is unimportant, but the focus of this book is on policy decisions made by the state (both local and central state) in relation to those actions which have been defined as criminal.

Having said that, readers will spot the lack of much discussion of the question of why some criminal behaviour is the focus of attention from policy makers and some, such as white-collar crime and domestic violence, is largely ignored: this is partly because policy makers have been largely uninterested in such issues for reasons which are touched upon briefly, but also because to write about these silences and inactivities, while undoubtedly valuable, would make this book several times its current length.

The book focuses primarily on England and Wales. Comparative history does provide important insights into the formulation and implementation of criminal justice policy: for instance, Palmer (1988) has shown the insights which can be gained from studying the early history of the Irish and the English police. Once again, space means that this dimension has been almost entirely omitted, but undoubtedly the work which Palmer has done could be repeated across the whole criminal justice system, and, indeed, could be broadened out: in looking at the police, for instance, the experiences of police in Scotland, the colonies of the British Empire and in the USA and, most recently, in Northern Ireland have fed into policing in England and Wales. Those willing to ignore this omission will nevertheless be annoyed if they live outside the south-east of England to find an apparent obsession with London (by which is meant not just the City of London, but also Westminster and other parts, such as Southwark, and the parts of Surrey, Kent, Essex and Middlesex which have been sucked into what people see as London). This can hardly be helped. London dominates the history of England and Wales during the period covered by this book. It was easily the largest and the richest city, and, of course, the capital; indeed, politically, economically and culturally it has long been a major world city. The problems which London faces are, therefore, focused on by politicians and the media based there, and issues of concern to the rest of the country often seem to be recognized only in so far as they have an impact on London. This may not be fair and it is intensely irritating to those who live in other parts of the country; however, the fact remains that London and its concerns have been of massive importance in the history of criminal justice policy. But, as with everything else in this book, that is only one person's opinion.

* * * *

Like so many others, I groan when an actor or actress at an award ceremony blathers on about those who have helped him or her to this particular peak, and yet I know why they do it. It is an important personal acknowledgement and should be seen in this light (rather than an attempt to spread blame which one suspects with writers it sometimes is). Although I hardly see myself in the same terms as Tom Hanks (I am taller) or Vanessa Redgrave (ditto, slightly), I also want to acknowledge the contribution that other people have made to the book: Tim Newburn and Brian Willan, who have shown remarkable patience, Allen Rawlings, who ploughed through a draft and also found Inspector Bucket, Kay Rawlings, Pamela Kissack, Belinda Bray, David Haskins, Richard Ireland,

Helen Palmer, Betsy Stanko, Anne Scully, John Lowry and Jill Peay. I would also like to thank the staff of the British Library, the Guildhall Library, Brunel University Library, the National Library of Wales and the Library at the University of Wales, Aberystwyth.

Note

1. Marcel Proust, *In Search of Lost Time* (Trans. C.K. Scott Moncrieff, T. Kilmartin and D.J. Enright), London: Chatto & Windus, 1992, vol. 2: 456.

Chapter 1

'The Very Hands and Feet of Every Kingdom'

An eighteenth-century criminal

John Sheppard was born to a poor family in Spitalfields in March 1702 and died aged 22 in November 1724. In appearance, lifestyle and death there was little to separate him from many other young men. He had rather large muscular hands which betrayed his six years as an apprentice to a carpenter called, appropriately, Wood, but otherwise he was small – only 5 feet 4 inches – and youthful looking: as one contemporary who knew him put it, he 'appears to be very young, having a perfect Boy's Countenance' (*Daily Post*, 4 Sept. 1724; *Parker's London News*, 11 Nov. 1724). His life, spent in and around Spitalfields and Drury Lane, was unremarkable and even the manner of his death, although certainly painful, slow and tragic, was not unusual, for, like thousands of others – a large proportion of whom were about his age – in the eighteenth century, he was strangled to death on the end of a rope at Tyburn in London, near the modern site of Marble Arch. The crimes which led to this judicial killing were also unremarkable: breaking into and stealing from houses. And yet by the time he died he was well known throughout London, indeed the whole country quickly got to hear of Jack Sheppard as ballads, biographies, newspaper articles, plays and pictures poured out. This certainly was unusual, and, what is even more curious, he is one of only a handful of criminals who lived at that time (Jonathan Wild, whom we shall encounter later, Captain Kidd the pirate, and Dick Turpin the highwayman spring to mind) whose fame has survived through into the late twentieth century. Sheppard has been the subject of several biographies, the most recent of which appeared in 1997, and in 1968 a film, *Where's Jack?*, loosely based on his life appeared with chirpy Tommy Steele as our hero and Stanley Baker as the evil Jonathan Wild, who, in true cinematic tradition, is ultimately thwarted as Jack cheats death (Rawlings, 1992a: 39–75). Whereas Wild, Kidd and Turpin acquired fame through their crimes, it was Sheppard's extraordinary ability to escape from prison that secured his reputation: in the summer and autumn of 1724 he escaped from three different prisons, including twice from a supposedly high-security cell in Newgate.

Biographies of notorious criminals sold well in the early eighteenth century, and one publisher, John Applebee, quickly recognized the commercial potential of Sheppard's story. After the first escape from Newgate and subsequent recapture, he commissioned a biography from Rev. Wagstaff, the Ordinary of Newgate's deputy[1] (*Daily Journal*, 16 Sept. 1724). However, Sheppard escaped again before the pamphlet could be published, so Applebee decided to produce a longer biography written by one of the hack writers for whom such work provided a steady income (possibly, Daniel Defoe, the author of *Robinson Crusoe*): this was *The History of the Remarkable Life of John Sheppard* (1724), which ran through three printings in two weeks. When Sheppard was recaptured and hanged, Applebee quickly published another account, *A Narrative of all the Robberies, Escapes, &c. of John Sheppard* (1724), which went to eight printings in a couple of months. Aside from these, another five or six biographies were produced by other publishers, as well as endless column inches in the newspapers.

The History is the best written of these accounts. It is not just a narration of the life of a thief and expert escapist, it also presents the metamorphosis of 'a promising young man' into 'an old Man in Sin' (Rawlings, 1992a: 48–9). What happened to him is briefly described at the start of the biography, in which Sheppard is said to have been:

> an early profficient, had a ready and ingenious Hand, and soon became Master of his Business, and gave entire Satisfaction to his Masters Customers, and had the Character of a very sober and orderly Boy. But alas unhappy Youth! before he compleated six Years of his Apprenticeship, he commenced a fatal Acquaintance with one *Elizabeth Lyon*, otherwise call'd *Edgworth Bess*, from a Town of that Name in *Middlesex* where she was Born, the reputed Wife of a Foot-Soldier, and who lived a wicked and debauch'd life . . . Now was laid the Foundation of his Ruin.
>
> (Rawlings, 1992a: 49)

Captivated by Lyon he quarrels with Wood and turns away from his apprenticeship to a life of idleness and extravagance which he can only support by crime. From that point – even though at the time of publication he was on the run – the inevitability of his death on the gallows looms over the story.

His ability to break into houses and out of prisons reveals his 'unheard of Diligence and Dexterity' (Rawlings, 1992a: 51), but also the waste of those talents: as another contemporary biographer put it, 'it was pity such an ingenious Fellow should be a Thief' (Rawlings, 1992a: 42). For a while each escape increases the terror among sections of the middling classes, including Mr Kneebone, who had helped John when he was younger:

> The People about the *Strand*, *Witch-street* and *Drury-Lane*, whom he had Robb'd, and who had prosecuted him were under great Apprehensions and

> Terror, and in particular Mr. *Kneebone*, on whom he vow'd a bloody Revenge; because he refus'd to sign a Petition in his Behalf to the *Recorder* of *London*.
>
> (Rawlings, 1992a: 57)

While Kneebone shakes, a carefree Sheppard drinks brandy, eats oysters and has his hair cut amidst his friends in the Cock and Pie alehouse on Drury Lane:

> it was thought all the common People would have gone Mad about him; there being not a *Porter* to be had for Love nor Money; nor getting into an Ale-house, for *Butchers*, *Shoemakers* and *Barbers*, all engag'd in Controversies and Wagers about *Sheppard.*
>
> (Rawlings, 1992a: 58–9)

He seems single-handed to have turned the social order on its head, with employers hiding from employees and all work having ceased. But it is implicit that this situation is only transitory. Sheppard's power cannot last; he will be caught and hanged, and order will be restored.

The pattern of this account of Sheppard's life is repeated in the biographies of countless dozens of others who were hanged at Tyburn in London in the eighteenth century. They endlessly replay the story of a young man, grown weary of his apprenticeship, who turns to crime (often under the influence of a woman) and is hanged. Nicholas Carter, an apprentice glover, was only about 14 years old when in 1690 he sat in the condemned cell at Newgate and told the Ordinary that, 'being Idle, and regardless of his Parents Good Admonitions', he had run away from work and turned to crime (Ordinary of Newgate, 26 Jan. 1690); the 'Flying Highwayman' William Hawke, hanged in 1774, became 'weary of [the] confinement' which his apprenticeship entailed and . . . turned to crime (Anon., 1774: 3); and Thomas Munn, the 'Gentleman Brickmaker', turned from work to robbery because '[I] did not have any Restraint laid on my whimsical Humour' and was hanged in 1750 (Anon., 1750c: 3. Generally, Bell, 1991; Faller, 1987; Rawlings, 1992a).

These biographies were popular because, rather than in spite, of their tendency to repetition. They touched on concerns which for their predominantly middling-class readers[2] ran deeper than the issue of crime – concerns about social disorder. At the heart of these was, typically, London, which was by far the largest city in England and so not suprisingly home to by far the largest number of criminals. The labouring poor[3] massed in its alleys and back lanes seemed beyond the control of the authorities and exposed to 'Temptations to Debauchery or Extravagance' of which London had a surfeit. For many writers London represented the worse features of a drift away from what they believed to be the stability, order and permanence of a rural economy towards the rootless existence of urban dwellers who depended on what seemed like more ephemeral occupations, such as manufacturing and service. In the country, the gentry, supposedly, took an active interest in the lives of the labouring poor. In London, they indulged themselves in elaborate clothes, wigs and endless socializing, leaving the labouring poor to idleness, immorality and indiscipline (Brown, 1757). The consequences of this could be seen at Tyburn, in the criminal biographies and in the engraving by the artist William Hogarth of the dead-end culture of *Gin Lane* (1751). Urban disorder and death could not stand comparison with the order and fecundity of the countryside: 'in London amongst the lower classes all is anarchy, drunkenness, and thievery; in the country good order, sobriety and honesty' (Shebbear, 1776. Also, Short, 1750). At the bottom of the criminal biographies and of this discourse about London – at once the centre of power, wealth and high culture, and of crime, disorder and disease – was an anxiety about the very basis of national prosperity: the labouring classes provided the workers, soldiers and sailors on whom England's economic and imperial power depended; if they did not work or fight or produce the next generation, what would happen?

The poor, the rich and the middling people

The relationship between the propertied and the labouring classes changed dramatically after the mid-sixteenth century (Lawson, 1986; Sharpe, 1982). Between the early sixteenth and mid-seventeenth centuries the population of England and Wales more than doubled and large-scale capitalist agriculture became dominant, and from the late seventeenth century manufacturing and mining developed rapidly. These changes had a major impact on the relationship between the different sections of society, creating a marked social polarization – and with it reduced mutual awareness and understanding, and increased tension – as the moral values of the better off and of the labouring classes diverged (Burke, 1988; Thirsk, 1967).

The rise in population led Robert Gray to warn in 1609:

> Our multitudes, like too much blood in the body, do infest our country with plague and poverty. Our land hath brought forth but it hath not milk sufficient in the breast thereof to nourish all these children which it hath brought forth.
>
> (Coward, 1994: 63)

For the wealthier landowners this provided a tremendous opportunity which they realized through the expansion of their property: swallowing up small farms, enclosing common and waste lands, cutting down woodland and draining wetland areas. As they became richer so they sought to distance themselves from their 'inferiors'. They built physical and social fences between themselves and the rest of society: to exploit their land, to ensure privacy and to emphasize their superiority. They ripped out whole villages and encircled their estates with walls, hedges and ditches; they turned vast tracts of farming land into landscaped gardens and views in an arrogant and ostentatious display of their wealth; they travelled in the privacy of coaches and sedan chairs; and contact with tenants and estate workers was left to their stewards. Much of their time was spent away from their country estates in London, or, by the eighteenth century, on the Grand Tour of Europe, which was regarded as an important part of any gentleman's education, or at one of the spa towns, such as Bath. Although most of the gentry were involved in local government as justices of the peace, few were active, as Lord Chancellor Harwicke bemoaned in 1754, ''Tis a common complaint in many counties, that, tho' great numbers are in the Commission, yet there are not acting justices enough to do the ordinary business of the country' (Beattie, 1986: 60; Landau, 1984).

The middling classes – particularly, the larger tenant-farmers, but also the richer villagers and, as manufacturing and mining expanded, the urban businessmen and merchants – also became richer. They began to aspire to the lifestyle of the gentry and to distance themselves from the labouring classes: 'everyone is flying from his inferiors, in pursuit of his superiors who fly from him with equal alacrity', lamented Soame Jenyns in the early eighteenth century (Langford, 1989: 67). By the eighteenth century the middling classes had grown in size, self-confidence and political independence. They were bolstered by the broad support for business which came from the gentry, who themselves invested not just in modernizing their farms, but also in mining, manufacturing and transport. They played a key role in the administration of justice and in the general regulation of their communities as constables, churchwardens, overseers of the poor, surveyors of the highways and so forth. By the end of the eighteenth century, although the government was still aristocratic, one historian has argued that England 'was not a nation of gentry, but a powerful and extensive middle class . . . [I]t increasingly decided the framework of debate and the terms of tenure on which the traditional politics of monarchy and aristocracy were conducted' (Langford, 1989: 68).

At the bottom of this pile were the labouring classes. As the gentry and the middling classes increased their wealth and improved their education, their housing, the clothes they wore and the stability and privacy of their family lives, so they viewed the labouring classes as increasingly alien: by turns comic, picturesque (Brewer, 1997), objects of sympathy and frightening. As land was swallowed up, the poor who might live on a piece of wasteland, graze some cattle on the common and gather fuel and hunt game in the woodland, but who had no documentation with which to prove any of these rights, or who could not afford to litigate, lost the means by which they could eke out a subsistence living. The landowners, who wished to enrich themselves, claimed that by removing these alternatives to waged labour they were performing a public service because, for instance, the commons sustained 'the idlers and beggary of the cottagers' and harboured robbers who preyed on travellers (Hill, 1996: 21. Also, Locke, 1993: 133). But the labouring classes did not simply stand by and watch their rights being destroyed, they sent threatening letters to rich farmers, maimed their cattle, poached their deer, set fire to their hay ricks and cut down the fences which enclosed common land. Of course, to the propertied such actions merely confirmed their opinion about the indiscpline and idleness of the labouring classes.

Stripped of the means of subsistence, the labouring classes were driven into complete dependence on waged labour. The shift was dramatic: in the mid-sixteenth century about 25 per cent of the population depended on waged labour, 300 years later it was 80 per cent (Beier, 1989; Rule, 1992: 4). Yet, as the early seventeenth-century puritan Richard Rogers acknowledged, often wage labour alone 'could not support a viable household' (Hill, 1996: 22): in late eighteenth-century Staffordshire about 10 per cent of families were unable to buy sufficient bread, rising to about 40 per cent in years when prices were high (Rule, 1992: 116). But to the eighteenth-century economist Sir James Steuart the shift to a dependence on wage labour was a natural and, therefore, inevitable process, 'Their parent, Earth, has in manner banished them from her bosom; they have her no more to suckle them in idleness; industry has gathered them together, labour must support them, and this must produce a surplus for bringing up children' (Linebaugh, 1991: 99).

The labouring classes were recognized as the root of the economic and colonial expansion on which the wealth of the minority was built. They were 'the very *Hands* and *Feet* of every Kingdom and State' (Braddon, 1721: 9); they '*get* Estates for the *Rich*, and then *Fight* to defend their *Persons* and *Properties*, from becoming a *Prey* to *any Invaders*' (Anon., 1722: 19).

> Our domestic safety and comfort, our private wealth and prosperity, our national riches, strength, and glory, are dependent upon an industrious and well-order'd Poor; a proper attention, therefore, to their morals and support must always be the concern of very wise and good administration.
> (Potter, 1775: 1. See also, Anon., 1765b: 53–4; Davenant, 1695: 144; Davenant, 1699: 51)

The problem was perceived as being that 'there are very few industrious poor (comparatively speaking) in the kingdom' (Anon., 1765b: 49). Society had a right to insist on their labour, for, as the novelist and magistrate Henry Fielding (1988a: 228) put it in 1751, 'having nothing but their labour to bestow on the society, if they withhold this from it they become useless members; and having nothing but their labour to procure a support for themselves they must of necessity become burdensome'. Idleness was, therefore, regarded as analogous to crime; indeed, it was believed to be the root of crime and social disorder: 'where *Idleness* prevails, it nurses Wantonness, Baseness, and Effeminacy, and almost every Vice', preached John Woodward in 1697, adding that the idle of London 'perplex the *Business* of the more Diligent, disturb their *Quiet*, pilfer their *Goods*' (Woodward, 1697: 11 and *vi*). The dramatist, Thomas Walker (1728: 16), was more direct: 'Idleness is the Road to the Gallows', and this was a key theme in the criminal biographies. While only a minority turned to crime, the rest where regarded as behaving only marginally less badly: 'the poor,

in general work only for the bare necessaries of life, and for the means of
a low debauch, which when obtained they cease to labour, till rounded
by necessity' (Anon., 1765b: 6–7). Frustrated economists and social commentators believed that, 'When wages are good [the poor] won't work
any more than from hand to mouth or if they do work they spend it in
riot or luxury' (Porter, 1990: 90). In the 1720s Bernard Mandeville noted
the habit of observing 'Saint Monday', that is taking an extra day off
each week:

> Everybody knows that there is a vast number of Journeymen Weavers . . .
> who, if by four Days Labour in a Week they can maintain themselves, will
> hardly be perswaded to work the fifth; When Men can shew such an
> extraordinary proclivity to Idleness and Pleasure, what reason have we
> to think that they would ever work.
>
> (Linebaugh, 1991: 263)

Complaints that the labouring classes worked short weeks or indulged in
the trappings of wealth – tea, sugar and white bread – were also expressions of concern about the development of a quasi-autonomous culture
with its own patterns of work and leisure which a freer market in labour to
some extent facilitated. While commentators endorsed the idea of a free
market in waged labour in so far as it advantaged the employer, they
did not approve of the element of choice it brought to the worker. The
labouring classes were, therefore, characterized as reluctant workers and
potential criminals. This legitimized the regulation of labour and leisure,
and the criminalization of unregulated methods of obtaining food or
income: the taking of perquisites (scraps of material and so forth) from
work, the hunting of game and gleaning (that is, gathering what was
leftover after harvesting). Making such activities illegal did not mean that
they were always punished: farmers often regarded gleaning as a useful
method of clearing a field, and the taking of perquisites was regarded as
legitimate by many employers, while others, who may have disliked these
practices, chose to do nothing in the interests of smooth industrial relations. The point is that it was believed important for the power of regulation to be in the hands of landowners and employers, even if they did
not make use of it (Emsley, 1996: 121–50; Linebaugh, 1991: 221–70; Styles,
1983a).

There was, it is true, some criticism of the failure by the gentry and the
middling classes to impose discipline. Defoe (1727: vol. 1, 160; Rawlings,
1992a: 20–1; Thompson, 1993: 36–8), himself not only a prolific writer
but also the proprietor of several failed business ventures, warned:

> Servants out of government are like soldiers without an officer, fit for
> nothing but to rob and plunder . . . [W]hat servants can a man expect when
> he leaves them to their own government, not regarding whether they serve
> GOD or the *Devil?*

And the same criticism was often made in criminal biographies. Jack
Sheppard was said to have remarked of his apprenticeship: 'I believe if

less Liberty had been allow'd me then, I should scarce have had so much Sorrow and Confinement after' (Rawlings, 1992a: 21). Of John Simons, a pickpocket hanged in 1693, it was claimed that, 'Had his Master . . . held a strict hand over him, he had not gone far astray from God, nor dared to have done evil Actions'; and forty years later, as William Shelton waited in the condemned cell, he too regretted that his master, 'being in a bad State of Health, was not able to give me such Correction as was absolutely requisite for young Sparks in my Lax way of Living' (*Ordinary of Newgate's Account*, 8 May 1693; 9 Oct. 1732). The frequent repetition of such complaints about the failure of employers to play a role in the moralization of the labouring classes suggests that they went unheeded, or that they were simply impossible to heed. However, the point is that, while much of this writing did not reject the economic benefits of a capitalist society, it did implicity grieve over the passing of what were imagined to have been more tightly structured social relationships which pertained under feudalism (Fielding, 1988a).

Controlling the labouring classes

Whatever the reason, by the eighteenth century neither the gentry nor the middling classes tended to see the regulation of the labouring classes as their responsibility, or, at least, they saw it as a matter which could properly be handled through the state and the law rather than through, for instance, the employment relationship; although, of course, the state (central and local) and its officers were the gentry (as judges, justices of the peace and members of parliament) and the middling people (as overseers of the poor, churchwardens and constables).

Legal regulation of the labouring classes took many different forms. For instance, campaigns against alleged immorality were routinely directed at them. A law-and-order panic in the 1590s provided an opportunity for radical Protestants (often lumped together subsequently as 'Puritans') to press for the deepening of the reform of the Church of England, which stretched to include the establishment of a new moral order based on subordination and work and opposed to the leisure activities of the labouring classes. This campaign continued right through the period up to the Civil War in the 1640s (Underdown, 1987; 1996). During the session 1597–8 seventeen bills on the poor and vagrants were introduced into Parliament with nine becoming law, and between 1601 and 1606 there were 25 bills on the regulation of alehouses (Power, 1985: 376–7; Underdown, 1987: 48). With varying degrees of enthusiasm, justices of the peace, manorial courts and church courts attacked, among other things, vagrancy, swearing, prostitution and drunkenness. Some of these actions were undoubtedly motivated less by a concern about morals *per se* than by a wish to avoid the payment of poor relief to a wandering pauper or an illegitimate child

(Sharpe, 1984: 84). Nevertheless, the result was the same, and the level of activity shows that these were not just the concerns of a handful of puritan zealots (Underdown, 1987).

This early seventeenth-century moral zeal was resisted in various parts of the country and its excesses produced something of a backlash when the monarchy was restored with Charles II in 1660. However, the underlying concerns which produced campaigns against immorality among the labouring classes were still there. Indeed, the flattening out of the rate of population growth in the late seventeenth century, as well as improvements in the economy and in wages, encouraged an even stronger and more independent popular culture. This was further facilitated by the decline of the church and the manorial courts, which had played major roles in the enforcement of morals: although restored along with the monarchy in 1660, the church courts never recovered the power they had previously enjoyed, and the manorial courts had declined over a longer period as a consequence of the disintegration of the feudal system of which they were a part. This is not to say that nothing was done. Charles II, in a monumental display of hypocrisy when one considers his own behaviour, issued a proclamation against vice in 1661 (reissued in 1663). There were more such proclamations under the reigns of the more ascetic monarchs Queen Mary and William III in 1690, 1698 (reissued in 1699) and Anne in 1702 (Amussen, 1985; Radzinowicz, 1948–68, vol. 3: 2–6 and 438–40), and these prompted the establishment of voluntary societies for the reformation of manners whose mission it was to enforce the criminal laws against prostitution, sabbath breaking, swearing, drunkenness and so forth. After a flurry of activity the societies collapsed amidst mob violence and accusations of divisive zealotry and class bias: 'Your Annual Lists of Criminals appeare/ But no Sir *Harry* or Sir *Charles* is there.' (Defoe, 1709. Also, Bahlman, 1957; Craig, 1980; Issacs, 1979; Portus, 1912; Shoemaker, 1991: 238–72).

This did not end action against immorality, indeed the societies were resurrected in 1757 with the support of the methodist leader John Wesley and the Bow Street (London) magistrate John Fielding, only to collapse in 1763 following a disastrous civil action (Radzinowicz, 1948–68, vol. 3: 144–6). Magistrates also launched periodic initiatives against immorality, particularly at times when crime was believed to be particularly high: when one such crime panic broke out in 1748, magistrates in London ordered raids by packs of constables and soldiers on gaming houses, brothels, vagrants and street prostitutes (see Chapter 2). Parliament continued to enact legislation as a result of pressure to control immorality. In 1735 the Middlesex justices compiled a report on gin drinking and then petitioned Parliament for regulation on the ground that it was undermining the health and working efficiency of the labouring poor. Their campaign drew support from the Society for the Promotion of Christian Knowledge, which had been associated with the societies for the reformation of manners, and from backbench members of Parliament concerned about disorder in London. The result was the controversial Gin Act 1736 which merely provoked protests from those who resented having their pleasures controlled (Anon., 1736; Clark, 1988: 72–7; Slyboots, 1726).

These examples of exhortation, legislation and enforcement might be multiplied. Almost without exception they were directed at the labouring classes, but, this was hardly remarkable since many among the gentry and the middling classes agreed with the view that in order to improve the economy, and at the same time, to reduce crime, it was necessary to moralize the labouring classes, and that this in turn meant an assault on popular culture. On the other hand, there was little desire to engage in national schemes which interfered with the power of local authorities or which enhanced the strength of the central state; nor was there much enthusiasm for spending large amounts of time and money on these issues, except during periods of crisis; and the memory of the religious excesses of the seventeenth century meant that attempts at moral policing were often coolly received. Moreover, the labouring classes were not necessarily willing just to fall into line with the latest interference in their lives and pleasures.

Potentially more effective were the poor laws (Slack, 1988). These had been codified by the Tudors into a national system based around the parishes and were a response to the perceived threat posed by what was believed to be the growing numbers of the mobile labouring poor. Providing for the needs of the poor enabled the state to dictate the terms upon which assistance would be given. In particular, it was linked to the suppression of the mobile poor. This was initially achieved by defining them as vagrants and then whipping them. The Settlement Act 1662 made things a good deal easier because it avoided the problems of definition by enhancing the powers of the parish officers to control the mobility of the poor, even if they were not vagrants. In brief, those who did not have a settlement through birth, marriage or long residence within a parish could be moved on and, because settlement brought entitlement to poor relief, parish authorities were keen to remove those who might become chargeable (Burn, 1797, vol. 3: 365–748). Not surprisingly, the poor laws gave the justices of the peace and the more substantial villagers who acted as poor law officials broad discretionary powers to define who qualified for assistance, the amount of that assistance and the form it took.

The rewards of crime and the thieftakers

As has been seen in relation to the campaigns against immorality, the criminal justice system potentially provided another mechanism for controlling the poor. Its structure left many of the key decisions to people from the community affected by a crime and the more important those people were the more influence they had. As a general rule it was left to the victim to decide whether or not to pursue an offender; the pre-trial process and the trial of petty offenders was in the hands of officials who were propertied people from the area within which the crime had been committed (for example, the constable and the justice of the peace); even though the trial of more serious offenders was presided over at the assize by a judge appointed by the monarch, the verdict of guilt or innocence was pronounced by a trial jury drawn from minor property owners within the same broad area; and while remission of the penalty imposed on those found guilty at the assize was in the hands of the monarch, the opinion of local people (once again, the propertied were more likely to be listened to) was often canvassed before a decision was made.

There were significant changes in the response to crime from the late sixteenth century which indicate an increased concern to define a broader range of activity as deserving punishment and a desire to increase the number of offenders who were caught. New offences were created, the number of capital offences increased and a broader range of penalties developed (see Chapters 2–4). There was a rapid increase in the number of indictments from the 1570s which put greater pressure on the court system and led to more judicial control of trials and a reduced role for juries in pursuit of greater expedition (Cockburn, 1985; Lawson, 1986; Samaha, 1974; Sharpe, 1982). The summary jurisdiction of the justice of the peace was continually expanded allowing him to deal (either on his own or with another justice) with minor offenders outside the full meeting of the quarter sessions and without the encumbrance of a jury. Justices also had the power to bind people over to keep the peace, or to be of good behaviour, or to do or refrain from doing particular acts. These powers gave them enormous discretion because the definition of what amounted to a breach of the peace or good behaviour was unclear. The establishment of houses of correction under the Tudor poor laws gave the justices another powerful weapon for the punishment of a broad range of loosely-defined deviants, such as runaway apprentices and people of 'ill fame'.

Efforts were made to encourage prosecutions. There was a range of sanctions and rewards to induce people to apprehend offenders. The hue and cry was an ancient requirement that people living in a hundred[4] pursue felons; it also gave the victim certain rights to compensation from the hundred (Radzinowicz, 1948–68, vol. 2: 27 and 164; 13 Edw. I, st. 2, c. 1 and 2 (1285); 27 Eliz. I, c. 13 (1585); 8 Geo. II, c. 16, s. 11 (1735)). This idea was extended in the eighteenth century: the Waltham Black Act 1723 (9 Geo. I, c. 22, s. 7) enabled the victim of various offences, including cattle maiming, arson and the cutting down of trees, to sue the hundred for up to £200 (also Riot Act 1715, 1 Geo. I, stat. 2, c. 5, s. 6). The flaw in this was exposed by the rather obvious fraud of a failed lawyer called Thomas Chandler, who sued the hundred of Sonning in Berkshire for £1,000 in 1748 representing losses sustained in a robbery. It then emerged that he had faked the robbery. He was convicted of perjury, and a statute was swiftly passed in 1749 (22 Geo. II, c. 24) which required two witnesses to the felony.[5] A constable[6] who failed to call out the hue and cry or to join in a pursuit could be fined, and, under legislation which rapidly multiplied from the sixteenth century, he could also be penalized for not enforcing laws on subjects ranging from sabbath observance and the control of alehouses to the sale of adulterated butter and giving false measures (Radzinowicz, 1948–68, vol. 2: 27 and 161–3). The effectiveness of such sanctions is difficult to judge. Legislators in the early modern period must have been aware that they went against the inclination of constables not to bring cases to court. To some extent this was the result of constables being corrupt, or neglectful, or intimidated by the possible reaction of the offender, but there was also a general expectation that petty criminals would not be brought to court unless other factors aggravated their offences, such as their being 'old offenders'. Legislation which penalized communities and constables tended to undercut such attitudes.

While the hundred and the constables were pressed into law enforcement by the prospect of penalties, individuals were encouraged to pursue offenders by the offer of inducements. By the eighteenth century courts had begun to pay some poor prosecutors their costs – a practice formalized by a series of statutes beginning in 1752 (Beattie, 1986: 41–8 and 130; Paley, 1991: 2 and 44). Rewards were also offered. Common informers received a share in any fine imposed for the breach of a large number of regulations enacted in the sixteenth to eighteenth centuries and concerned with subjects such as selling gin without a licence, giving false measures and depositing rubbish in the streets of London (Radzinowicz, 1948–68, vol 2: 139–46). With more serious offences like theft, rewards might be offered by victims, and these probably became more common as a result of the growth of newspapers: the first reward advertisements appeared in 1657 in the *Publick Advertiser* and *The Weekly Information from the Office of Intelligence* and by the eighteenth century they were an important part of the income of newspapers (Styles, 1989; Thomas, 1978: 779). It is true, however, that such advertisements tended to be directed towards the return of stolen property rather than the prosecution of an offender, even though several statutes were passed in the eighteenth century to stop the practice: Horace Walpole, a son of the former Prime Minister Sir Robert Walpole, who had a watch stolen in Hyde Park in 1750, later negotiated with the robber, 'Gentleman' James Maclean, for its return. The state also offered rewards in connection with certain serious offences, and from 1688 this became part of the effort to encourage the prosecution of offenders. The preamble to an act of 1692 which promised a £40 reward for the conviction of a highway robber (4 Will. & Mar. c. 8, s. 7) explained:

> the Highways and Roads within the Kingdom of *England*, and the Dominion of *Wales*, have been of late Time more infested with Thieves and Robbers than formerly, for Want of due and sufficient Encouragement given.

Similarly, the reorganization of government finances in the 1690s was propped up by capital offences and rewards (6 & 7 Will. III, c. 17, s. 9

(1695); 10 & 11 Will. III, c. 23, s. 2 (1699)). These precedents were added to in the eighteenth century, and reached their peak with the Offences Against the Customs Act 1746 (19 Geo. II, c. 34) which promised the enormous sum of £500 for the conviction of members of smuggling gangs (Winslow, 1977). The state also offered rewards on particular occasions (advertised public rewards), such as in response to the activities of a particular offender like Dick Turpin in the 1730s, or a particular category of offence like street robbery in London (Radzinowicz, 1948–68, vol. 2: 84–98 and 133–7. Also Paley, 1989b: 317–23). Individual government departments advertised rewards: after a mail robbery the Post Office invariably promised a £200 reward (Beattie, 1986: 156–7). Aside from cash,[7] both statutory and advertised public rewards normally offered immunity from prosecution to accomplices who gave evidence against an associate (Radzinowicz, 1948–68, vol. 2: 33–56),[8] and this was regarded as a particularly valuable weapon for breaking-up gangs (Fielding, 1988b: 158–63; Radzinowicz, 1948–68, vol. 2: 43–5; Wilson, 1722).

Rewards and immunities to accomplices were criticized. It was argued that those who were given immunities in exchange for evidence against other gang members generally returned to crime, and cases like that of James Dalton, the leader of a gang of street robbers, seemed to confirm such claims. Following the offer in March 1728 by the government of a reward and immunity for the conviction of London street robbers, Dalton, whose activities probably prompted the reward, was arrested and persuaded to give evidence against his comrades 'for the Preservation of my own Life'. As a result, six of his friends were hanged. Dalton was attacked in court and fled abroad. But, doubtless because he had no means of earning his living, he soon returned to London and was himself hanged in 1730 for robbing John Waller in Bloomsbury. Dalton went to his death denying the crime, and it is possible that the relatives of his late comrades, from whom he had presumably fled, were behind the Waller accusation. In 1732 Waller was convicted of having falsely accused another person with the aim of obtaining a reward. Put in the pillory at Seven Dials in London, he was killed by a crowd led by Edward Dalton, James's brother, who was then convicted of murder and hanged. The story has one further twist. Dalton's original arrest in 1728 was the result of a confession by Martin Bellamy, a marginal member of the Dalton gang. Bellamy had been tricked into confessing to a journalist from the *Daily Journal*, who posed as an official with the power to offer him immunity. Once his statement had been published, the authorities seem to have decided to use it to pressure Dalton because, as the gang's leader, it was presumably felt that his evidence would be more likely to get a conviction. Bellamy's cooperation was no longer needed and he was hanged (Rawlings, 1992a: 77–109). It was cases like these that led even the people who believed that immunity for accomplices was an important weapon in the fight against gang crime to concede that they should be transported (Radzinowicz, 1948–68, vol. 2: 53). Others attacked the whole idea of immunity, arguing that it tainted the criminal justice system and so reduced its authority (Radzinowicz, 1948–68, vol. 2: 53–4). Yet, in spite of such reservations offers of immunity remained an important part of the criminal justice system. In 1826 Chitty justified them in his book on criminal law:

> The law confesses its weakness by calling in the assistance of those by whom it has been broken. It offers a premium to treachery, and destroys the last virtue which clings to the degraded transgressor. Still on the other hand, it tends to prevent any extensive agreement among atrocious criminals, makes them perpetually suspicious of each other, and prevents the hopelessness of mercy from rendering them desperate.
>
> (Radzinowicz, 1948–68, vol. 2: 54)

More generally, informers were regarded with disgust and suspicion. In the early seventeenth century Edward Coke, the Lord Chief Justice, called common informers 'viperous vermin' (Radzinowicz, 1948–68, vol. 2: 139), and they were routinely assaulted. In 1702 and 1709 constables employed by the societies for the reformation of manners were killed by a London mob (Anon., 1732b; Woodward, 1702). When the rewards offered by the Gin Act 1736 'unleashed a tidal wave of informing' against unlicensed premises, the informers were attacked by London crowds encouraged – if encouragement were needed – by officials like Thomas De Veil, the Bow Street magistrate, who denounced the act for having let 'loose a crew of desperate and wicked people who turned informers merely for bread' (Clark, 1988: 80; Rude, 1974), and all around the country magistrates were reported to be refusing to convict under the Gin Act if the only evidence was from professional informers (*Gentleman's Magazine*, 1738–9).[9]

Yet, in spite of such reactions, Parliament saw rewards as a useful mechanism for ensuring the enforcement of law: in 1738 it was made an offence punishable by transportation to assault a Gin Act informer (11 Geo. II, c. 26, s. 2). Moreover, there was no shortage of people willing to risk the dangers of informing, indeed many made it a profession. In the early eighteenth century Jonathan Wild built a profitable business by, on the one hand, organizing the theft of goods which would be returned to their owners for a fee and, on the other hand, informing on the thieves for the reward – he was, for instance, involved in the arrest of John Sheppard (Howson, 1987). This prompted an outburst from Daniel Defoe, who as usual cut to the heart of the issue:

> this willingness of the Government to detect Thieves, seem'd to be a kind of Authority, for *Jonathan* in his vigorous pursuit of those who he thought fit to have Punished.
>
> (Defoe, 1725)

Wild went too far, but thieftaking for the rewards offered was important in terms of its impact on the structure of the criminal justice process in the eighteenth century. In a study of the middle of the century, Paley (1989b) has shown how extensive thieftaking was, how thieftakers pressed reluctant victims to prosecute and how the Bow Street magistrate, Henry Fielding, relied on them when constructing his plan to deal with robbery (see Chapter 2). Nevertheless, the suspicion was that thieftakers committed perjury in order to obtain the reward, and this seemed adequately supported by cases such as those involving Waller and his imitators in the 1750s the Macdaniel gang (Cox, 1756; Paley, 1989b: 323–9). Thieftakers may, however, have blackmailed far more felony suspects than they brought to trial because of the costs involved in a prosecution and because of the risk that an accused would be acquitted or convicted of a lesser charge for which no reward was offered (Paley, 1989b: 309–10 and 322–3).

The credibility of those who gave evidence as professional thieftakers or as accomplices presented a serious problem, but the Bow Street magistrates Henry and John Fielding argued that these people played a key role in the administration of justice, and criticized the way their evidence was constantly challenged by judges and treated with caution by juries (Beattie, 1986: 371–2). After Waller's conviction, the government did decide not to offer rewards over and above those in statute (Beattie, 1986: 52–3). This resolve vanished in the face of the next crime panic and proclamations offering a reward for the conviction of London street robbers like that which broke the Dalton gang were issued in 1735, 1744, 1749 and, finally, 1750 (Radzinowicz, 1948–68, vol. 2: 98–104). It continued to be accepted practice for the professional constables attached to the Police Offices which grew up in London after the mid-eighteenth century (see Chapter 2) to receive rewards, and so the problem of perjury did not vanish: indeed, in 1816 several police officers were arrested for conspiracies similar to those carried out by Waller and the Macdaniel gang (Anon., 1816). In the early nineteenth century an attempt to abolish statutory rewards and to replace them with a better system of awarding costs to prosecutors was watered down (58 Geo. III, c. 70 (1818)), and the courts were left with a discretion whether or not to order payment of a statutory reward. This was extended in 1826 (7 Geo. IV, c. 64) when the courts were given the power to award payments to those who had been actively involved in apprehending people guilty of any of a fairly broad range of offences (Radzinowicz, 1948–68, vol. 2: 74–82).

* * * *

In the early modern period the criminal justice system remained, as it always had been, primarily organized and controlled locally, and the social, demographic and economic pressures which came to a head in the seventeenth and eighteenth centuries encouraged the placing of a broader range of legal instruments (the poor law, the criminal law) into the hands of the gentry and the middling classes. Yet, it is also true that the situation had changed, or, at least, carried within it the possibility of change. The trend towards legislation which offered rewards to those who assisted in the enforcement of the law and which penalized those who did not suggests that there was a concern in the seventeenth and eighteenth centuries to make the decentralized criminal justice system more effective.

These reforms came at the same time as changes in the criminal law (see Chapter 3) during a period from the late seventeenth to the mid-eighteenth century when party political divisions between Whigs and Tories raged and plots were hatched to overthrow the regimes which had followed the deposition of James II in 1688. The apprehension caused by these conflicts was magnified by the undermining of what were regarded as the stabilizing influences both of religion, as its certainties decayed in the face of advances in science, and of the foundation of wealth on land, as other means of acquiring wealth emerged (finance, manufacturing and so forth). In part these concerns found expression in criticism of the labouring classes and were translated into efforts to improve the efficiency of the criminal justice system as a means of securing social discipline. However, some of these efforts encouraged the involvement of thieftakers and criminals. This undermined the emphasis on discretion and control in the hands of local people and officials which had always been seen both as another important guarantee of stability and as a crucial defence against the tyranny of central government. The idea of prompting people into action did build on the tradition that the criminal justice system should be invoked by individuals and communities, not state officials, but, in practice, rewards encouraged professionalism and detachment from victims and communities. These tendencies were to be exploited by Henry and John Fielding at Bow Street in London and placed by them at the core of their approach to the criminal justice system (see Chapter 2), so that by 1821 one writer was complaining, 'nothing is well done that is not paid for specifically' (Radzinowicz, 1948–68, vol. 2: 167). The abuses committed by informers and thieftakers were well known, but no mechanism existed for exposing them, and, because of their importance, there was no real desire to create one. Jonathan Wild, John Waller and Stephen Macdaniel were part of the mainstream, they simply went too far (was it just that they were caught?), and, rather like the response today when a corrupt police officer is exposed, punishing them simply conveyed the impression that it was these individuals who were corrupt and not the system.

Further reading

There are a large number of general social, political and economic histories of the period: see, for instance, Berg (1994), Burke (1988), Coward (1994), George (1966), Langford (1989), Porter (1990), Rule (1992) and Thompson (1968; 1993). On the seventeenth-century anything by Christopher Hill and David Underdown is worth reading. Finally, Slack (1988) provides a succinct discussion of poverty and the poor laws in the sixteenth and seventeenth centuries. Crime in the eighteenth century has been a major interest of historians over the past two decades, so much so that bibliographical essay writing has become something of an industry (Emsley and Knafla, 1996; Innes and Styles, 1986; Rawlings, 1990), and all history journals regularly publish work in the field. A good example of the way in which the study of crime has had an impact on the writing of social history is Linebaugh's book (1991). He displays a breathtaking range, and, while he has been criticized for distorting eighteenth-century society by looking at it from the viewpoint of its criminals, his point is that for the most part those hanged at Tyburn did not form a separate criminal class, they were simply labouring people struggling like their friends and family to get by. It should be remembered that the study of crime is for him a means to the objective set by Thompson (1968: 13), 'I am seeking to rescue the poor stockinger, the Luddite cropper, the "obsolete" hand-loom weaver, the "utopian" artisan, and even the deluded follower of Joanna Southcott, from the enormous condescension of posterity.' Flawed though criminal records are as an historical source, they are, neverthe-less, an important way of getting over the lack of information about the labouring classes. Other historians have been centrally concerned with crime and criminal justice and indirectly (if at all) with broader social and political processes. Beattie (1986) is a fine example of this type of work. His collection and analysis of data represented an important new stage in the subject. Reading of his book should be supplemented by looking at Shoemaker (1991), in which there is a careful examination of the treatment of petty offenders. It is possible to catch up with these debates through Sharpe (1984) and Emsley (1996). While Sharpe's book is now in need of updating, both books are written by leading historians in the field and are much more than simply excellent summaries of other work. Not surprisingly, the student is likely to find access to primary materials (contemporary records and texts) difficult: Rawlings (1992a) reprints a handful of criminal biographies with annotations and introduct-ory essays, and several notebooks of eighteenth-century justices of the peace have been published (Paley, 1991). Statutes and reported cases are widely available but underused sources. Finally, although many have tried to write modern biographies of eighteenth-century criminals, only Gerald Howson (1973, 1987) has really succeeded with his books on Dr Dodd, the cleric and forger, and Jonathan Wild.

Notes

1. Newgate was the prison in which those condemned at the Old Bailey were held prior to execution. The Ordinary of Newgate was the prison chaplain, and from the late seven-teenth century the holders of that post published brief biographies of all those prisoners who had been hanged (Rawlings, 1992a: 113–19).

2. The likelihood that the bulk of the readers did not come from the poorer, labouring classes is based on the level of literacy required to read them and on their price (Faller, 1987; Rawlings, 1992a).

3. The division of society into the landed (aristocrats and gentry) classes, the middling classes (farmers, professional people such as lawyers, doctors and shopkeepers) and the labouring classes (from the relatively well-paid skilled artisans to the indigent living off poor relief), is crude and forces people into categories and associations with which they would

have been uncomfortable. However, for the purposes of this book such shortcuts are necessary. It should also be noted that 'poor' was a term applied broadly to the labouring classes.

4. A hundred was a sub-division of a county.

5. The liability of the hundred was not abolished until 1827 (7 & 8 Geo. IV, c. 31).

6. The constable was unpaid and was chosen from among those who met certain property qualifications. Refusal to serve was punishable by a fine. While some constables were conscientious, it is hardly surprising that a good many were not since they still had to earn a living and they had to live in the communities in which they served.

7. Usually rewards were in cash, although one statute in 1699 (10 & 11 Will. III, c. 23, s. 2) offered the 'Tyburn ticket', a certificate which gave exemption from parish office. Aside from rewards, there were provisions for compensation where someone was killed or injured while apprehending a person later convicted of certain offences: for example, under the Black Act (9 Geo. I, c. 22, s. 12) death or the loss of an eye or the use of a limb was to be compensated for by the payment of £50.

8. The most extreme example is in 5 Ann., c. 31, s. 4 (1706) which offered anyone convicting two other people of burglary or housebreaking a pardon for all previous felonies committed, except murder or treason.

9. Attempts in the nineteenth century to use hatred of the common informer to persuade Parliament to abolish the right to share in fines failed, and the common informer continued until 1951 (Radzinowicz, 1948–68, vol. 2: 153–5).

Chapter 2

Peace and Police:
The 1748 Crime Panic

It is shocking to think what a shambles this country is grown! Seventeen were executed this morning, after having murdered the turnkey on Friday night and almost forced open Newgate. One is forced to travel even at noon as if one was going to battle.

(Horace Walpole in Lewis, 1960: 312)

The panic

[handwritten marginalia: Crime wave. The panic led to a greater push to control crime, to do something about it.]

The crime wave, about which Horace Walpole was complaining, came with the ending of the War of the Austrian Succession in 1748. It led to such alarm that George II felt obliged to urge action from Parliament, and it provided the opportunity for Henry and John Fielding, magistrates at Bow Street, to secure government finance for radical plans to resolve the problem of crime by the creation of a specialist, permanent bureaucracy.

Reports of robberies in one leading newspaper, the *Whitehall Evening Post*, rose dramatically through 1748: a rough comparison between January to April and September to December shows a three-fold increase. The situation became so bad that the editor took the unprecedented step of leading with an article on the subject:

> The Frequency of audacious Street Robberies repeated every Night in this great Metropolis, call aloud on our Magistrates to think of some Redress; for, as the Case is now, there is no Possibility of stirring from out habitations after dark, without the Hazard of a fractured Skull, or the Danger of losing that Property People are sometimes obliged to carry about them.
>
> (*Whitehall Evening Post*, 17 Jan. 1749)

Things were no better the next year. Walpole, bemoaning the lack of political intrigue, remarked that, 'Robbery is the only thing that goes on with any vivacity' (Lewis, 1960: 199). And he spoke from experience having himself been shot at and robbed in Hyde Park by James MacLean. The crime wave continued into 1751: in September the *Gentleman's Magazine* (1751: 423) reported that, 'So many robberies were committed this morning and the night before, on passengers from *London* to *Wandsworth*, *Putney*, and *Richmond*, that this evening most of the people returning thence to *London*, assembled at *Wandsworth*, and came home in companies.' Alarmed newspaper readers might have supposed the whole country to be under siege from robbers: people in Carlisle could not leave home 'without Danger to our Persons or Effects'; Kingston in Surrey was 'greatly infested by several Highwaymen'; and travellers leaving Maidenhead went 'in Parties armed' (*Penny London Post*, 3 Feb. 1748; *Whitehall Evening Post*, 22 Sep., 10 Dec. 1748). Not surprisingly, the courts were busy. In January 1748 it was reported that the forthcoming Old Bailey session 'will be one of the smallest known for some Time past', but at the session for August 1749, 'There is the greatest Number for capital Offences that has been known for Years past' (*Whitehall Evening Post*, 12 Dec. 1748, 31 Aug. 1749). The story was the same elsewhere: at Winchester in February 1749 'the County Gaol there was scarce ever known to be so full of notorious Criminals as it is at present'; in March the assizes in Rochester in Kent were 'the largest known in the Memory of Man'; and later that same month in the counties around London it was reported that 'the Gaols have hardly ever been fuller' (*Whitehall Evening Post*, 25 Feb., 9 Mar., 28 Mar. 1749).

Peace also brought economic dislocation. Dockworkers at the naval yards were laid off; merchant seamen, who had enjoyed high wages, suddenly found the market saturated with ex-Royal Navy men and either lost their jobs or had to accept pay cuts; and there were similar stories in other industries. The lifting of a ban on the export of grain to France allowed dealers to take advantage of the high prices there forcing up prices in England and leading to rioting among consumers, sometimes with tragic consequences: at Penryn two Cornish tinners were shot dead by soldiers (*Penny London Post*, 13 Jul., 5 Aug., 24 Aug. 1748; *Whitehall Evening Post*, 14 Jan., 9 Feb., 5 Mar., 10 May, 14 May, 19 May, 12 Nov. 1748).

The belief that there was a link between demobilization at the end of a war and crime was already well established (Anon., 1701). In early 1748 there were about 120,000 soldiers and sailors, this figure was more than halved by the end of the year. Peace meant both the return of young men who had no work and the end of a useful means of getting rid of troublesome youths (ordering them into the army or navy). Troubles associated with demobilized soldiers and sailors dominated news reporting from mid-1748. The location of the ports on the south coast, the archaic system of payments by the Navy Board which often required sailors to go to London, and unemployment meant that many travelled to the capital: 'this – P[eac]e has stocked the Town so full of gay young Fellows' (Anon., 1750b: 8). In 1748–9 sailors rioted over the failure to pay wages and prize money, laying siege to George II at St James's; they also rescued a colleague who was being taken to London's Newgate Prison, attacked tax collectors on Portsmouth Common, demolished bawdy houses in the

Strand and Goodman's Fields (London), assembled at Tyburn to protect the bodies of hanged comrades from being taken by anatomy teachers, and were identified as the perpetrators of numerous serious crimes – more than half of the 44 people hanged at Tyburn in 1749 were sailors.[1]

The reaction

There has been a tendency to view such panics about crime merely as media or political constructions (which they sometimes were) and to ignore the impact which they have on policy. Considering the disruption which large-scale demobilization caused, it seems not unlikely that there was a real rise in crime (Beattie, 1986), but, whether or not this was the case, the panic in the years from 1748 to the mid-1750s undoubtedly had an important impact and put crime firmly on the national political agenda.

There was a variety of responses to this apparent surge in crime, although most avoided spending the sort of money that was lavished on the victory celebrations (Brewer, 1997: 25–8). Some sailors and soldiers were sent off to deal with smugglers in Kent, Sussex and Suffolk (*London Evening Post*, 3 Jan. 1749; *Whitehall Evening Post*, 19 May, 11 Jun., 29 Dec. 1748, 7 Jan. 1749; Winslow, 1977); some were given land in Nova Scotia – an idea which, it was hoped, would both get rid of the men and subjugate the troublesome Acadians. The government also resorted to some well-tried strategies. In January 1749 a reward and immunity to accomplices was offered for the conviction of robbers operating in London; within six weeks, 'So many highway-men and street-robbers are in custody on the impeachment of their accomplices that the prisons are quite full'. The reward was renewed by the government in January 1750 following the robbery of several aristocrats, including Horace Walpole, and again in December 1750.[2] The numbers hanged in London increased (*London Evening Post*, 26 Mar., 17 May, 4 Oct. 1750):[3] 'Robberies were so frequent . . . that the Administration found it necessary to execute the utmost Severity of the Law' (Allen, 1750: 19). In part, this was doubtless linked to the offer of additional rewards: thieftakers were encouraged to bring felons to court, this seemed to confirm the crime wave, which, in turn, encouraged courts to convict and the government to leave more of the condemned to hang (Paley, 1989b: 325–8). Pressure for more severe punishment led to the Murder Act of 1752, which required murderers to be hanged soon after the trial and their bodies either dissected or left on a gallows. However, the low level of murder convictions made this a largely symbolic gesture: three out of 163 hanged in London and Middlesex in 1749–51 were condemned for murder, the bulk of the rest had been convicted of theft, housebreaking and robbery.

There was plenty of criticism in London about the efficiency of the street patrols conducted by watchmen and of the magistracy. 'The Watchmen', remarked one pamphleteer, 'are either infirm, old, or indigent People, who serve their Offices for Hire, are often in Fee with the Public-Houses' (Anon., 1751b: 22), and the magistrates were berated for their failure 'to think of some Redress' (*Penny London Post*, 4 Jan. 1748; *Whitehall Evening Post*, Jan. to Feb. 1749). Parishes did take on extra patrols, and parliamentary interest in the reform of the police[4] in London was hinted at as early as December 1748. In March 1749 Islington raised money to employ soldiers to patrol the area, and in the following winter the government used soldiers to watch roads around London in the evenings (*Penny London Post*, 29 Jul. 1748; *Whitehall Evening Post*, 13 Dec., 29 Dec. 1748; 21 Jan., 4 Mar., 7 Mar., 5 Oct., 17 Oct. 1749). Some parishes, such as St George's Hanover Square, Edmonton and Tottenham, offered rewards. Merchants on the Thames raised £1,100 to fund rewards and the costs of prosecuting thieves,[5] and between 1749 and 1751 approximately 24 people were hanged at Tyburn alone for crimes connected with the river and a greater number were transported. Then, in 1751 the merchants obtained an act making it a capital offence to steal on rivers goods worth forty shillings.[6]

As the panic continued into 1750 and beyond so writers began to consider the roots of the problem by linking this crisis to long-standing concerns about the morality and discipline of the labouring poor and the impact of gin drinking, gaming houses, alehouses, brothels, prostitution and so forth. Magistrates were urged to take action: 'The *Ax* must ... be laid to the Root of the Tree', wrote one pamphleteer who claimed they were being bribed not to raid gaming houses. Magistrates did make a number of well-publicized raids on gaming houses: as early as February 1748 soldiers and constables smashed their way into a gaming house in the Strand, and in October magistrates in Middlesex and Westminster resolved to meet regularly to review the situation.[7] There were frequent general searches ordered by the magistrates to clear London's streets of 'idle disorderly Persons, and reputed Thieves and Pick Pockets'; vagrants and street prostitutes were arrested in large numbers and whipped until their backs bled or put to work in a house of correction. There seems to have been less enthusiasm for suppressing bawdy houses – the action of the vestry of St Mary, Whitechapel against them in June 1748 and the shutting of a house in the Strand in July were rare exceptions. In the end it was the sailors themselves who demolished several houses in the Strand and Goodman's Fields in the summer of 1749, although they were motivated not by morality but by the wish to avenge the robbery of a comrade.[8]

A major turning point in the crisis came when George II, doubtless prompted by the robbery of several of his friends, intervened by referring to the crime wave in speeches to both Houses of Parliament in January and November 1751. He called on Parliament:

to consider seriously of some effectual Provision to suppress those audacious Crimes of Robbery and Violence, which are now become so frequent, especially about this great capital; and which have proceeded, in a great Measure, from that profligate Spirit of Irreligion, Idleness, Gaming, and Extravagance, which has of late extended itself, in an uncommon Degree, to the Dishonour of the Nation, and to the great Offence and Prejudice of the sober and industrious Part of my People.

                    (Torrington, 1972–8: sess. 1747–48 to 1753: 388; also 334)

As a result, a large select committee under Sir Richard Lloyd was established and the pamphlet writers were given a new lease of life.[9]

The novelist Henry Fielding, who was appointed as a magistrate at Bow Street in 1748, had been deliberating on the problem for some time, and his pamphlet, *An Enquiry into the causes of The Late Increase of Robbers* (1751), appeared just before the king first addressed the issue (*London Evening Post*, 19 Jan. 1751; Battestin, 1989: 513–21; Cross, 1918, vol. 2: 255; Zirker, 1988: lviii–lix). He argued that the end of feudal discipline and the wealth brought by trade had made the labouring classes relatively independent. They were able to indulge in goods and entertainments which previously they could not have afforded. These diverted them from work, encouraged their natural tendency to idleness, and, as a result, increased the likelihood that they would slip into crime. Not averse to over-indulgence himself, he did not seek to eradicate the luxury of the rich, indeed, like Bernard Mandeville (1924) in *The Fable of the Bees* thirty years before, he saw economic advantage in this expenditure:

for as riches are the *certain* consequences of trade, is luxury the no less *certain* consequence of riches; nay, trade and luxury do indeed support each other . . . To prevent this consequence therefore of a flourishing commerce is totally to change the nature of things, and to separate the effect from the cause. A matter as impossible in the political body as in the natural. Vices and diseases, with like physical necessity, arise from certain habits in both; and to restrain and palliate the evil consequences is all that lies within the reach of art.

                                                  (Fielding, 1988b: 71)

He believed the solution lay chiefly in increasing the powers of magistrates to regulate 'places of pleasure', such as gaming houses and alehouses. However, the last part of the pamphlet is concerned with what he terms 'encouragements to crime' in the justice system. He called for stronger measures against receivers of stolen goods, and for magistrates to be given the power to detain suspicious persons, thereby preventing the mobility which made criminals so difficult to find. Fielding defended thieftakers and was critical of juries for convicting felons of non-capital offences thereby depriving thieftakers of rewards which were payable only on a capital conviction. He suggested that poor prosecutors should be paid their costs, that the rule requiring corroboration of the evidence of an accomplice-turned-informer be abandoned because it made it difficult to obtain a conviction, that pardons be less frequently given because they

[handwritten margin note: Hanging changed to private execution]

encouraged people to commit crime in the expectation that, even if caught, they would not hang, and that because the public hanging had lost its terror it should be replaced by a private execution.

The links between this pamphlet and the Lloyd Committee have been thoroughly chewed over. While claims that Fielding was 'the man behind the scenes' of the committee have now been discarded,[10] it would seem strange if Fielding, as the chair of the Westminster and Middlesex Quarter Sessions and as someone who was regularly in contact with government ministers, had not been consulted. In any case much of what he wrote was uncontroversial, as indicated by the general praise heaped upon it at the time.[11] He did have his critics. Most notably, the great scholar and conversationalist Dr Samuel Johnson believed that it was the large number of capital offences which discouraged victims from prosecuting and so encouraged crime. Others agreed with Fielding's view that there was a link between morality and crime, but attacked both his suggestion that magistrates be given more powers and his frequent use of soldiers to support the civil authorities as threats to liberty (Johnson, 1969, vol. 2: 114; Battestin, 1989: 521): such ideas, it was argued, showed, 'no Plan of Government but Force, and no Coercive but what is founded on Fear, Cruelty and Violence':

> unless there is a general Disposition in the Body of the People, to co-operate with the Magistrate in the Suppression of Vice and Immorality and in the execution of the Law against publick Offenders, that it is out of the Power of any human Legislature, to contrive Laws, that can make that People honest, happy, or free.
>
> (Anon., 1751c: 5)

This writer argued that the solution lay in moral reformation and in citizens taking responsibility for apprehending offenders, not in paying others to do this work.

Although the Lloyd Committee made a number of recommendations, only one statute was passed – the Disorderly Houses Act 1752 (25 Geo. II, c. 36).[12] This did, however, cover a fair number of issues. It created an offence of advertising for the return of stolen property where a promise was made that no questions would be asked; it required 'Places of Entertainment for the lower Sort of People' to be licensed by a magistrate; it gave courts the discretion to grant a poor prosecutor's costs in a felony case; and it allowed a magistrate to detain a suspicious person for up to six days without charge so that victims of crime could come forward (*Covent Garden Journal*, 30 May, 2 Jun., 13 Jun., 11 Nov. 1752. But *Gentleman's Magazine*, 1752: 30–1). Separately from the Lloyd Committee another moral hazard was attacked in 1751 when the Gin Act was rapidly enacted to tighten up licensing laws. It was the result of 20 petitions which had themselves been prompted by a sermon preached by Issac Maddox, Bishop of Worcester, in February 1751. The petitions claimed that gin drinking injured 'the Health, Strength and Industry of the Poor' and 'inflames them with Rage and Barbarity, and occasions frequent Robberies and Murders' (Maddox, 1751; *Commons Journals*, vol. 26: 55, 77, 84–5, 88, 94, 106–7, 114, 117, 133 and 219).[13]

New policing strategies: the Fieldings

Alongside these legislative changes, new policing strategies were being developed, especially in London and, more particularly, from 1748 by the magistrates at Bow Street – Henry Fielding, his devoted step-brother John, and Saunders Welch (Rawlings, 1995). The effect of their work was to challenge the notion that the enforcement of the criminal law was a personal decision which should be left to the victim. The Fieldings did not represent a decisive break with previous practice rather an acceleration of existing tendencies. Eighteenth-century magistrates were already acquiring more power within the criminal justice system. There had been a shift of work from manorial and church courts to the magistrates' courts in the seventeenth century, and from jury to summary trials held before one or two justices in the eighteenth. In London changes in policing had also enhanced their position. In 1737 magistrates in the City of London opened a rotation office where they were available to the public at regular times, and this idea was adopted at Bow Street by Sir Thomas De Veil in 1739 (Anon., 1748; Beattie, 1986: 65–72; Leslie-Melville, 1934: 143–4; Pringle, 1955: 60–76). A regular, paid watch was established in the City under statutes starting in 1705, and this practice spread to other parishes over the next forty years (Emsley, 1991: 20–1; Rumbelow, 1971: 83–6; Tobias, 1979: 36–43).

In one sense, then, the Fieldings were simply part of a process of continual change. Nevertheless, they had an important impact. They (in particular John) tried to bring system to the collection of information about crime and criminals, and they regularized their relationship with a group of thieftakers. Thieftakers had long been associated with magistrates in London, however, at Bow Street instead of the thieftaker deciding which cases to pursue and how to undertake the task, they were directed by the Fieldings. They could still claim rewards, and they were paid retainers or were given jobs – as, for instance, gaolers – to ensure a regular income. In other words, although these Bow Street thieftakers were never entirely above suspicion – indeed, there was a connection between the Macdaniel gang and Henry Fielding – 'a process of professionalization had taken place' which increased their respectability, or at least created an impression of their efficiency (Paley, 1989b: 336–7).

Publicity was central to the Fieldings' work. They recognized the limitations of simply relying on the public bringing information to the office at Bow Street. Moreover, pamphlets, such as *The Discoveries of John Poulter* (1754), showed that criminal gangs operated across large areas: Poulter and his gang travelled to fairs and markets all over England committing confidence tricks and opportunist thefts (Rawlings, 1995: 139–77). The Fieldings believed that the justice system had to be equally flexible. It was Henry Fielding (admittedly, elaborating the practice of Sir Thomas De Veil) who in 1753–4 devised a system for the collection of information about London crime and suspected offenders at his office in Bow Street, but, ill health forcing his resignation in that year, its execution was left to John Fielding. The aim was to deter potential offenders by 'the Certainty of speedy Detection'. This was to be achieved through 'the drawing of all Informations of Fraud and Felony into one point [namely, Bow Street], registering Offenders of all Kinds, quick Notice and sudden Pursuit, and keeping up a Correspondence with all the active Magistrates in England' (Fielding, 1769: vi and v; also Fielding, 1755, 1768). Although these early plans were focused on London, the Fieldings recognized that the mobility of offenders like the Poulter gang was a problem, and there is plenty of evidence that John Fielding was supplying information and assistance to other magistrates from the 1750s. But it was not until 1772 that a fully-worked out national strategy appeared – the General Preventative Plan (Styles, 1983b). In this he encouraged magistrates and gaolers around the country to supply Bow Street with information about offences and offenders, together with warrants which could be forwarded to any place in which a suspicious person had been apprehended. He secured government finance for the plan enabling him to publish information through *The London Packet or New Lloyd's Evening Post*, which was then sent out free; from autumn 1773 this purpose was served by his own newspaper, *The Hue and Cry*, which flourished long after his death and spawned the enormously popular *Police Gazette* in the nineteenth century. There was widespread support for Fielding's plan, possibly because the demobilization following the peace of 1763 and end of transportation to America in 1775 prompted further crime panics (Hewitt, 1779, 1783). However, Fielding's suggestion in 1775 that salaried high constables actively pursue offenders was less well received, partly because it was seen by provincial magistrates as an overreaction to what, in most places, was a relatively small problem. Aside from this strategy for the collection of information, both Fieldings believed magistrates should be active in solving cases, and they both engaged in lengthy examinations of suspects and witnesses. They were also keen for that aspect of their work to be widely reported, and both men either published or had interests in newspapers.[14] This publicity was important for their plans, encouraged government funding and enabled John Fielding to engage in the self promotion that led to a knighthood in 1761 (Fielding, 1758: 15–16; Fielding, 1754: introduction; Fielding 1755: 1–2; Leslie-Melville, 1934). It also allowed them to attack those aspects of the criminal justice system which they felt obstructed their work (Anon., 1765a: 18; Beattie, 1986: 369–73; Fielding, 1988b: 158–62; Langbein, 1983: 96–100). Running through their work the Fieldings implicitly asserted that specialist skills and full-time officials were needed to detect the most serious offenders (*Gentleman's Magazine*, 1751: 38; *Whitehall Evening Post*, 8 Jan. 1751). They made large claims: in 1770 John Fielding boasted that no street robber had escaped justice for 20 years (Committee on Fielding's Plan, 1770. Also, Fielding, 1768).

The Fieldings did shift the emphasis of discussion towards themselves as magistrates proactively directing the criminal justice process. Before the mid-eighteenth century the focus of crime reporting in newspapers and biographies was the offender's life, crimes, trial and execution; from the 1750s it typically included – and sometimes concentrated on – the process of detection, and often this would involve a reference to John Fielding gathering information and organizing the pursuit of suspects (Anon., 1765a; Bevell, 1765; Hewitt, 1779, 1783; Rawlings, 1992a: 25).

* * * *

Although many of the ideas which the Fieldings paraded in their endless publications were familiar, their organization of the thieftakers and their use of publicity to press forward their vision of the role of the magistrate had an important long-term impact on the criminal justice system. In effect, they believed that crime control was achievable through the combination of a detection system and a tighter control on the morals of the labouring classes, but that this required a powerful (in terms of legal, financial and human resources) bureaucracy headed by active magistrates. In what they saw as a fractured post-feudal and increasingly urban society it was their view that the individual was unable to detect offenders or to provide the programme of moralization required for a long-term solution to crime. A criminal justice system which relied on the initiative of individual victims had no real response to the sort of violent gang crime which, the Fieldings claimed, was commonplace. They wanted a law enforcement system which was more consistently proactive rather than one which passively responded to the needs of individuals and communities. The implication of their work was that law enforcement was a realizable goal and that it should be the defining objective of the criminal justice system since this was a means by which people could be deterred from crime. This was both to put the pre-trial detection process at the heart of the system, rather than the victim or the trial or punishment, and to present it as a technical, bureaucratic, apolitical process operated by full-time experts in which popular involvement was confined to providing information on terms dictated by that bureaucracy. The Fieldings seem not to have wanted to do more than build on existing models of local justice; they did not wish to construct a centralized system. And yet John Fielding saw Bow Street at the centre of a national effort against crime, a clearing house for information and the coordinator of magistrates all around the country, and by also seeing crime detection as a technical exercise, which might well be placed in the hands of honest thieftakers, his vision necessarily implied the disconnection of crime control from individual victims and from local interests.

Further reading

Many of the works mentioned at the end of Chapter 1 are also relevant here. There are a large number of police histories which purport to cover the period before 1829, but rarely give it much space and so end up presenting it as the *hors d'ouevre* before Peel's main course. Rumbelow (1971) is an interesting exception in that he is largely concerned with policing in the City of London before 1800. The best biography of Henry Fielding is Battestin (1989), unfortunately from the point of view of the historian of crime John Fielding is the more interesting of the two, but has not had a biography since Leslie-Melville (1934), which has long been out of date. Paley (1989b) has brilliantly dissected the relationship between the Bow Street magistrates and the thieftakers, and the best recent study of John Fielding's plan for policing is Styles (1983b); there is also Rawlings (1995) in which some of the ideas discussed in this chapter are developed further. Henry Fielding's 1751 pamphlet is typically left out of collected editions of his works, fortunately Zirker (Fielding, 1988b) has produced a book which includes that essay and others on social issues, all annotated with a splendid introduction; he has also written an excellent full-length study of these pamphlets (Zirker, 1966).

Notes

1. *Penny London Post* 3 Aug., 2 Sep., 16 Dec. 1748; *Whitehall Evening Post* 9 Jan., 10 Dec. 1748; 4 Jul., 6 Jul., 8 Aug., 19 Oct. 1749 and *passim*; Baugh 1965, 1977; Linebaugh 1975: 659; Linebaugh 1977; Merriman 1961.

2. *Gentleman's Magazine* 1749: 88, 1750: 41–2 and 378, 1751: 38; *Whitehall Evening Post,* 4 Feb., 7 Feb., 16 Feb. 1749, 8 Jan. 1751; *London Evening Post,* 5 May, 8 Dec., 13 Dec., 15 Dec. 1750, 14 May, 23 May 1751.

3. The London sheriff Sir Stephen Janssen later produced statistics showing that capital convictions and hangings were higher in the years of peace between 1749 and 1756 than in the years of war (1756–63) which followed (Howard, 1777; Select Committee on the Criminal Law, 1819: appendix).

4. In the eighteenth century the term 'police' referred to the whole civil administration, it was not until much later that it became confined to the narrow idea of the body of state officials charged with various duties connected to law enforcement. However, in this book the word is used in its latter sense even in the discussion of the eighteenth century.

5. Collaboration between the river's merchants went back to patrols undertaken in 1711 and, more recently, to some joint action against thieves in 1743.

6. Wilson, 1749: 11–12, 1743: 4; Radzinowicz, 1948–68, vol. 2: 353–7; Historical Manuscripts Commission, 1920–23, vol. 1: 85–6; *Commons Journal,* vol. 26: 212; Philopatriae, 1756; *London Evening Post,* 16 Oct. 1750, 22 Jan. 1751; Linebaugh, 1975: 502; *London Evening Post,* 19 Jan., 26 Mar., 4 Apr., 9 Apr., 13 Apr., 20 Aug. 1751; *Whitehall Evening Post,* 22 Jan. 1751; Purland: 184–5.

7. *British Magazine,* 1750: 188; *Covent Garden Journal,* 9 Jun., 23 Sep. 1752; *General Advertiser,* 24 Oct. 1748; *Gentleman's Magazine,* 1751: 87 and 185; *London Evening Post,* 19 Jan. 1749, 21 Apr. 1750, 14 Feb., 23 Mar., 24 Apr., 13 Jul. 1751; *Penny London Post,* 29 Jan., 29 Jul., 5 Aug., 17 Oct., 24 Oct., 7 Nov. 1748; *Westminster Journal,* 26 Mar. 1748; *Whitehall Evening Post,* 2 Feb., 17 Jun., 2 Jul. 1748, 21 Jan. 1749. Also, Battestin, 1989: 502–3, 510–11 and 522; Brittanicus, 1750: 4–11.

8. *Whitehall Evening Post,* 14 Jun., 28 Jun., 2 Jul. 1748, 7 Oct. 1749; *Penny London Post,* 29 Jan., 29 Jul., 5 Aug., 17 Oct., 7 Nov. 1748; Purland: 343.

9. The committee was set up on 1 Feb. 1751 and its membership increased on 12 Feb., 28 Mar. and 1 Apr. (*Commons Journals*, vol. 26: 27, 39, 155 and 158). Its terms of reference were extended (ibid: 123). George II's speeches were still being recalled in 1763 (Mildmay, 1763: iii).

10. Fielding, 1967: 153; Cross, 1918, vol. 2: 268 and 280, vol. 3: 339; Dudden, 1952, vol. 2: 794–6; Jones, 1933: 236–9; Rogers, 1979: 190–1. But, Amory, 1971; Zirker, 1966: 32–42.

11. Anon., 1751a; Anon., 1751b; Battestin, 1989: 519–21; Civis, 1752; Cross, 1918, vol. 2: 223–300; *Gentleman's Magazine*, 1751: 3–4; Jones, 1752; Paulson and Lockwood, 1969: 239–49; Philonomos, 1751; Philo-Patria, 1751; *The Monthly Review*, 1751: 229–39.

12. *Commons Journals*, vol. 26: 159, 190, 220, 236, 260–1, 266, 268, 270, 283, 286, 287, 289, 344–5, 381–2, 458–9, 490 and 588; *Lords Journals*, vol. 28: 101; Lambert, 1975, vol. 1: 46, vol. 9: 357–67; *Gentleman's Magazine*, 1752.

13. Perhaps as effective were Hogarth's engravings which compared the fat, prosperous *Beer Street* with the emaciated, moribund *Gin Lane* (1751) (*London Evening Post*, 14 Feb. 1751; British Museum, Add. Mss 27, 991, fo. 49b; see also Chapter 1 above).

14. In addition to books and pamphlets (for lists of which see, Battestin, 1989; Leslie-Melville, 1934), Henry Fielding produced *The Covent Garden Journal* (1752), and John Fielding had an interest in the *Public Advertiser*, which took his advertisements and featured his work at Bow Street, as did the *Daily Gazetteer* in the 1760s and *Lloyd's Evening Post* in the 1770s (see also, Styles, 1983b).

Chapter 3

Legal Massacres:
Capital Punishment
in the Late Eighteenth-Century

More crime panics: the 1770s and 1780s

Throughout the period to the mid-nineteenth century the spectacle of the public hanging played an important role in the criminal justice system. The number of people hanged declined and yet Parliament continued to add capital offences to the statute book right into the early nineteenth century. However, the second half of the eighteenth century did witness changes in attitudes to the gallows and a shift away from its use as a spectacular means of deterring people from offending.

The panic which began in 1748 largely subsided on the outbreak of the Seven Years' War in 1756 (Mildmay, 1763) as vast numbers of the young, labouring classes joined or were pressed into the services. However, the same fears about crime surfaced on the conclusion of the war in 1763. In 1765 one newspaper remarked that at the Old Bailey there was 'the largest Session of Gaol-Delivery that has been known in the Memory of the oldest Man living' (Purland: 571). Magistrates in Middlesex and Westminster opened more public offices along the lines of those already established in the City and at Bow Street, government funding was obtained for the Bow Street Horse Patrol, improvements were made to street lighting in some of the main thoroughfares in Westminster, and in 1768 John Fielding presented to a select committee his detailed plans for improving contacts between justices of the peace throughout the country (Fielding, 1768; Committee on Fielding's Plan, 1770; Leslie-Melville, 1934: 142–66 and 259–74; Styles, 1983b). The 1760s were also troubled by the most serious rioting of the century to date, a flavour of which was given by a bemused Benjamin Franklin writing in 1769:

> I have seen, within a year, riots in the country, about corn; riots about
> elections; riots about workhouses; riots of colliers, riots of weavers, riots of
> coal-heavers; riots of sawyers; riots of Wilkesites; riots of government
> chairmen; riots of smugglers, in which custom house officers and excisemen
> have been murdered, the King's armed vessels and troops fired at.
>
> (Porter, 1990: 17)

In London the government sent soldiers and sailors to deal with strikes among Spitalfields silk weavers and Thames coalheavers; several people were killed in the clashes which followed and many others hanged. The capital was also riven by conflict around the battle-cry of 'Wilkes and Liberty', which centred on the controversies provoked by John Wilkes' criticism of government policy, and which led, among other things to a fortnight of rioting in 1768, and across the country there were food riots as harvests failed in the mid-1760s (Linebaugh, 1991: 311–18 and 321–3; Randall, 1985; Shelton, 1973). Some of these problems diminished in the early 1770s, but by the summer of 1775 newspapers were again reporting crime in terms which recalled the late 1740s: 'Perhaps there never were more numerous or formidable Gangs of Housebreakers than have lately infested, and do still infest, this City and its Environs' (Purland: 1877). That September more felons were awaiting trial at the Old Bailey 'than for a long Time past', and at the September 1777 session 170 people were tried – 'so great a Number has not been known for some Time' (Purland: 1885, 2105, 2119).

A number of factors explain the unusual circumstance of a crime panic occurring in the late 1770s when Britain was in the midst of the American War of Independence (1775–83). America had been the destination for transported felons, so the start of the war meant convicts had to be incarcerated in England, but there were no facilities to do this. Then in 1780 London was paralysed for five days by the Gordon Riots, which led to a large number of casualties, the execution of 25 rioters and the widespread destruction of property, including at the home of Lord Chief Justice Mansfield, the magistrate's office at Bow Street, the Bank of England and Newgate prison. Although nominally led by Lord George Gordon as a protest against Catholic toleration, the riot contained elements of what a contemporary called 'Republican phrenzy' and a 'levelling spirit' in its attacks on the rich and the Bank of England (Linebaugh, 1991: 333–60; Castro, 1926; Hibbert, 1958). It seemed that the London poor were out of control and the authorities were impotent. Harriet Frankland, who was visiting London at the time, wrote to her family in Wales:

> the soldiers refused to fire despite orders, then fired over heads, only when officers threatened to shoot them did they fire on [the] mob . . . It is said that the Soldiers are much on the side of the Populace & tell people that they ought to read Fox's Book of Martyrs, & that then they would see whether the Papists ought to be tolerated.
>
> (NLW Mss, Harpton Court C/230)

In the short term, the authorities improved their ability to respond to any future riot in London, and when in 1794 a crowd attempted to free people seized by press gangs, constables, the militia and the army responded rapidly (Linebaugh, 1991: 413 and 436; Rogers, 1990). Nevertheless, the Gordon Riots remained a powerful image in the minds of politicians for several generations. There was also political instability caused by the collapse in 1782 of Lord North's administration as a result of the defeat in North America, and the loss of the colonies led to a more general questioning of the competence of aristocratic government. There followed calls for parliamentary reform, and also a range of voluntary initiatives on social problems: societies for the prosecution of felons[1] were set up in huge numbers, the Sunday School movement emerged in 1783–4, and a reformation of manners movement was begun in the 1780s (Innes, 1990b).

The fact that there was concern about law and order even before the war ended meant that when the preliminary peace treaty was signed in 1782 the crime panic which followed was more intense than any experienced during the eighteenth century. The *Whitehall Evening Post* (27 Mar. 1783; Hay, 1982; Madan, 1785: appendix) warned that, 'the reducing of the navy, army, and militia, will cast a number of men adrift, many of whom are idly inclined, and may become obnoxious to the laws'; in November 1783 the *Gentleman's Magazine* (1783: 974), reporting at the end of the Old Bailey Sessions, commented, 'Villains increase so fast, that a bare recital of their names and atrocious crimes would more than fill our Magazine.' The picture was the same elsewhere: at the Gloucester Assizes thirteen people were condemned, 'a melancholy proof of the profligacy of the times' (*Whitehall Evening Post*, 5 Apr. 1783). The *Public Advertiser* (Oct. 1784) reported that, 'highway robberies are . . . committed at noonday, in a public road, in the sight of several passengers . . . [W]ho is safe from their depredations? Sun-shine is now no security'. In the Commons, Sir Archibald Macdonald, the Solicitor-General, spoke of 'the alarming height to which depredation and outrage had arrived', and a petition from the City of London to George III in 1786 complained of 'the rapid and alarming increase of crimes and depredations in this city and its neighbourhood, especially within the last three years' (*Parliamentary History*, vol. 25, c. 888; *Gentleman's Magazine* 1786: 263).

Alongside crime, there was rioting: in February 1783 at Wapping sailors rioted and in April the Horse Guards had to be called out when several hundred sailors protested in London at the non-payment of wages and prize money; that month there were also mutinies at Portsmouth when sailors were told they would be sent to North America rather than being discharged and a regiment in Wakefield surrounded the house of General Tottenham demanding to be discharged (*Whitehall Evening Post*, 11 Feb., 19 Apr., 3 Apr., 10 Apr. 1783). Unemployed ex-Royal Navy sailors protested in St James's Park against the practice of employing foreign sailors on low wages, and later unrigged several outward bound ships on the Thames (*Whitehall Evening Post*, Mar.–Apr. 1783). Sailors were also reported to be involved in robberies in Hampshire, through which many passed on their way from Portsmouth to London, and, although the grave of an unidentified murdered sailor in Thursley churchyard in Surrey serves to remind us that sailors who had just been paid were also targets for robbers, it was as criminals that they were generally depicted: 'since such a number of soldiers and sailors have been discharged, it is dangerous for people to be from home after dark, as robberies are very frequently committed by them' (*Whitehall Evening Post*, 20 Mar. 1783). The problem of unemployment among men discharged from the services did prompt the creation of *ad hoc* work and food subsidy programmes (*Whitehall Evening Post*, 13 Mar. 1783, 24 Jan. 1784), and the *Whitehall Evening Post* (13 Mar. 1783) urged the gentry to undertake such projects in terms which indicate the depth of the crisis:

> If the gentlemen in the different counties do not exert themselves . . . in providing employment for the numbers that will shortly be turned adrift, they must relinquish the comfort of enjoying [their] property in security.

The disorder was not simply associated with sailors. When hand-bills began to circulate in London in March 1783 calling on the people to arm and 'to take upon themselves the vindication of their own rights', the government, fearing a repetition of the Gordon Riots, called out the army and the City of London Military Association (*Whitehall Evening Post*, 29 Mar. 1783). The harvest failed in 1782 causing high prices and food riots: Stephen Barlow was hanged after a Newcastle crowd had stopped a boat loaded with cheese and flour – his distraught wife killed herself the next day; two more were hanged after a crowd had marched in columns of twos into Halifax market, seized corn and sold it at what they considered a fair price (*Whitehall Evening Post*, 18 Mar., 25 Mar., 3 Apr., 1783; Styles, 1980). But in spite of such repression food rioting was widespread from Wrexham market, where Welsh colliers sold corn they had stopped from being exported, to Whitby, where the townspeople removed corn from a sloop in the harbour (*Whitehall Evening Post*, 4 Jan., 25 Mar. 1783; Rude, 1964: 37).

The death penalty in the 1780s

[handwritten margin note: Magistrates would give orders]

Familiar responses to the crime panic were tried. As sailors arrived in London in large numbers in February 1783, the magistrates gave orders 'for reputed bad houses to be searched every night, and disorderly persons to be taken up' (*Whitehall Evening Post*, 13 Feb. 1783). Those who tramped the country in search of work were viewed with suspicion and harassed: following a rash of robberies and burglaries in 1786 the Quarter Sessions in Cardiganshire and in Worcestershire ordered constables to keep a watch out for strangers (NLW Mss, Radnorshire QS, Order Book 2). In London a revival of the ideas promoted by the Fieldings was demanded:

> Our gangs of thieves are grown too numerous, and the individuals which compose them too desperate and dangerous, to be controuled by the comparatively feeble powers of the private magistrate, or of the common parochial constable . . . [N]othing but active magistrates, who devote their whole time to the one single object of the police – and bands of stout,

able, and resolute officers, whose only business is to execute the warrants of those magistrates – can insure any tolerable quiet to the metropolis and its *environs*.

(Madan, 1785: 133–4)

In 1782 the government decided to deny pardons to robbers, burglars and housebreakers, and the number of people hanged rose to levels not seen before in the eighteenth century. In September 1783 at the Old Bailey 58 people were condemned and a further 24 in the following sessions: 'Two such sessions . . . were hardly never known in London' (Knapp and Baldwin, 1809, vol. 3: 459–61). In all 173 were sentenced to death at the Old Bailey in that year, the highest annual total of the century – a rise of more than 60 per cent on 1782 and more than double the figure for 1750 or 1751. The number who were hanged also increased. Between 1756 and 1781 of those condemned at the Old Bailey on average 29 were hanged each year. Between 1782 and 1787 that figure rose to 65 (Hay, 1975: 513–16; Radzinowicz, 1948–68, vol. 1: 147–8), with almost 100 hanged in 1785 and again in 1787. The percentage of the condemned who were hanged increased from around 30 per cent to about 65 per cent between 1783 and 1785, rising to just over 80 per cent in 1787. This pattern was repeated outside the Old Bailey: for instance, on the Home Circuit (the assizes for the counties around London) the number condemned more than trebled, as did the number executed.

The 'Bloody Code'

During the eighteenth century there was an increase in the number of people condemned to death, but, in spite of what happened in the 1750s and 1780s, the number who were hanged declined when compared with the end of the sixteenth century. In the late sixteenth century one in four of those tried for felony was hanged, by Anne's reign (1702–14) it was about one in ten and the rate generally continued to fall (Jenkins, 1986: 51–71; Sharpe, 1984: 65). A number of explanations for this phenomenon have been advanced: a drop in serious crime; a general dwindling of concern over serious crime; the operation of the benefit of clergy,[2] by which felons could escape execution, and the widening of its application to include women; the manipulation by prosecutors and jurors of the value placed on goods stolen in larceny cases where this defined the distinction between capital and non-capital felonies (for instance, in a shoplifting case, which was a capital offence if the goods stolen were worth five shillings, the jury often found a defendant guilty of taking goods worth four shillings and ten pence); more precision in the rules of criminal procedure and the laws of evidence; a stricter interpretation of capital statutes by judges in cases of ambiguity which made conviction more difficult; and a greater willingness to use the prerogative of mercy, possibly

[handwritten marginal note: DROP IN CRIME LEVELS.]

encouraged after 1718 by the institution of a system for the transportation of offenders which was regarded as providing a suitable alternative punishment (Beattie, 1986; Hay, 1977; Radzinowicz, 1948–68, vol. 1; Sharpe, 1984: 65–70).

This decline in the use of the death penalty seems at odds with the fact that a large number of statutes were enacted after 1688 which created new capital offences (Innes and Styles, 1986: 420–30; Rawlings, 1993):

> Even as late as 1688, despite the exceptionally rigorous laws which had been enacted during the reigns of the Tudors and Stuarts, no more than about fifty offences carried the death penalty ... In the eighteenth century, however, their number began to spectacularly increase.
>
> (Radzinowicz, 1948–68, vol. 1: 4)

Counting how many capital offences were created is difficult because of issues such as whether or not the principal offence also included accessories, but Blackstone estimated that by the 1760s there were 160 capital offences; in 1819 the figure was put at 223, and the modern historian Professor Radzinowicz plumped for 240 (Radzinowicz, 1948–68, vol. 1: 3–8). Radzinowicz is clear that this build up was the result not of a plan, but of a combination of factors: a liberal criminal procedure and a willingness to use the prerogative of mercy reduced the likelihood that an offender would be hanged and, therefore, encouraged Parliament to enact extreme penalties as a deterrent in the knowledge that their use would be limited; the lack of an effective police force or a satisfactory alternative punishment to the death penalty; and a conservatism which led to a reluctance to abolish capital offences. Against this view, Hay (1977) has argued that the eighteenth-century ruling class was primarily concerned to use the gallows to protect not its property but its authority. Having a large number of capital offences gave the gentry the opportunity to demonstrate their grip on the ultimate manifestation of power, the capacity to decide between life and death. This was a calculation which had to be finely judged: to hang too many risked popular outrage; to hang too few meant the message would not get through.

Both Radzinowicz and Hay do agree that the number of new capital offences created in the eighteenth century put the criminal law on to a different level of theoretical severity from previous centuries (even if in practice fewer people were hanged): it was in the eighteenth century, so historians tell us, that the 'Bloody Code' was created. There are several problems with this portrayal. First, there is the complex question of counting the number of capital offences. The general policy was to create narrowly-defined offences. For instance, there was no general act on larceny, such as was enacted in the nineteenth century, just a patchwork of statutes attaching the death penalty to a range of larcenies defined by the thing stolen, or by its value, or by the relationship between the victim and the thief, or by the place where the theft occurred, or by a combination of these: shoplifting goods worth five shillings was capital

(3 & 4 Will. & Mar., c. 9, s. 1), as was stealing property to the value of forty shillings from navigable rivers (24 Geo. II, c. 45), embezzling goods to the same value from an employer (12 Ann., c. 7, s. 1), and stealing sheep, cattle (14 Geo. II, c. 6, s. 1) or deer (9 Geo. I, c. 22, s. 1). Second, the new capital offences were generally built on principles laid down in the sixteenth century (Williams, 1979: 217–52). So, for instance, although new offences were created, the statutes more typically broadened the range of capital larcenies to items of property not previously covered: for instance, stealing horses had long been capital, but eighteenth-century statutes extended that penalty to cattle and sheep. Third, the number of capital laws was inflated by poor drafting. The forgery of an Exchequer bill was made capital by three statutes (3 Geo. I, c. 8, s. 40, 8 Geo. I, c. 20, s. 20 and 2 Geo. II, c. 25, s. 1), but omissions or errors in these had to be corrected by a further three statutes (7 Geo. II, c. 22, s. 21; 31 Geo. II, c. 22, s. 78; 18 Geo. III, c. 18, s. 1). The practice of making legislation only temporary also led to more capital statutes: the Act against Theft and Rapine in the North, originally passed in 1661 (13 & 14 Car. II, c. 22), was renewed six times and only made permanent in 1757 (31 Geo. II, c. 42, s. 1). Fourth, it is worth remembering that comparing the period after 1688 with the period before is bound to give a false impression since the changed constitutional structure meant that Parliament sat more often and for longer periods; it is hardly surprising, therefore, that it passed more legislation. Fifth, some capital offences were repealed: for example, the Witchcraft Act (1 Jac. I, c. 12) in 1736 (9 Geo. II, c. 5), and in 1773 (13 Geo. III, c. 59) the punishment for frauds involving marks on silver and gold plate was changed from death to transportation. Sixth, some legislation which created capital offences also provided for an alternative punishment: in 1745 (18 Geo. II, c. 27) judges were given the discretion to sentence someone who had stolen cloth from the drying grounds to death or to transportation; and in 1753 (26 Geo. II, c. 19) plundering goods from a wreck was made a capital offence, but the prosecutor was given the discretion to prosecute for a non-capital petty larceny if the amount was small (no amount was specified) and there was no violence.[3] Finally, while new offences relating to forgery, cattle theft and riot claimed a number of victims, most of the capital laws enacted in the eighteenth century were never used, and the bulk of those condemned were convicted of offences, such as robbery, housebreaking, burglary, rape and murder, which were capital before 1688.

Historians have also claimed that Parliament gave little or no consideration to capital legislation: according to Radzinowicz, 'It is significant that practically all capital offences were created more or less as a matter of course by a placid and uninterested Parliament. In nine cases out of ten there was no debate and no opposition' (Radzinowicz, 1948–68, vol. 1: 38; Hay, 1977: 20). This suits a major theme in his book that Parliament acted carelessly rather than with cruelty until woken up by the arguments of those reformers who wished to see a reduction in the number of capital offences. However, reports of debates on any subject from the period before 1750 are rare, and the mere fact that a lot of bills on criminal law failed suggests that they were not simply nodded through. The passage of the Waltham Black Act in 1722 illustrates this point. Edward Thompson, having found no reports of debates, wrote of the act, 'At no stage in its passage does there appear to have been debate or serious division; a House prepared to debate for hours a disputed election could find unanimity in creating at a blow some fifty new capital offences' (Thompson, 1977: 21). Yet, there is good reason to suppose that there was a considerable amount of discussion in the Commons. Unusually, a committee of the whole House took two sittings to consider the bill and made several amendments, one of which was rejected by the House; and there was another amendment at the third reading stage. Subsequent events also suggest that the act was controversial, or at least became so: the Tory opposition named the act when calling for 'the redress of specific grievances perpetrated upon the people by the administration since 1714' (Foord, 1964: 34; Lambert, 1975). There is evidence that throughout the eighteenth century backbench MPs took a lively interest in the whole range of social policy, including criminal law (Innes, 1990a), but the majority of bills which they introduced did not pass, and the suggestion that backbenchers could obtain criminal legislation 'for the mere asking' (Hay, 1977: 20) is not accurate. Capital punishment seems to have been seen as usually only appropriate in legislation with a broad national significance and not where merely narrow local issues were involved. Most of the capital laws were introduced by members of the government or by those who had a close link to government, and they were typically concerned with government matters, such as the defence of the realm,[4] the establishment of the succession,[5] and the protection of the revenues and public credit.[6]

Focusing on capital offences also tends to lead to the conclusion that non-capital laws were of little significance, and yet it was far more common for criminal offences created in the eighteenth century to impose a lesser penalty, such as a fine. The Transportation Act 1718 also proved significant. It enabled the courts to transport those convicted of a non-capital felony and those capital felons who had been pardoned. The act was part of a package of measures – including the Riot Act, various treason laws and the Waltham Black Act – drawn up by Robert Walpole's Whig government at a time, following the accession in 1714 of George I, when the security of the Hanoverian succession was by no means certain, although it is also true to say that Walpole saw political advantage in promoting the impression of a country under threat from Tories and Jacobites (supporters of the family of the deposed James II) and criminals. The Transportation Bill was introduced by William Thompson, the Solicitor-General and an Old Bailey judge, and the government provided the finance to make transportation succeed. The act had an immediate impact on sentencing: in Surrey before the act almost 60 per cent of men convicted of non-capital felonies were branded on the thumb and discharged, whereas afterwards almost 60 per cent were transported and less than 9 per cent branded and discharged. It, therefore, bridged the gap between a penalty that was often considered too severe (capital punishment) and one that was thought too light (branding on the thumb or whipping): it 'created a penal system that could never again operate without a centrally dominant secondary punishment' (Beattie, 1986: 502–13).

Debating the 'Bloody Code'

Yet, it is clear that the public hanging played a significant role within the criminal justice system. In spite of the offers of rewards (see Chapter 1), it seems likely that not many of those who committed offences were brought before the courts, and, therefore, it was regarded as important to convey the impression of omnipotence through theatrical displays in the punishment of both petty (whipping, the pillory) and serious offenders (the gallows). However, a debate on the effectiveness of capital punishment had been running throughout the century and was energized by the publication in 1767 of *An Essay of Crimes and Punishments*, a short book by Beccaria, an Italian economist, and by the legal carnage of the 1780s.

Beccaria argued that capital punishment was inefficient in dealing with the problem of crime. It drew attention from the crime to the criminal and by constant repetition prevented any useful lessons being learnt by the spectators because they either sympathized with the condemned or became hardened to suffering. Moreover, the link between the crime and the punishment could not be established in the minds of the public if there was a possibility that those who were convicted might be pardoned, and yet the severity of capital offences meant that the power to pardon was necessary (Beccaria, 1769: 77 and 176; Eden, 1771: 317, 319–20 and 328–31; *Public Advertiser*, 27 Jul. 1768). The answer, therefore, was a punishment less than death involving a longer period of public exposure of the criminal, which would always be invoked and which linked the crime to the punishment. Beccaria rejected transportation and imprisonment because they hid criminals from view, for him the most effective punishment was public labour: 'there is no man, who upon the least reflection, would put in competition the total and perpetual loss of his liberty, with the greatest advantages he could possibly obtain in consequence of a crime' (Beccaria, 1769: 107).[7]

Beccaria's book met with an enthusiastic response across Europe. In Britain *Thoughts on Capital Punishments* appeared in 1770 (Anon., 1770) and in the same year William Meredith proposed to the House of Commons that a select committee be set up to inquire into the criminal laws (*Parliamentary History*, vol. 16, c. 1124–7); the following year William Eden (1771) published his *Principles of Penal Law* and in 1772 Henry Dagge's

Considerations on Criminal Law appeared (Dagge, 1772). Beccaria's book was also criticized, but there was a surprising amount of agreement among the critics about his identification of the key problems. For instance, there was a general attack on the role of discretion in the criminal justice system, particularly the exercise of mercy after conviction, which culminated in the decision of 1782 to deny a pardon to certain types of capital convicts. Martin Madan, who was not a supporter of Beccaria, argued that crime was only likely to be reduced 'when the fears of severe punishment duly operate on the minds of those whom no other consideration can restrain'. He believed that the laws were sufficiently severe, so the reason they were not effective in deterring people from committing crimes was that they were not put into effect. He attacked the use of the pardon: 'it is illegal, arbitrary, and unconstitutional; tending to overturn the true distinction between the *legislative* and *executive* powers'. The proposition that the legislature enacted laws expecting them not to be fully enforced seemed curious to him: it 'appears to me to be giving themselves a very needless *trouble*, which might have been *spared*, by not enacting such Laws at all' (Madan, 1785: appendix, 3, 42n, appendix, 54). In the Commons in 1785 Alderman Townsend agreed, 'it was to no purpose to multiply penal laws if they were not put in force' (*Parliamentary History*, vol. 25, c. 903), and his view was supported in the following year by a petition from the City of London (*Gentleman's Magazine*, 1786: 264). More generally, the societies for the prosecution of felons, which began to appear in large numbers in the 1770s and 1780s, usually made it a condition for reimbursement of expenses that members prosecuted any felon they detected and pressed for the full punishment to be inflicted (Manchester Committee, 1772).

Madan's view was not simply an apologia for the 1782 policy of full enforcement or a response to the work of Beccaria and his English followers, it also amounted to a criticism of those who broadly defended the *status quo*, such as William Blackstone, Edmund Burke and Archdeacon Paley. Blackstone, the first Vinerian Professor of English Law at Oxford University and later a judge, was certainly inspired by Beccaria when writing about criminal law in his enormously influential book *Commentaries on the Laws of England* (1765–9). Unlike Beccaria, he did not denounce the use of capital punishment and he defended the use of the prerogative of mercy, but he did argue that capital punishment should not be attached to 'slight offences' because, 'Where the evil to be prevented is not adequate to the violence of the preventive, a sovereign that thinks seriously can never justify such a law to the dictates of conscience and humanity.' Severe punishments caused people not to prosecute, jurors not to convict and judges to recommend pardons, all of which led offenders to the dangerous expectation that they would never be hanged even if they were caught. Blackstone was forthright in his criticism of Parliament: 'It is a kind of quackery in government, and argues a want of skill, to apply the same universal remedy, the *ultimum supplicium*, to every case of difficulty' (Blackstone, 1795, vol. 4: 10 and 17). Burke, writing in the 1770s, agreed.

He argued against the creation of new capital offences. In part this was an expression of his conservatism; in part it was the more radical proposition that '*capital* punishments are not more certain to prevent Crimes than *inferior* penalties'; and in part it was his opinion that, 'Whenever an inferior offence is once raised to an higher penalty; it becomes a reason for raising all others and on this Analogy all Crimes will become Capital' (Burke, 1996a). Like Blackstone, Burke defended the pardon as a useful instrument of government. For instance, when writing about the treatment of the Gordon rioters in 1780, he argued for the careful selection of whom to execute. First, he thought that many Londoners 'rather approve than blame the principles of the Rioters' and so the government needed to be careful not to aggravate them by 'an injudicious severity' or encourage them by 'weak measures'; so, the number of executions 'ought to be such as will humble; not irritate'. Second, 'it is certain, that a great havock among Criminals hardens rather than subdues the Minds of people inclined to the same Crimes; and therefore fails of answering its purpose as an example'. If the government treats human life with compassion by only executing carefully selected individuals then, Burke argued, potential criminals will value their own lives and not put them at risk. Third, 'the least excess in this way excites a tenderness in the milder sort of people which makes them consider Government in an harsh and odious light' (Burke, 1996b).

The most comprehensive expression of conservative thinking was by Archdeacon William Paley in *Principles of Moral and Political Philosophy* (1785). This was based on lectures he delivered at Cambridge between 1768 and 1776 – that is, shortly after Beccaria's book was first published in Britain, and indeed the chapter on criminal law is entitled 'Of Crimes and Punishments'. While Beccaria argued that punishments should be 'in proportion as they are destructive of the public safety and happiness, and as inducements to commit them are stronger' (Beccaria, 1769: 21), Paley's view was that the punishment should be sufficient to prevent a particular crime in the future and, therefore, should be adjusted to take account of the ease with which an offence could be committed and the difficulty involved in its detection: so because it was hard to detect those who stole cloth from the bleaching grounds or sent anonymous letters it was necessary to make them capital offences. For him having a large number of capital offences worked well since deterrence did not require the execution of all offenders, but only 'a few examples of each kind': 'By this expedient, few actually suffer death, while the dread and danger of it hang over the crimes of many' (Paley, 1833: 161). The use of the pardon was, therefore, essential. Acknowledging that his approach might lead to a high rate of execution, Paley argued it was better than the alternative, a pervasive policing system which would undermine the 'liberties of a free people' (Paley, 1833: 165).

In 1786 Samuel Romilly entered the debate, which was to occupy an important part of the rest of his life, in a pamphlet written primarily as a response to Madan, but which also amounted to a critique of Beccaria and some of his English followers (Romilly, 1786). To Madan increased crime required more executions, to Romilly a high level of executions demonstrated the failure of that approach. He dismissed Madan's argument about the unconstitutionality of the use of the pardon by drawing on Paley's view that Parliament had indicated approval of selective enforcement by failing to take action against it. From Beccaria he took the idea that the need to exercise mercy so frequently proved that Parliament had attached excessive penalties to certain crimes. He did not believe people were deterred by executions for theft: 'they imagine they see revenge sanctified by the legislative, for to what other motive can they ascribe the infliction of the severest penalties for the slightest injuries?' (Romilly, 1786: 31–2). It was the certainty of punishment that was the best deterrent, and so measures were needed to encourage convictions, including reducing penalties where their severity deterred victims from prosecuting and jurors from convicting. He also believed that, while capital punishment was appropriate for crimes such as murder,

> death cannot be inflicted for a mere invasion of property, consistently with reason and justice, nor without a gross violation of the laws of nature, and the precepts of our religion. Between a sum of money and the life of an individual, there is no proportion, or, to speak more accurately, they are incommensurable.
>
> (Romilly, 1786: 25, also 32–4)

Many of the key participants in this debate were, as might be expected, lawyers – Blackstone, Eden, Romilly – and their criticisms emphasized what they saw as the irrational and unsystematic nature of statute law when compared with the rationality of the common law as outlined in Blackstone's *Commentaries*. As Romilly put it, the capital laws 'have been, for the most part, the fruits of no regular design, but of sudden and angry fits of capricious legislators' (Romilly, 1786: 15, also 15–22). Even arch-conservatives, such as Lord Ellenborough, the Lord Chief Justice, found something in this view. In 1803 he piloted through an act (43 Geo. II, c. 58) which, while it created several new capital offences, repealed the Infanticide Act 1624 (21 Jac. I, c. 27). Blackstone had written of this act that it 'savours pretty strongly of severity' in that it reversed the normal burden of proof. Under the act, where a baby was found dead and the mother was unmarried, it was assumed that she was guilty of infanticide unless she could prove that the child had been still born. The statute seemed to have been concerned more with tackling immorality than with infanticide: it was assumed that such women were likely to murder their children to avoid censure and a severe law, it was thought, might resolve the problem by deterring them from having sexual intercourse outside marriage (Malcolmson, 1977). By the mid-1720s it was being disregarded: 'it has of late years been usual with us in England, upon trials for this offence, to require some sort of presumptive evidence that the child was born alive before the other constrained presumption (that the child whose death was concealed had, therefore, been killed by the mother) is admitted to convict the prisoner' (Blackstone, 1795, vol. 4: 197–8; East, 1803, vol. 1: 228; Hoffer and Hull, 1984; Malcolmson, 1977). To lawyers like Ellenborough – who adhered broadly to Paley's line – it was not the harshness of the punishment that offended him, it was that the statute was archaic and irrational when measured against the changes in judge-made criminal procedure and evidence over the previous hundred years or so, changes which imported scientific methods of proof and rendered the 1624 act obnoxious.[8]

The controversy over capital punishment did not, then, consist of two clearly-defined camps divided by their relative assessments of the cruelty of the law. Blackstone was critical of the fact that there were so many capital offences, but was less clear on whether there should be repeals; Romilly was in favour of repealing certain capital laws, but in many respects supported the *status quo*; and Ellenborough did not merely favour continuing the policy of having a large number of capital offences, he wanted more, and yet he also introduced one of the first repeals.

The force of tradition and the political uncertainty of the 1790s drove many of those who had favoured reform towards loyalism and conservatism (see below, Chapter 4; Gatrell, 1994: 237–38 and 321). But a strong, if disparate, opposition had built up by the early nineteenth century of those who believed that the capital laws were ineffective in preventing crime because their severity meant they were not being enforced (victims, it was claimed, were reluctant to prosecute and jurors to convict where the offender might be hanged), of lawyers who sought a more rational and efficient criminal justice system, of political radicals who sought to eradicate the manifestations of aristocratic government (Brewer, 1980), and of Evangelicals and Quakers who believed that individuals could be reformed and who, therefore, supported a penal policy which focused more on the criminal than on deterring prospective offenders. Furthermore, public attention was being drawn to the issues of capital punishment by campaigns concerned with the fairness of the criminal justice system or, as Gatrell (1994) puts it, 'the *casualness of justice*'. These campaigns focused on individual cases. The unprecedented nature of the clamour to save Dr Dodd from death in 1777 showed how much things had changed and laid the background for attacks which were to follow. Dodd was a fashionable London preacher, a patron of the Magdalen Hospital, which 'rescued' prostitutes, and of other charities, and author of *Beauties of Shakespeare*, which remained in print right into the twentieth century, as well as a Beccarianesque tract, *The Frequency of Capital Punishment*, although the distaste which he expressed for capital punishment seems to have been only theoretical for in 1772 he was the chief witness against a robber who was later hanged. Dodd's crime was to have obtained money by means of a forged bond allegedly drawn by the Earl of Chesterfield, to whom he had been a tutor. He was arrested, convicted and condemned. There then began a massive campaign to save his life, but all to no avail, and he was hanged in June 1777 (Howson, 1973; Radzinowicz, 1948–68, vol. 1: 450–72). Dodd's was not an isolated case, several others around that time led to fierce criticism of the criminal justice system: there was, for instance, the execution of Daniel and Robert Perreau for forgery eighteen months earlier on the evidence of Caroline Rudd, who some commentators – but certainly not all – regarded as the instigator of the offence (Anon., 1775a; *cf.* Anon., 1775b); and also the execution of John Donellan in 1781 for the murder of Sir Theodosius Boughton (Anon., 1781a; *cf.* Inge and Webb, 1781. See also, Gatrell, 1994: 328 *et seq.*; Watkins, 1815). These controversies included implicit and even explicit attacks on the use of capital punishment, although they often amounted to arguments that it should not be (or have been) used in a particular case not that it should be abolished for that offence.

It was to restore the credibility of the criminal justice system and to make it more efficient that Robert Peel introduced his reforms of the criminal law when he was Home Secretary in the 1820s. Rather than an enthusiastic abolitionist, he was a pragmatist who wanted to ensure the survival of aristocratic government by removing those capital offences which, because they were rarely used, discredited the criminal law and thereby the system of government of which it was a part. At the same time he proved himself keen to enforce those capital offences which remained (Gatrell, 1994: 568–9).

The spectacle of the public hanging

Looked at in terms of their achievements in the late eighteenth century, those who sought to reduce the number of capital laws seem on first sight to have failed (Hay, 1977). Yet, while few laws were repealed, the debate showed that attitudes had shifted, and from mid-century there were important changes in the organization of capital punishment.

For much of the eighteenth century there had been concern about the impact of the public hanging. In 1752 the *Covent Garden Journal* (18 Jul. 1752), noting that a daring street robbery had taken place the day after eleven people had been hanged at Tyburn, commented that this was 'an Instance of the little Force which such Examples have on the Minds of the Populace'. Equal despair was expressed the year before when Solomon Smith was arrested for picking a pocket 'within seven Yards of the gallows' and in 1748 when a pickpocket was caught at work as the procession to Tyburn passed by (Purland: 189; *Penny London Post*, 22 Jun. 1748). Some blamed the condemned's behaviour at the gallows for this lack of deterrent effect. In 1725 Mandeville was shocked to see them 'either drinking madly, or uttering the vilest Ribaldry, and jeering others, that are less impenitent', with the result that the spectators take away the impression, '*That there is nothing in being hang'd, but a wry Neck, and a wet pair of Breeches*'

(Mandeville, 1725: 19 and 37). In April 1752 the *Covent Garden Journal* (28 Apr. 1752) reported the hanging of five people at Tyburn: one man threw an orange at the constable who had arrested him, joked with the crowd and asked them to protect his body from the anatomists; three of the others behaved in a similar fashion. The newspaper commented, 'No Heroes within the Memory of Man ever met their Fate with more Boldness and Intrepidity, and consequently with more felonious Glory . . . to the great Encouragement of all future Heroes of the same Kind.' Twenty years later a London newspaper was still asking, 'How are we to punish Criminals who fear not Death?' (Purland: 1757).

There were various attempts to resolve this problem. *Hanging, Not Punishment Enough* (Anon., 1701. Also, Ollyffe, 1731; Jones, 1752: 7–14; Philo-Patriae, 1735: 21–2 and 25) suggested torturing people to death by breaking on the wheel, whipping to death or roasting over a slow fire, so that the condemned might be '*made to feel himself die*' and thereby make an appropriate impression on the spectators. The Murder Act 1752 (25 Geo. II, c. 37) did something to meet such suggestions. It aimed to provide 'some further Terror and peculiar Mark of Infamy' and 'to impress a just Horror in the Mind of the Offender, and on the Minds of such as shall be present, of the heinous Crime of Murder' (preamble). The threat of being dissected after death by the surgeons was presumed to be a great aggravation to the penalty: 'Every one knows how great an aversion most people have against being anatomized' (*Gentleman's Magazine*, 1751: 464–5). This seemed confirmed by the efforts to which the condemned and their friends and family had always gone to prevent the surgeons' assistants grabbing a corpse at the gallows for their masters' anatomy classes: in 1750 William Smith begged for money to pay for his burial, 'I cannot refrain from anxiety, when I think how easily this poor body, in my friendless and necessitous condition, may fall into the possession of the surgeons, and perpetuate my disgrace beyond the severity of the law' (Knapp and Baldwin, 1809, vol. 2: 332; *Gentleman's Magazine*, 1750: 426; Linebaugh, 1977).

Yet, in spite of the Murder Act there was generally a shift away from such calls for increased severity by mid-century. Francis Hutcheson in his influential book, *Inquiry into the Original of our Ideas of Beauty and Virtue* (1725), argued that sympathy for the suffering of others was a natural inclination: there is 'a universal determination to benevolence in mankind even toward the most distant part of the species' (Fiering, 1976: 207. Also, Brewer, 1997; Gatrell, 1994; McGowen, 1986, 1987, 1994). It became common to argue that such feelings meant many spectators were disgusted both by the hanging and by the behaviour of the crowd. As one newspaper commented,

> It is impossible . . . for a Man of humane Feelings to view a Procession to the public Place of Execution, without being inspired with a Wish to prevent the Necessity of exhibiting such horrid Spectacles.

> (Purland: 1427)

The Times (24–30 Jun. 1788) led a brief campaign against the burning of women for petty and high treason (men were hanged for these offences) following the burning of the coiner Margaret Sullivan in June 1788. Although the newspaper did not oppose capital punishment for such crimes, it did oppose the method of carrying it out:

> Must not mankind laugh at our long speeches against African slavery – and our fine sentiments on Indian cruelties, when just in the very eye of the Sovereign we roast a female fellow creature alive.

The practice was abolished in 1790 (Campbell, 1984).

It was also claimed that the frequency of executions hardened and degraded the crowd: one newspaper in 1768 attacked 'the Frequency of our Public Executions, when Human Creatures are monthly convey'd to the Gallows, with as little seeming Concern, as if they were so many Oxen fatted and fitted for Slaughter' (*Public Advertiser*, 27 Jul. 1768. Also, Purland: 1370 and 1907). A pamphleteer expressed concern at the failure of the increase in executions after 1748 to stem the crime wave:

> Considering the Number and Frequency of Executions in this Metropolis, the almost infinite Multitudes that resort to these shocking Spectacles, with a kind of unnatural Eagerness, one would be tempted to imagine, that Hanging is become a Sport; and publick Justice executed on the most atrocious Criminals, is looked upon by the Inhabitants of the Cities of *London* and *Westminster*, as a mere pastime . . . [E]ither the Morals of the People are so much debauch'd, and their Hearts so hardened, that they cannot understand the Design of these Wretches being brought to suffer in their Sight; or Executions are become so frequent, that they have lost the Force of Novelty to make them operate on the Minds of the People, according to the wise Intention of the Legislature.
>
> (Anon., 1750a: 2)

But the writer also went on to suggest that, while some spectators became hardened by the spectacle, others regarded the condemned 'with Compassion, Simpathy, and Pity' and 'They condemn the Severity of the Law, than express their Horror at the Crime . . . [I]t has brought Theft, Robbery, Pilfering, and the lowest Vices, into some kind of Repute' (Anon., 1750a: 2 and 3. Also, Anon., 1765a: 19–20). Many feared that criminals were being seen as heroes and heroines, their fame promoted by being exposed on the gallows and in the pages of a newspaper or criminal biography: Jack Sheppard, Dick Turpin, 'the Gentleman Highwayman' James MacLean, 'Sixteen-string' Jack Rann, Mary Young ('Jenny Diver') and 'the Flying Highwayman' William Hawke all became famous. The Rev. Parker, preaching in York after the hanging of John Ryley in 1783, warned, 'To whatever degree you may indulge pity for his distresses, and his family, take care to cherish an equal hatred to his guilty actions' (Parker, 1783: 13). Such views led Henry Fielding (1988b: 169–70; Mandeville, 1725) to suggest that a greater terror might be attached by holding the execution in private since this would avoid the element of familiarity and remove the support of the crowd from the condemned.

In fact, it was events around the gallows that forced the authorities into action. There were confrontations at Tyburn and elsewhere between those who wished to bury the bodies of the hanged and the surgeons' assistants, who wanted them for their masters' anatomy lessons (Linebaugh, 1977; Anon., 1749b: 24; Anon., 1761: 28; Wilson, 1739: 14; *Annual Register*, 1761: 89–90; *Gentleman's Magazine*, 1739: 213; *Penny London Post*, 19 Apr. 1748; *Whitehall Evening Post*, 26 Mar. 1754). These battles were facilitated by the sheriff's men withdrawing once the condemned had been hanged rather than waiting for the customary hour to elapse and then supervising the cutting down of the body. When in 1736 Thomas Reynolds was taken down from the gallows and put in a coffin, he promptly 'thrust back the Lid, and . . . clapt his Hands on the Sides of the Coffin in order to raise himself up'. The authorities had already withdrawn and the crowd was able to prevent the hangman from hanging him again, although efforts at revival ultimately failed (*London Evening Post*, 27 Jul. 1736. Also, *Ordinary of Newgate's Account*, 20–22 Dec. 1738). In the wake of the 1748 crime panic the sheriff, Stephen Janssen, who was in charge of executions at Tyburn, was faced with problems of order maintenance caused by the hanging of large numbers of people – and more particularly of sailors, whose colleagues were famous for their willingness to riot. Janssen decided that his officers should supervise the cutting down of the bodies and their handing over to relatives so that a battle might be avoided (*London Evening Post*, 17 May 1750).[9] Incidentally, this did also enable Janssen to use dissection as a form of aggravated punishment, for instance, to punish those who attempted an escape from Newgate – 'as a Terror to other Offenders' (*General Advertiser*, 24 Mar. 1752).

Janssen's action put an end to the battles over the bodies of the London hanged, but it did not end feelings of sympathy for the condemned and revulsion at the behaviour of the crowd. As a result of these views there were changes in the organization of the hanging in London in the second half of the eighteenth century which reduced the emphasis on its public nature, and meant it largely lost its original purpose as a spectacle and became solely a means of killing people. In 1759 the permanent gallows at Tyburn were removed, and instead a mobile scaffold was erected before each hanging day: the triple tree was, therefore, no longer a constant reminder of the ultimate penalty for crime and of state power (*Whitehall Evening Post*, 4 Oct. 1759; Purland: 874). Next came the abolition of the procession from Newgate to Tyburn in 1783. There was a history of executions being held at other places in London in order to make a deeper impression on spectators: those guilty of offences at sea were hanged at Wapping; a murderer might be hanged near the scene of the crime; seven striking coalheavers were hanged in their own neighbourhood in Sun Tavern Fields, Shadwell in 1768; and in 1769 two silkweavers – Doyle and Valloine – were hanged in the heart of the silkweaving district of Bethnal Green at the request of the employers. By the time of the Gordon Riots rather different considerations were evident: the hangings of 25 rioters were dispersed around London and held on five different days, not to increase their impact, but to reduce the likelihood of any reaction (Linebaugh, 1991: 280–1, 321 and 363–4). Similarly, it was no coincidence that the decision to abolish the procession to Tyburn in 1783 occurred in the midst of the legal massacres which followed the ending of the American War of Independence. It was against this background that the objections of property developers and wealthy residents in the West End of London around Tyburn made an impact: they had complained that the streets became blocked by the crowds of spectators and by workmen building and then removing the mobile gallows. Employers were also annoyed that workers took hanging days off. The switching of the place of execution to outside Newgate prison enhanced the amenities for the wealthy who lived around Tyburn in the West End and meant that the hangings could take place early – usually at 8 a.m. – rather than at midday, so the working day would not be lost. Dr Johnson was aghast at the decision:

> they object that the old method drew together a number of spectators. Sir, executions are intended to draw spectators. If they do not draw spectators, they don't answer their purpose. The old method was most satisfactory to all parties: the public was gratified by the procession: a criminal was supported by it. Why is all this to be swept away?
>
> (Boswell, 1931, vol. 2: 473)

But his view of hanging as a spectacle which should draw a crowd had been discarded. The *Public Advertiser* (11 Dec. 1783) approved the reform in a comment which revealed how much had changed: 'No longer will thoughtless Youth neglect their Employments to attend Tyburn Executions' (*Gentleman's Magazine*, 1783: 1060; *The Times*, 1 Aug. 1788; *Daily Universal Register*, 7 Nov., 9 Nov. 1786; 15 Oct., 15 Dec. 1787, 5 Jan., 7 May 1788).

The trigger for the ending of the procession to Tyburn was the sharp rise in executions in 1783, but the fact that this had not been the outcome of the rise in the 1740s and 1750s shows there had been a shift in the perception of the function of the gallows. Until mid-century the presence of a large crowd was still seen as important, and the main problem was to create the right impression on the spectators; after that time a large crowd came to be seen as a threat to order and the public execution both as criminogenic and as disgusting to the 'Man of humane Feelings'. Tyburn was no longer a place where the state demonstrated its power and the crowd watched in awe. Instead, the spectators were horrified, or gawped with curiosity, or committed the very crimes for which people were hanged, or cheered those who, eschewing repentance, died a 'brave death'. Rather than uniting society, Tyburn became an expression of its division and cruelty.

Although the new form of execution was still in public (and remained so until 1868) and continued to draw large crowds, it took place outside Newgate. Detailed arrangements were made which aimed to keep the condemned out of sight of the crowd for as long as possible and get the hanging over with quickly. The spectators were separated from the condemned by the height of the platform and the presence of officers. The condemned emerged from a hidden passage directly on to the scaffold and were, therefore, not visible until the last moment. They were given time to pray, but were not encouraged to deliver a dying speech. Instead of taking several hours and being played out through the streets of London, the hanging took minutes and was hidden as far as was possible. When Henry Fauntleroy was hanged at Newgate in 1824 it was remarked that,

> The whole of the ceremony was performed with humane dispatch, and from the time of the culprit leaving his cell to the moment when he was launched into eternity, scarcely more than three minutes elapsed. The glimpse which those near the scaffold caught of his face was but momentary. The clergyman stood before him and concealed his person from the gaze of the multitude until he had fallen.
>
> (British Library Broadsheets, 29)

Although the changes which began with Janssen's intervention had brought control of the execution back into the hands of the state, its function as an instrument for teaching the people lessons about state power had been abandoned, or rather the lessons being taught were quite different.

* * * *

The debate on capital punishment was less oppositional than is often supposed. After the mid-eighteenth century there was much common ground between those who wanted to reduce the number of capital offences and those who wanted broadly to retain the *status quo* about the objectives of the criminal law, the need to improve its efficiency in achieving them, and the desirability of presenting 'a more pleasing image of justice' (McGowen, 1983: 96) which was in tune with contemporary attitudes to human suffering and would, therefore, draw greater support for the legal and political order. While there were no substantial repeals of capital statutes in the eighteenth century, by the 1780s it was clear that there had been a change in the perception of the purpose of the gallows. The abolition of the procession and later the reduction in the number of capital offences were expressions of a shift away from the principles which underpinned the 'Bloody Code', and they paved the way for other administrative changes with new agendas, such as the reform of the police and the prisons (McGowen, 1983).

Further reading

An important starting point for further reading is Beccaria's book (1769); in its day it was one of the most influential works to emerge from the

Enlightenment. In terms of historiography, the pioneering work of Sir Leon Radzinowicz (1948–68, vol. 1) has been criticized, however, his book led the field, is packed with information and provided much of the groundwork upon which those who attacked him in the 1970s based their accounts. The most important of these revisionist histories is Hay, Linebaugh, Rule, Thompson and Winslow (1977) and the key essay (if only in terms of the attention which it has received) in that book is Hay (1977). These revisionist histories have themselves since been criticized and revised (Brewer and Styles, 1980: 11–20; Langbein, 1983, whose essay provoked further controversy). While Hay (1977) presents a fascinating discussion of why the 'Bloody Code' was constructed and how it survived, the revision of Radzinowicz's account of reform has been undertaken by McGowen (1983, 1986, 1987, 1988, 1994) and Gatrell (1994). Potter (1993) discusses the role played in debates on capital punishment by the clergy; on the abolition of public executions see also Cooper (1974). Incidentally, reading Radzinowicz, then Hay, then Gatrell (which is the way to do it) reveals a lot about the changing context within which these three historians worked.

Notes

1. These were voluntary associations of people who subscribed a regular sum into a general fund from which, when they were victims of crime, they could claim the costs of tracing and prosecuting the alleged offenders (King, 1989; Philips, 1989).

2. The benefit of clergy was originally a device to save the clergy from being hanged, but had long been generally available to anyone who could prove the ability to read a short passage from the Bible. By the early eighteenth century the requirement that the person be able to read had been virtually dropped and the benefit of clergy became available to all those (including women) convicted of capital crimes, unless legislation had withdrawn the right to plead benefit as increasingly became the case in the eighteenth century.

3. In practice, the judges always had an important influence on whether or not a condemned felon was hanged and also the prosecutor could frame a charge so that it was non-capital.

4. 22 Geo. II, c. 38, one of the statutes on discipline in the armed forces, included some 22 capital offences.

5. For example, the capital offences contained in legislation against those who associated with the deposed James II and his family (the Jacobites): 9 Will. III, c. 1, sections 2, 5 and 7 (correspondence with James II); 3 & 4 Ann., c. 14, sections 1–4 (traitorous correspondence); 17 Geo. II, c. 39, sections 1–2 (correspondence with grandsons of James II); 20 Geo. II, c. 46, sections 1–3 (relating to the Jacobites of the '45). There were also capital offences designed to protect those on the throne and their families, such as, 13 & 14 Will. III, c. 6, section 15; 4 & 5 Ann., c. 8, section 1, 10 and 16; 6 Ann., c. 7, section 10; 5 Geo. III, c. 27, sections 14 and 21.

6. For example, 6 Geo. I, c. 11, *Commons Journals*, xix: 255; 23 Geo. III, c. 70, *Commons Journals*, xxxix: 511, 516 and 702; 25 Geo. III, c. 50, *Commons Journals*, xl: 372 and 374.

7. The Lloyd Committee had suggested that felons be put to hard labour in the dockyards, but its bill was lost (also, Anon., 1754: 26).

8. The changes in procedural and evidential rules and practice included allowing lawyers for both sides, the development of rules on hearsay evidence and the requirements that a confession be both corroborated and voluntary (Beattie, 1986: 113–24, 346, 350, 352–62, 364–74, 378–88, and 395–6; Green, 1985: 267–317; Langbein, 1978, 1983: 96–100; Malcolmson, 1977: 197–8; Shapiro, 1983: 163–93).

9. If no one claimed the body it might still go to the surgeons (*London Evening Post*, 4 Oct. 1750, 26 Mar. 1751).

Chapter 4

Transportation and the New Prisons, 1750–1790

Transportation and its problems

After the Transportation Act 1718 the principal method of disposing of those felons – the majority – who were not hanged was by transportation (Beattie, 1986: 450–519; Ekrich, 1987), but to some contemporaries the crime wave of the 1750s seemed to show that this was failing to deter offenders. It was believed that this was because either the North American colonies were too attractive as a destination, or convicts found it easy to return to England (Rawlings, 1992a: 94–8). Moreover, the colonists were becoming less enthusiastic about receiving the convicts. In any event, the courts were sentencing fewer to transportation by the mid-century, and yet there seemed to be no satisfactory alternative: the Murder Act of 1752 was irrelevant to the large bulk of crime; the Hard Labour Bill proposed by the Lloyd Committee in 1751 had not been passed, probably because its idea of a penal colony in England was regarded as too radical; an experiment with transportation to the coast of West Africa in 1769 had failed, and other possible destinations in Africa and the East Indies had been rejected (Ekrich, 1987: 224–9; Committee on Fielding's Plan, 1770). The issue was eventually forced by the American War of Independence (1775–83).

A few convicts were landed in North America during the war, and as late as 1785 it was hoped that it would continue as a destination (*Commons Journals*, vol. 40, 954–60 and 1160–4). In the meantime solutions had to be found at home, although some convicts were sent to Africa (Ekrich, 1987: 232–7; Shaw, 1966: 45–8). The problem was that local prisons were barely suitable for holding people before trial. The number of prisoners held in them before the war shows how little emphasis was placed on imprisonment and, therefore, how unprepared they were to take on a major role in punishment: according to John Howard's (1777) survey of prisons in England and Wales in the mid-1770s there were only 653 prisoners, of whom almost 60 per cent were debtors, 16 per cent were undergoing punishment for petty crimes and the rest were awaiting trial, execution or transportation (Rule, 1992: 240). Under pressure from county quarter sessions, who, along with the sheriff, were responsible for the gaols, the government began sending felons to the hulks – worn out battleships moored off naval dockyards in the south of England – where they worked either on the docks or dredging out rivers and where, perhaps to reassure the public, they were exposed to view (Hard Labour Act, 1776, 16 Geo. III, c. 43; *London Magazine*, 2 Jul. 1777). This was a key moment in penal policy and administration: although government had spent large sums on transportation since the Transportation Act 1718, it now became involved in the administration of large prisons in this country for the first time, even if, initially, the day-to-day running of the hulks was in the hands of a contractor and nominally under the supervision of the Middlesex Quarter Sessions (Branch Johnson, 1970: 3–4; Holford, 1826).

Workhouses and prisons

Although the hulks were regarded as little more than a convenient solution to a problem which, it was hoped, would be resolved at the end of the war by the resumption of transportation, there was a developing interest in prisons. The enthusiasm with which some embraced them as a means of punishing and reforming offenders did not represent as much of a revolution as has been supposed since there had been interest in the development of workhouses for the poor and houses of correction for vagrants, petty criminals, runaway apprentices and the like since the late seventeenth century.

The political and social uncertainty caused by the revolution of 1688 and by the see-saw of war and peace which followed led to a series of crime panics between 1690 and 1720 that enabled thieftakers like Jonathan Wild to prosper, prompted the establishment of the societies for the reformation of manners, led to the development of transportation and created renewed interest in the possibilities of the workhouses and houses of correction. Although the history of both of these institutions stretches back to the Tudors, it was after John Cary established a workhouse at Bristol in 1696 that interest was revived in their role as a mechanism for reforming those who claimed poor relief. Cary's hope was that the poor would acquire skills which would enable them to find work and would in the meantime produce goods to pay for their own upkeep (Cary, n.d.). A number of other parishes obtained local acts in order to follow Cary's example. Then in 1723 a statute was passed which authorized all parishes to build workhouses, but it placed deterrence above self sufficiency and allowed relief to be withheld from those who refused to enter the workhouse. This reflected the prevailing view that indigence was the result of the poor's disinclination to work and that this required a punitive response. It was claimed that the new workhouses would introduce 'among the Poor, Habits of *Sobriety, Obedience,* and *Industry,* [and would] secure any Parish from an Entail of *Poverty* and *Idleness*' (Anon., 1725: 6). However, there was no compulsion on parishes to build workhouses, and the costs tended to frighten off ratepayers as did the reaction of the poor who resented being treated like criminals (Muskett, 1980; Potter, 1775: 16; Webb, 1922: 141–2).

The debate over workhouses did raise an issue which later became important in the development of the prison, namely, the idea that incarceration presented opportunities to alter the inmate's character. A commentator on workhouses writing in 1732 might have equally been describing the programmes which were still being put forward by prison reformers a hundred years later:

> They may be made, properly speaking, Nurseries of Religion, Virtue, and Industry, by having daily Prayers and the Scriptures constantly read, and poor Children Christianity instructed. And as the *Publick* will certainly receive a Benefit from their Work, so the *Poor* can have no Occasion to complain, because every one has therein *Food* and *Raiment* suitable to their Circumstances; their Dwelling is warm, sweet and cleanly, and all proper Care is taken of them in Age and Sickness. Their reasonable Wants of every kind are supplied; and therefore they ought to be *content* and *thankful,* and do their Duty, that is, all they can do, in that State of Life wherein it has pleased God to place them. It is indeed a Sin for them to murmur and complain or to refuse to work . . . Idleness and Sloth are Immoralities as well as Publick Nuisances: and, as the Apostle commands, They who are guilty of them ought *not to eat, if they will not work.*
>
> (Anon., 1732a: iii–iv)

At the same time as Cary's Bristol workhouse was creating interest and imitators, new houses of correction were being constructed to deal with the roots of crime – idleness, immorality and vagrancy: 'all-purpose places of confinement for people who it was thought should be kept off the streets'. In 1706 courts were empowered to put felons in the house of correction, and, although this did not lead to a wholesale shift towards imprisonment of such offenders, magistrates routinely incarcerated a wide range of people from petty thieves and prostitutes to runaway apprentices and 'suspicious persons' under vagrancy laws (Shoemaker, 1991: 175 and 166–97. Also, Beattie, 1986: 492–500; Innes, 1983). But confidence in the ability of the houses of correction to reduce crime tailed off as crime panics continued into the mid-eighteenth century.

There was less interest among magistrates in prisons than in workhouses or houses of correction simply because their role was narrower: as John Howard had shown, the county gaols were principally filled with debtors and those who were awaiting trial or the execution of a sentence. So, the attempts throughout the century to introduce changes in prisons met with limited success. Legislation in 1670 had sought to separate debtors from felons, and in 1702 a committee of the Society for the Promotion of Christian Knowledge under Thomas Bray recommended, among other things, the segregation of different categories of prisoner (Harding *et al.*, 1985: 99–100; McGowen, 1995: 83). In 1696 and 1701 inquiries were held into the Fleet prison in London and vain attempts made to reduce various abuses, including overcrowding. A parliamentary select committee conducted another investigation into the Fleet and also the Marshalsea prison (London) in 1729, but the blame for the abuse of prisoners was placed on the staff and no substantive reforms were effected. As a result of his experience on that committee, James Oglethorpe, established Georgia as a debtor's colony, although the experiment failed. Some time later, in 1753, he headed another, similarly fruitless, inquiry into the King's Bench prison in London (Harding *et al.*, 1985: 98–102; McConville, 1981: 55). In the 1730s the poor law reformer, William Hay, introduced several bills to promote new prisons and headed a committee which recommended reforms in gaols and houses of correction (Harding *et al.*, 1985: 101). Many others worked hard to stop abuses and overcrowding and to improve the health of prisoners, but the apathy and parsimony of the authorities and the claims of vested interest, such as from the keepers who earned their living by exploiting prisoners, stood in their way.

John Howard and prison building from the 1770s

In the 1770s a coincidence of circumstances – the end of transportation to America and the work of John Howard (1726–90) – raised awareness in imprisonment (Freeman, 1978: 15–51; Whitfield, 1991). Although Howard made no suggestions that could be said to have been really new, he came along at the right time and indulged in a kind of philanthropy which was in tune with the Age of Sympathy and the Age of Reason (Howard, 1958; Ignatieff, 1978: 47–59; McConville, 1981: 84–8; Ramsay, 1977). His interest developed late in life when he was appointed as high sheriff of Bedfordshire in 1773 and, therefore, took on a degree of responsibility for the county's gaols which he found to be in an appalling state. A deeply religious man, he took to his work with a missionary zeal, travelling extensively both at home and abroad – indeed, he died while undertaking a study of the poor in Russia. His great survey of prisons, *The State of the Prisons in England and Wales* (Howard, 1777), expressed the horror he felt at the moral and physical health of prisoners. It also represented an important shift in methodology. Eschewing the purely intellectual approach adopted by Beccaria, Howard sought to justify his conclusions by the presentation of empirical data: he visited prisons, measured the cells, counted the prisoners, noted the fees they had to pay to the gaoler and the diet the poor prisoners received. Nevertheless, his religious beliefs directed his conclusions and pointed him towards the view that an individual could be reformed by being given the opportunity (or forced) to seek her or his own salvation in prison.

Howard's first major ally was Alexander Popham, MP for Taunton. Popham had obtained an act in 1773 permitting justices to appoint a salaried chaplain for county gaols (13 Geo. III, c. 58), and two other statutes in 1774 – on the payment of the fees of prisoners who had been acquitted or discharged (14 Geo. III, c. 20) and on sanitary conditions in prisons (14 Geo. III, c. 59). This last issue was of major concern to Howard. There had been little inclination to do anything about the poor physical conditions endured by prisoners: an act of 1700 (11 & 12 Will. III, c. 19) had allowed magistrates to raise money for rebuilding because, according to the preamble, prisons had become 'prejudicial to the health of prisoners and insufficient for the safe custody of them'. Some new prisons were built, but many counties did not regard this as a priority (Beattie, 1986: 292–4). So most remained in a poor state, and this, along with poor diet, allowed a form of typhus known as gaol fever to kill more prisoners than the gallows (Creighton, 1965: ii, 88–102; Lettsom, 1794; Mason Good, 1795; Whitfield, 1991: 193). The keeper of the Poultry Compter in London noted in 1670 that most gaols were 'so stifled up and subject to annoyances, infection, contagion, sickness and disease' that the justices were reluctant to enter them and even the gaolers were wary of going to some parts of their own prisons (Harding et al., 1985: 99). Things had changed little fifty years later. In 1720 prisoners were 'dying in Newgate like rotten Sheep', and at the Marshalsea prison eight to ten were dying each day in the winter of 1729 from fever and starvation (*Original Weekly Journal*, 30 Apr. 1720; *Commons Journals*, vol. 21, 378. Also, H., 1705). The Ordinaries of Newgate regularly noted the poor health of prisoners – the result of a mixture of disease, bad diet and the conditions – although this interest seems to have been motivated not by any wish to criticize the authorities, but by a desire to explain to a disappointed reading public why they had been unable to extract some juicy confession out of a prisoner for publication. In 1700 John Cooper 'was ill with the Distemper, which is a violent Fever, attended with a delirious Light-headedness, and so was not in a capacity to give any Account of himself' (*Ordinary of Newgate's Account*, 24 May 1700). In 1739 John Adamson was 'miserably poor and nak'd, neither was there any body to relieve him: He seem'd to me to be foolish, or a little craz'd'. In 1740 Thomas Hawkins was:

> lame of his Legs, which Lameness after Conviction increased till his Irons were taken off, then he fell sick and feverish, and at Times was out of his Senses; he was very poor and naked, and his Cell became so loathsome, by Reason of his illness and nastiness, that one cou'd scarce go within the Door.

At the same time William Morris was so ill that he could not walk, but he had been sentenced to hang and so was carried into the cart for the journey to Tyburn. In March 1740 the Ordinary noted that of the 31 condemned prisoners, nine became sick, of whom two died. In 1741 the Ordinary found that Mary Harris had gone blind, and that John Dean's 'Feet and Legs, through nakedness and cold, swelled so, that he was not able to walk'. In April 1742 all eight condemned prisoners were 'very much Subject to Illness' (*Ordinary of Newgate's Account,* 14 Mar. 1739: 6, 18 Mar. 1740, 13 Feb. 1740: 5 and 19, 16 Sept. 1741: 7, 13 Jan. 1741/2, Part I: 4–5, 12 Jul. 1742: 4, 12 Jun. 1742: 5). The situation was no better outside London. At the Surrey county prison in Southwark at least eight prisoners died each year between 1721 and 1740; this rose to 40 a year between 1740 and 1742 as a result of gaol fever and an increase in bread prices which reduced the amount of food the fixed prison allowance would buy (Beattie, 1986: 301–6).

Local authorities were reluctant to spend money on measures to improve the health of prisoners. It was only when gaol fever spread outside Newgate, killing some judges, lawyers and jurors at the Old Bailey in 1750 that any real interest was shown in conditions at the prison – the fact that 62 prisoners had died that year went unnoticed. Yet even then the authorities did not rebuild the prison, they merely improved the ventilation (Beattie, 1986: 304; Evans, 1982; Harding *et al.,* 1985: 93–6). This did not end the problems: in 1767 the *Gentleman's Magazine* (1767: 340) attacked 'the horrid neglects of gaolers, and even of sheriffs and magistrates whose office it is to compel gaolers . . . to do their duty'. The report of a select committee of 1774, before whom Howard had made an impressive appearance, led to the Health of Prisoners Act 1774 (14 Geo. III, c. 59) which authorized the construction of ventilation schemes, baths and sick rooms, the regular cleaning of the prison, and visits by a surgeon. However, it fell short of the rebuilding which Howard urged.

What really concerned contemporary commentators was often less the physical health of the prisoners than the internal order of the prisons. It was by linking together issues of discipline, security and health at a time when alternatives to transportation were being sought (both because of a concern about its effectiveness and because of the American War) that reformers like Howard were able to make headway. In 1725 Mandeville had complained of the anarchic state of prisons:

> The licentiousness of the place is abominable, and there are no low jests so filthy, no maxims so destructive to good manners or expressions so vile and profane, but what are utter'd there with applause, and repeated with impunity. They eat and drink what they can purchase, everybody has admittance to them, and they are debarr'd nothing but going out. Their most serious hours they spend in mock tryals, and instructing one another in cross questions, to confound witnesses; and all the strategies and evasions that can be of service, to elude the charge that shall be made against them.
>
> (Mandeville, 1725)

Underpinning this account is Mandeville's concern at the existence of a vigorous tradition of self governance among the prisoners which was facilitated by the actions of the keepers, who, as private contractors, had an interest both in keeping down the costs of policing the prison and in selling privileges to prisoners, such as a better cell, food, drink and access to visitors (Innes, 1980; Sheehan, 1977).

The neglect of the fabric of prisons created security problems. Although local authorities had to maintain the building, responsibility for escapes lay with the keepers, even if they were the result of disrepair. For the keeper often the only solution was to put prisoners in chains. The escapes of John Sheppard in 1724 illustrate the difficulties. The keepers of the New Prison complained on at least five occasions between 1720 and 1725 about the state of the building. Nothing was done and Sheppard escaped in 1724. He later broke out of Newgate prison which was also in a poor state of repair. Its keeper, William Pitt, had already been prosecuted over the escape of Jacobites in 1717, and so he advertised a reward of 20 guineas for Sheppard's recapture. When Sheppard was retaken Pitt loaded him with chains which were bolted to the floor – even so Sheppard managed one further escape (Rawlings, 1992a: 71 and 73; Sheehan, 1975; Beattie, 1986: 296–8).

The Penitentiary Act 1779

The halting of transportation and the search for alternatives provided the chance to put some of the suggestions made by Howard and others into effect. The Penitentiary Act 1779 (19 Geo. III, c. 74) was the opportunity to work with a blank canvas. This act was promoted by Howard, Blackstone and Eden, and drew on the experience of foreign institutions, such as the *Spinhuis* in Amsterdam and the *Maison de Force* in Ghent. Section 5 attacked transportation and then summed up the programme which many prison reformers were to pursue over the next two hundred years:

> if many Offenders, convicted of Crimes for which Transportation hath been usually inflicted, were ordered to solitary Imprisonment, accompanied by well regulated labour, and religious Instruction, it might be the means, under Providence, not only of deterring others from the Commission of the like Crimes, but also of reforming the Individuals and inuring them to Habits of Industry.

There were to be two penitentiaries – one for men and one for women – run by salaried officers and subject to a committee of supervisors. The prisoners were to be put to labour 'of the hardest and most servile Kind', which made the hope that costs would be met out of that labour unrealistic. Prisoners would, so far as possible, be separated while at work and sleep in a solitary cell, and they would wear uniforms 'as well to humiliate the Wearers as to facilitate Discovery in case of Escapes'. They were to be rewarded for good behaviour and punished for bad through a system of grading, payment and remission. The penitentiary was, therefore, seen not just as a place for separating prisoners to secure good health and to prevent moral contamination, it was also a means of achieving an improvement in the morals of the prisoners and of deterring others from crime (Smith, 1778: 103–5).

In the end no penitentiary was built. Blackstone complained that the act did not resemble the original proposal, but more disastrous was the quarrelling among the commissioners appointed to build the prison. By the time the death of one commissioner, Fothergill, and the resignation of another, Howard, had resolved these squabbles, the government had lost enthusiasm because of the projected cost (Semple, 1993). From its point of view the most pressing problem was not the moralization of prisoners, but prison overcrowding caused by the loss of the penal colonies. However, this was regarded as only a short-term problem that would be resolved by the recommencement of transportation, which in spite of criticism still had the advantage of removing offenders from England. In the meantime the hulks seemed a satisfactory and cheap expedient. In 1784 the Penitentiary Act was allowed to expire, while legislation, to continue the imprisonment of convicts on the hulks was passed and the power to transport renewed (24 Geo. III, sess. 2, c. 56; Blackstone, 1795, vol. 4: 371–2; Ignatieff, 1978: 93–6; Commons Journals, vol. 39: 1040–6; Smith, 1778: 103–5; Ekrich, 1987: 232–7; McConville, 1981: 107–8).[1] But problems with the hulks became public by 1785 when Mansfield, the Lord Chief Justice, was alarmed to receive a report which revealed overcrowding and insufficient work for the convicts, and also that the county gaols were still full of prisoners waiting to be transferred to the hulks (Gentleman's Magazine, vol. 55: 916–7). The hulks were shown to have appallingly high mortality rates, and in 1786 a riot on a hulk moored at Portsmouth ended only after eight prisoners had been shot dead and another 36 wounded (Commons Journals, vol. 36: 926–32, vol. 37: 306–15; Beattie, 1986: 593; Gentleman's Magazine, vol. 56: 260). These problems together with the work of Howard and others maintained interest in the possibilities offered by carefully designed prisons.

Local enthusiasm for prison building

The criticism of prisons in the 1770s and the need for more accommodation did prompt some local authorities to rebuild along lines which were close to those set out in the Penitentiary Act: Josiah Dornford declared in 1785 that 'Were our prisons new modelled, it would be one considerable step toward reform of the lower orders of the people' (McGowen, 1995: 85. Also Hanway, 1776). An attack by Howard on the Sussex prisons in 1774 had produced action because of the enthusiasm of one of the magistrates for the county, the Duke of Richmond. He initiated the building of a new county prison at Horsham in 1775 (completed in 1779) which, it was hoped, would achieve an improvement in the health and morals of prisoners through a combination of architecture (the physical separation of different categories of prisoner) and inspection (a salaried gaoler was required to meet criteria set by the justices). Another new prison was built at Gloucester (under 25 Geo. III, c. 10). It was started in 1785 and opened in 1791, and, as in Sussex, was the brainchild of an enthusiastic and powerful individual, Sir George Onesiphorous Paul (1746–1820). Like Howard, he became interested in prisons after his appointment as high sheriff, but, unlike Howard, he was able to turn his enthusiasm into grim reality (Whiting, 1975). Gloucester exemplified the effort to combine security, physical health, reformation of character and terror. Kid Wake, a Gosport bookbinder imprisoned in 1795 for shouting 'No George, no war' at the king, gave a flavour of the regime:

> I was taken to the bath; and, being stripped of all my clothes, compelled to put on the parti-coloured dress of a convicted felon. My head was shaved; an iron ring put around my leg; and I was shut into my solitary cell.
> (Wake, 1801: 9)[2]

Although a limited amount of association was allowed, solitary confinement formed the core of the regime. The belief was that this would be terrifying, and, therefore, a deterrent; that it would reform prisoners by forcing them to face up to their crimes; and that it would prevent moral and physical contagion. Encouraged by general powers in the Gaol Acts 1784 and 1791, a number of local authorities followed the examples of Sussex and Gloucester by building new prisons in the 1780s: in all, 42 new gaols and houses of correction were built between 1779 and 1787, many designed by Howard's friend William Blackburn (Cooper, 1981; Evans, 1982; Semple, 1993: 98).

It is tempting to focus on these new prisons, but prison reform was still a matter for local authorities and many remained unenthusiastic. Backbenchers did initiate enabling legislation, such as the Gilbert Act of 1782 (22 Geo. III, c. 64), which empowered local authorities to rebuild houses of correction on the new principles of supervision and classification. However, that act was permissive, and, although Sussex used it to reconstruct their house of correction at Petworth, few other authorities seem to have taken up this opportunity (McConville, 1981: 92–5). Justices, who already faced a mountain of administrative regulation, were, perhaps, not keen to increase their workload, or were more worried about the cost of a new building than the physical or moral condition of the prisoners. There was the conflict with the sheriff's role in the administration of prisons: while the justices controlled the houses of correction and had important powers in relation to the building and organization of county prisons, the sheriff was the authority for the prisons and he appointed the gaoler (Harding *et al.*, 1985: 96–8). There was also the gaoler who typically paid for the office and was in effect self-employed, living off fees and the sale of privileges to prisoners. The office was a form of property and as such there was a reluctance to interfere: the House of Lords, for example, refused to pass a bill that would have reduced overcrowding in the King's Bench prison because it would have affected the income of the officers (Harding *et al.*, 1985: 101). So, while Howard may have been disappointed to find that, in spite of having sent copies of Popham's 1774 acts to every county gaol, only 15 out of 130 had implemented them, but he surely cannot have been surprised (McConville, 1981: 88). Even at the height of the post-war crime panic in the mid-1780s with prisons filling up and their poor conditions becoming even more obvious, the reforming authorities remained in the minority (Evans, 1982: 135–87). The assumption was that transportation would soon be resumed and that, in any case, the punishment of felons was a problem for central government. The use of the hulks and the landing of convicts in Australia from 1788 suggests that government agreed.

To read descriptions of prisons at the end of the eighteenth century, it seemed as though little had changed. Newgate remained notorious: in 1781 it was described as 'the horrible prison of Newgate: a building so contracted, loathsome, and dark, that it baffles all description' (Anon., 1781b: 12). Many local authorities simply maintained the fabric of the buildings, although some did not even manage that much, and if changes became unavoidable, they often did only the minimum necessary. When in 1790 Radnorshire Quarter Sessions decided that a new house of correction was required, they ordered the conversion of an existing building (Harding *et al.*, 1985: 124). Even Howard's own county of Bedfordshire delayed rebuilding until 1797 with the new prison opening in 1801 – eleven years after his death. But reforming counties did not always get it right. Dorset rebuilt its prison in 1783, but Howard was so scathing in his criticism of the new building that the justices started again (McGowen, 1995: 91).

Yet, this view of magistrates should not be taken too far. Landau has shown that during the eighteenth century they were becoming less paternal and more patrician: 'He was less the "natural leader" of his neighbourhood and more its administrator' (Landau, 1984: 359. Also Davey, 1994: 110–19). This detachment and heightened sense of professionalism undoubtedly had an impact. At the end of the eighteenth and the beginning of the nineteenth centuries a good deal of legislation was passed enabling magistrates to take greater control over the prisons and to reform them. Of course, such legislation could be – and was – ignored, but it was passed by gentlemen in Parliament who were from the same social class and shared the same values as the magistrates – indeed, they were usually magistrates themselves – and we should treat with caution the remarks of zealous reformers such as Sir George Onesiphorous Paul, who wrote of the prison legislation, 'I have reason to think that in no one county of England have the powers of the three acts of the 22nd, the 24th and the

31st George III, been fully carried into effect' (McConville, 1981: 223–4). New prisons were certainly built and some enthusiastic magistrates did lavish large sums of money on them. Other benches, it is true, did little or nothing. Most fell between these two positions, stopping short of major rebuilding programmes, but beginning to use the powers given to them. The changes at the end of the eighteenth and the start of the nine-teenth centuries were as much about subtle shifts in the way in which magistrates, generally, viewed their role in prison administration as about the building work which they did or did not undertake. An indication of this is that by the early nineteenth century the inviolability of the keeper's domain was given less emphasis as magistrates saw intervention in the prisons as a natural part of their work.

*   *   *   *

The view that in 1800, while ideas about reforming the criminal justice system were being debated, little real change had occurred is untenable. Certainly, people were still hanged and whipped in public, and the large-scale repeal of capital laws lay in the future, as did the use of imprison-ment as the principal form of punishment for serious offenders; moreover, victims, unpaid officials and local communities remained at the heart of the criminal justice system. Yet change had been taking place through-out the eighteenth century. The development of transportation, houses of correction and prisons created alternative punishments for a range of offenders that were acceptable to magistrates, prosecutors and juries, and they sat alongside efforts to encourage the pursuit of offenders through rewards, awards of costs to prosecutors and the reorganization of the police. Yet this was not a smooth, continuous change. The enthusiasm for new ideas was likely to dwindle during wars, when crime was perceived to be less of a problem and when there existed the easy option of putting trouble-some young men into the army or navy (Conway, 1985; Radzinowicz, 1948–68, vol. 4: 79–104), only to revive during peace, or because an enthusiastic and powerful magistrate joined the bench.

While individuals like John Fielding and John Howard were import-ant, the opportunity they got to promote their ideas reflects the growing administrative capabilities of the local and central state. Significantly, up until the mid-eighteenth century reformers had tended to focus on fairly narrow issues, such as the inquiry into the abuses at the Fleet and Marshalsea prisons in 1729, whereas by the late eighteenth century they were more willing to see problems and solutions in broader terms, as, for instance, in Howard's *State of the Prisons*, or the Gaol Acts of 1784 and 1791. But, although the central state was increasingly becoming involved in certain aspects of the criminal justice system – such as funding trans-portation, rewards, the hulks and the Bow Street experiments – this was not regarded as inevitably leading to the elimination of the local author-ity's role; such an idea, had it been suggested, would have met with fierce resistance on account of its cost and its interference in the autonomy of local authorities.

Further reading

The only history of prisons from the medieval to the modern period is Harding, Hines, Ireland and Rawlings (1985), although Morris and Rothman (1995) is a valuable collection of essays on prison history which looks across international borders (also Spierenberg, 1991). McConville (1981) provides a comprehensive account of prisons in the eighteenth and nineteenth centuries, and that work usefully supplements and restrains the more thematic treatment by Ignatieff (1978) – Ignatieff (1983) has also provided a critique of his own work. Dobash, Dobash and Gutteridge (1986) correct the assumption that the treatment of men and women in prisons was essentially the same, although the book is stronger on the period after 1800 than before. Foucault (1977) uses a broad discussion of punishment in Europe during this period as a launch pad for his work on power and knowledge – however, his grasp of history is often rather wobbly (Garland, 1985). Evans (1982) has written an encyclopedic study of the important connection between architecture and prison discipline that began to emerge in the late eighteenth century and which reached its zenith with Pentonville in 1842. The history of transportation to North America is discussed in Ekrich (1987), and Branch Johnson (1970) provides the only history of the hulks. The most obvious need is for a thorough history of the prison before the 1770s along the lines of the fine studies of the King's Bench prison and the bridewells by Innes (1980, 1983).

Notes

1. For a critique see the letter from 'J.H.' (John Howard?) in *Public Advertiser*, 1 Jan. 1784.

2. Twenty years later, Elizabeth Fry was to express her view that the cutting of women prisoners' hair was useful in establishing 'that humiliation of spirit, which, for persons so circumstanced, is an indispensable step to improvement and reformation' (Dobash, Dobash and Gutteridge, 1986: 54).

Chapter 5

Establishing a New Police, 1792–1856

Radicalism, reform and the free market

By the late eighteenth century the criminal justice system was changing, but there were countervailing forces of conservatism. Among some the French Revolution (1789) encouraged the hope of a new dawn in civilization, but this waned as Revolution turned to Terror in France, and in truth among the English, loyalism seems to have been more commonplace than radicalism. Nevertheless, the fear of radicalism was magnified by the outbreak of the French Wars (1793–1815), and by periodic food shortages and economic slumps which stretched into the immediate postwar years and which found expression in a confusing mixture of protests, some motivated by economic demands (cheaper food, better wages, job security), some by the desire for political reform and many by a mixture of the two: there were food riots, particularly in 1795–6 and in 1800–1; the Luddites protested in the midlands and the north between 1811 and 1818, by, among other things, breaking machinery; there were demonstrations against the Corn Law Bill 1815, a measure which, it was believed, would keep food prices high; in 1816 agricultural workers in East Anglia rose up in the 'Bread and Blood' riots and there were riots in Spa Fields, London in the same year; in 1817 the Hampden Clubs, which promoted political reform, presented a national petition to Parliament demanding manhood suffrage, secret ballots and annual parliaments; in that year also the Blanketeers marched from Manchester to demand parliamentary reform, and there were risings in Huddersfield and the midlands; mass meetings were held in 1816–9 at which peaceful crowds met to demand political reform, such as that at St Peter's Fields in Manchester in 1819 which was bloodily broken up and ironically named 'Peterloo'; in 1820 the Cato Street conspirators plotted to assasinate the cabinet, and there were riots among the distressed weavers in Glasgow and woollen workers in the West Riding; in 1820–1 London was in turmoil over the treatment of Queen Caroline. Perhaps, not suprisingly governments throughout this period were ready to see conspiracies everywhere. Troops were poured into the north and the size of the yeomanry was almost doubled (Palmer, 1988: 189–90). A maze of statutes was enacted making it treason to speak or write against the constitution, restricting the right to hold meetings, outlawing the administering of oaths, proscribing certain organizations, censoring newspapers, and periodically suspending habeas corpus. The nervousness of the government and its implacable opposition to reform was particularly evident in the attitude of the mediocre Viscount Sidmouth, who was Home Secretary from 1812 to 1821, and who showed little desire to look much beyond the alarmist reports of government spies (Archer, 1990; Belchem, 1981; Booth, 1977, 1983; Colley, 1992; Hall, 1989; Jones, 1989; Palmer, 1988: 163–92; Randall, 1982; Thompson, 1968; Wells, 1988).

During the food crises when prices rose and consumers rioted, although the paternalism, which had been relatively commonplace in the eighteenth century (such as the establishment by local authorities of mechanisms to keep prices down), was still in evidence, there also emerged new attitudes to these problems. In part, these were fuelled by the apparent failures of the old system of poor relief to resolve the problem of poverty in spite of huge increases in spending – the poor rates trebled in the 25 years to the early 1780s, doubled over the next 20 years and doubled again in the 20 years which followed (Malthus, 1798; Rule, 1992: 24). The new political economists, such as Adam Smith and Thomas Malthus, provided the intellectual justification to those who resented these taxes and who saw poor relief as an expensive way of encouraging indigence by paying the poor for making decisions (such as having a family before they could afford to do so) that locked them into a cycle of deprivation from which they had no incentive to escape. Radical reform of the poor laws was difficult given the social and political tensions of the period. However, changes were evident in moves away from the tradition of protecting food consumers and employees through the regulation of the market. Legislation against forestallers (those who stockpiled food in the expectation that prices would be driven up) was repealed in 1772 as was the Assize of Bread (a mechanism for food price fixing) in 1815. Moreover, Parliament resisted requests from working people to regulate minimum wages, and, indeed, repealed existing wage laws and also the apprenticeship clauses in the Elizabethan Statute of Artificers. In 1799–1800 the Combination Acts were passed placing restrictions on trade unions in general which had previously been applied on an industry-by-industry basis (Rule 1992: 209–13; Thompson, 1968: 543–69). Not all of these measures met with universal approval among the ruling elite. The judges decided that forestalling was an offence at common law, but prosecutions seem to have been rare. And when faced by the reality of unrest, local authorities continued to respond to food crises by regulating the market or providing some kind of subsidy, most famously in the Speenhamland system of 1795, which was a wage supplement linked to the price of bread that drew its name from one of the places at which the practice was adopted. Evidence of a conflict over these issues between some local authorities and central government emerged during the 1800–1 food crisis when the Home Secretary, the Duke of Portland, not only did his best to discourage either assistance to consumers or the regulation of food prices, he also sent troops to deal with food rioters in Oxford, contrary to the wishes of the local magistrates, on the grounds that they constituted, in Portland's words, 'a violent and unjustifiable attack on property' (Thompson, 1993: 250–2 and 279–80; Thwaites, 1991).

The danger of the situation that prevailed in the late eighteenth and early nineteenth centuries was compounded by criticism of government emanating from the increasingly prosperous, and increasingly restless, middling classes. By the 1780s the feeling was growing that the interests of trade were being neglected by an unreformed government which essentially favoured landed interests and whose incompetence seemed self evident after the loss of the American colonies. Trade pressure groups were formed and there was agitation for political and legal reform. Although this did not mean the middling classes favoured extending reforms, such as the vote, to the labouring classes, there was, at least for a short while, apparently common cause between people from these different classes in their support for the radicalism of the French Revolution (Evans, 1983: 70–4). The middling classes largely drew back from this following the execution of King Louis and the outbreak of the French Wars in 1793, but after the wars the enactment of the Corn Law Act 1815 revived resentment because it contravened free market principles and blatantly discriminated in favour of the landed interest by boosting prices. However, fear of crime and disorder after about 1812, especially in manufacturing districts, and the revival of trade by 1820 did cool passions. Moreover, while the Corn Laws continued to rankle, the middling classes welcomed the willingness of government in the 1820s to embrace broadly free trade policies.

Nevertheless, the tensions which might explode into revolution seemed to many never to be far beneath the surface. In 1829 the *Quarterly Review* warned, 'if the social plague of poverty and degradation among the peasantry is not stayed . . . it will inevitably draw after it a strong and dreadful explosion' (Evans, 1983: 146). The failure of the harvest that year led to high bread prices in 1830, there was a downswing in trade with its accompanying choruses of unemployment and wage cuts, and pressure for parliamentary reform rumbled on among the middling classes. The revolutionary spirit which was scything its way through Europe in 1830 threatened to cut through England when the Swing Riots broke out among agricultural workers in the south and east. The government responded savagely, hanging nineteen and transporting 481 to Australia (Hobsbawm and Rude, 1973: 265–7. Also, Reaney, 1970). But the threat of revolution encouraged parliamentary reform, although it was also bound up with the unfavourable reaction of Ultra-Tories to Catholic emancipation in Ireland. The riots which were sparked by the rejection of the first Reform Bill

(Citizen, 1832) enabled the government to force through a second bill in 1832. Reform went some way towards placating the middling classes and preventing the possibility of an alliance with the labouring classes, thereby ensuring the survival of aristocratic government, albeit in a modified form. Indeed, in the 1830s and 1840s when the Chartists sought the vote for all adult men, the middling classes were not just unenthusiastic about the idea, they rushed to join the special constabulary.

The long war, popular radicalism, economic changes and demographic growth did encourage greater efficiency in government (including local government). The broader base of parliamentary representation led to the translation of some aspects of bourgeois thinking into social reforms. Such reform was also being pressed by the Evangelicals. This religious movement, while critical of various aspects of aristocratic government, was itself based on wide support from the political and economic elite, and had at the heart of its agenda the objectives of moralization and spiritual regeneration (Innes, 1990b). Governments took on limited programmes of reform in order to control its impact: for instance, Robert Peel, when Home Secretary in the 1820s, headed off criticism of the criminal justice system by a programme of reducing the number of capital offences, although he rigidly enforced those that were left (Gatrell, 1994). Social reform was also increasingly conducted by business-like and government-directed inquiries rather than by individual enthusiasts, and from the 1830s these inquiries tended to rest their conclusions on large amounts of oral evidence and data gathered through questionnaires. Although this information was often carefully deployed in the final report so as to support particular policies, such an approach gave the appearance of an apolitical, rational, scientific and bureaucratic process whose objective was an efficient system of administration.

Ideas about crime in the early nineteenth century

Statistics became an increasingly important part of any inquiry into crime or proposal for reform. The indefatigable Patrick Colquhoun, a Glasgow merchant who became a Middlesex stipendiary magistrate, wrote two influential books on crime, *A Treatise on the Police of the Metropolis* (1st edn 1797) and *A Treatise on the Commerce and Police of the River Thames* (1800), both of which relied heavily on statistics – although his methodology is often obscure and his accuracy open to doubt (e.g. Colquhoun, 1806: 341). Then in 1805 government-collected crime statistics were published, although this was a one-off chiefly concerned with the use of the death penalty. It was only in 1810 that criminal statistics began to be published annually. That series ended in 1818 (brief tables were published in 1819 and 1822 and fuller statistics in 1825), only to be revived in 1827 in a very generalized form with more detailed figures appearing from 1834

(Radzinowicz and Hood, 1986: 91–112). Whereas Colquhoun's statistics presented a static picture, the regular publication of criminal statistics seemed to show that crime was increasing rapidly. These figures also had another effect. Aside from personal knowledge, the only source of information in the eighteenth century about crime had been newspaper reports of incidents and the publication of the trials and biographies of individual criminals. The statistics of the nineteenth century presented crime as a mass phenomenon and, therefore, as even more frightening. Added to these impressions was the view, pressed by Howard and his followers, that criminality was a contagion that could, like gaol fever, be passed on easily. It all created an alarming picture of society apparently on the verge of moral collapse: crime became, as Martin Weiner (1990: 11) has argued, 'a central metaphor of disorder and loss of control in all spheres of life'. Crime was no longer just an individual or local issue, it was a national problem. This suggested a role for central government, although in the early nineteenth century it was by no means clear what that might be. During the first thirty years of the nineteenth century interventionism became commonplace across a range of social policy (Roberts, 1969) as a significant shift occurred from eighteenth-century views of central government as a threat to liberty and from the prioritization of the individual over the state. Both because it was able to provide a national overview and because it could fund and coordinate a national response, central government now represented a potential source of protection for individuals rather than of oppression, and liberty, instead of being defined in the language of rights and freedoms from government intervention, was to be guaranteed by the state's protection of property (Gatrell, 1990).

Views about the roots of crime had not greatly changed since the eighteenth century. The blame was still primarily placed on the shoulders of the poor, although there was some willingness to acknowledge the problems which they faced. A select committee in 1817 reported that boys got involved in crime as the result of parental neglect, poor education, lack of employment, gambling and sabbath breaking, but added that, 'All these may be considered as the principal incitements to crime, impelled into extraordinary action, during the last few years, by an increased population, and by the distresses among the lower orders, arising from the want of employment' (Committee on the State of the Police, 1817b: 327; also, 1818: 32; Select Committee on the Police, 1828: 7). While Jeremy Bentham thought criminal statistics might provide a moral barometer, in vain the radical John Wade cautioned in 1833 against reading too much into them:

It would be . . . erroneous . . . to infer that our national character has depreciated in consequence of the increase of metropolitan and manufacturing wealth and population . . . The truth, is that both virtues and crimes increase with riches, the former I conceive in a faster ration than the latter; unfortunately we have only statistical returns of the evil, not the good deeds of wealthy and civilised communities.

(Jones, 1982: 13–14)

Such caveats were, however, relatively rare and the more influential view was that social problems, including crime and indigence, were symptoms of a natural inclination to immorality and idleness among the labouring classes. So, for instance, Edwin Chadwick, the great apostle of Jeremy Bentham, wrote of crime:

> We find the whole ascribable to one common cause, namely, the temptations of the profit of a career of depredation, as compared with the profits of honest and even well paid industry . . . The notion that any considerable proportion of the crimes against property are caused by blameless poverty or destitution we find disproved at every step.
>
> (Royal Commission, 1839: 67)

While this seemed somewhat like the views of eighteenth-century commentators, the consequences were rather different because of the altered perceptions of the seriousness of the problems of crime and disorder and the threat which they represented in the context of post-1815 politics and society. In the wake of the apparent chaos of that period, the constant need to fall back on the army and the yeomanry, and the rising levels of crime, the criticism that the old criminal justice system was inefficient and ineffectual now made an impression.

Colquhoun (1806: 311–14) argued that,

> Offences of every description have their origin in the vicious and immoral habits of the people, and in the facilities which the state of manners and society, particularly in vulgar life, afford in generating vicious and bad habit.

He regarded the task of moralizing the poor as more important than the detection of crime and reflected this view in the fairly minimal treatment he gave in *A Treatise on the Police of the Metropolis* to the question of establishing a new system of law enforcement officers. But there were significant implications for the criminal justice system. Crime prevention was the great objective and if it was believed that moralization was the best means of achieving that goal, then offenders had to be caught early and educated before they committed more serious crimes. This did not fit with a system which focused on the wishes of the victim.

Reforming the police

As has been seen, the criminal justice system did undergo change in the eighteenth century: in London many of the parishes professionalized their street patrols, information gathering as organized from Bow Street was generally good (Committee on Westminster Nightly Watch, 1812: 4–6), and thieftakers were not confined by parish boundaries. Nevertheless, the thieftakers were largely only interested in offenders whose conviction would bring them a reward, and the fractured nature of the parish watches and their lack of funding had been exposed by events such as the Gordon Riots in 1780 and the crime panic of the mid-1780s (Select Committee on the Nightly Watch, 1812: 39–41). William Pitt had half-heartedly attempted to reorganize the London police in 1785, but failed, partly because of the cost and partly because of the belief that this was an attack on local autonomy and, therefore, on liberty. He had also met with implacable opposition from the City of London, which resented what it saw as an attack on its privileges – the experiment was foisted on Dublin in the following year (Palmer, 1988: 89–92). The next major attempt at reorganization was less ambitious. Taking as its model Bow Street, the Middlesex Justices Act 1792 set up a network of Police Offices in London run by stipendiary magistrates who commanded a small group of professional constables. These officers did not replace the parochial watchmen and constables, nor was the act an attempt to unify policing arrangements, indeed it was more concerned to deal with the problem of finding adequate numbers of able and enthusiastic magistrates to serve in the metropolis. There was no intention to separate the stipendiaries from the local communities in which they worked or to centralize power; however, the lack of suitable local candidates did force the government to appoint outsiders who tended to lack interest in the sort of local affairs that the rest of the magistracy saw as at the core of their work, and this created a distance between them. Then criticism of the handling of the investigation of the murder of seven people in Ratcliffe Highway, East London in December 1811 led the Home Secretary to make it a firm practice to appoint barristers from outside the local community as stipendiaries (Paley, 1989a: 109–11; Radzinowicz, 1948–68, vol. 2: 123–37).

Private police forces were also set up, the most important being the Thames River Police which was formed in 1798 by a group of merchants. But the distinction between private and public forces was fluid: for instance, the Thames River Police was taken over by government in 1800 (Colquhoun, 1800; Palmer, 1988: 144–5) and elsewhere in the country some private forces were later adopted by local ratepayers (Philips, 1989: 131; Storch, 1989: 227–31). But private security forces did not disappear with the spread of the state police: the propertied had their servants, and the warehouse, factory and dockyard owners had their watchmen. Indeed, the spread of private police continued as the state police failed to meet the desire for property protection by concentrating on an agenda which, as will be argued, saw the prevention of crime in terms of the moralization of the poor and the detection of offenders rather than the guarding of property.

By the early nineteenth century there were two models of public policing in London. The first built on the tradition of communal self-policing: here the parish paid for and regulated officers. The second was the stipendiary model of Bow Street and the Middlesex Justices Act which was funded by government and where professional magistrates controlled a small body of officers whose work was not confined to particular parishes. The fact that Peel chose neither model when he set up the Metropolitan Police in 1829 provides an important clue as to his intentions for this force (Palmer, 1988: 164–5).

The proposition that a radical reform in which the parish system – and later the constables attached to the Police Offices – would be abolished did not seem particularly likely in the years running up to 1829. On the other hand, while six select committees between 1812 and 1822 reported their general satisfaction with the parish police arrangements in London and their opposition to radical reform (e.g. Select Committee on the Nightly Watch, 1812: 1), the fact that there were six inquiries suggests a groundswell in favour of change. The problem was that while Sidmouth remained Home Secretary there was little enthusiasm within government. His departure and Peel's appointment in 1822 changed this situation. Driven by his sense of alarm at the ineffectiveness of the civil authorities in dealing with a series of incidents in London culminating in the Queen Caroline Riots of 1820–1, Peel actively pursued an issue which had previously been left to backbenchers and indeed chaired the 1822 committee. There is some danger of redecorating this whole debate in modern colours. The three reports of the Committee on the State of the Police of the Metropolis (1817a, 1817b, 1818) and even the report from the Select Committee on the Police of the Metropolis (1828), which led up to the 1829 reform, were, like Colquhoun's influential books, less concerned with the reorganization of police officers than with the prevention of crime through the moralization of the labouring classes. So, for example, the reports of 1817 and 1818 concentrated on alehouse licensing, the causes of juvenile delinquency and the better management of prisons.

The main argument against a shift from parochial policing lay in the old belief that it would give too much power to central government and so threaten liberty, which was assumed to depend on power remaining in the hands of local authorities; although, in practice, what this often meant was that the parish wished to retain control over expenditure and rates. In 1822 a select committee famously concluded:

> It is difficult to reconcile an effective system of police, with that perfect freedom of action and exemption from interference, which are the great privileges and blessings of society in this country; and Your Committee think that the forfeiture or curtailment of such advantages would be too great a sacrifice for improvements in police, or facilities in detection of crime, however desirable in themselves if abstractedly considered.
>
> (Select Committee on the Police, 1822: 9. Also,
> Committee on the State of the Police, 1818: 32–3)

At the same time, this conclusion was not absolute since the committee was prepared to make an exception in the case of the Bow Street patrols' work of identifying and harassing habitual offenders, and did recommend the funding of a small daytime patrol.

The Metropolitan Police Act 1829

Peel began introducing reforms to the Police Offices as soon as he came to office in 1822, and he remained convinced throughout the 1820s that radical changes were needed to cure the muddle which he saw in London's policing arrangements (Palmer, 1988: 290–4). In 1828 Peel set up another inquiry, and this time it produced the result he wanted. In introducing the Metropolitan Police Bill in April 1829, Peel gave three principal grounds for the establishment of a single police force for London (excluding the City of London) which would be accountable to the Home Secretary. First, he used the criminal statistics to demonstrate that crime was rising and he argued that this increase was due, not to deprivation amongst the poor, but to the depravity of 'trained and hardened profligates' who were encouraged to commit crime by the inefficiency of the parochial police. Second, he contended that the geographical limitations on parochial police forces were anachronistic in the face of criminals who did not confine themselves within such boundaries. Third, he claimed that many parochial watches were inadequate, and those that did have good arrangements merely displaced offenders into less well-policed areas. The logic of this argument was forgotten when it came to excluding the City of London from the measure, but Peel wanted it to creep quietly through Parliament and he was aware of the fate suffered by Pitt's bill (*Parliamentary Debates*, (new series) vol. 21, c. 867–84; Palmer, 1988: 193–217 and 286–93). These arguments were hardly new, but they had a particular strength in 1829. Major reforms were underway, such as, Catholic emancipation in Ireland, pressure for a broader franchise in England which eventually yielded the Reform Act 1832, and the abolition of a large number of capital offences in the 1820s. On the other hand, there was the radicalism and popular disturbances of the preceding twenty years. It all led to support for a balance to reform: 'an attempt to brake the pace of political and social change' (Palmer, 1988: 293–4).

In his speech on the Metropolitan Police Bill Peel did not raise the question of controlling the poor in general, doubtless recognizing that his argument was more likely to succeed if it played on fears about crime by demonstrating that both statistics and anecdotal evidence indicated that the parochial police were unable to cope. However, other evidence suggests that opponents of his plans were right in claiming that Peel was creating a quasi-military force to occupy poor areas (Paley, 1989a). Peel's approach to his job as Home Secretary and to policing in particular was strongly influenced by his work as Chief Secretary for Ireland (1812–18), where he had set up the Peace Preservation Force in 1814 – the Duke of Wellington, who was Prime Minister from 1828–30, had also held that post (Palmer, 1988: 193–217). His Irish experience had made Peel mistrustful of local authorities, and he brought this attitude to his design for the Metropolitan Police: locally-based policing was by its very nature uncoordinated, myopic and vulnerable to the parsimony of the parishes. But his plan was more than simply the product of a dissatisfaction with the parishes. There was plenty in the organization of the new police to justify the view that this was a standing army in all but name. One of the two commissioners put in charge of the new police was an army colonel, Charles Rowan, who had himself been in Ireland, and before his appointment Peel had written, 'It has occurred to me that if there were a military man conversant in the details of the police system in Ireland, he might possibly be usefully employed here' (Ascoli, 1979: 79). There was also the predominance of military men in the senior ranks, the uniforms, the drilling of the officers, the beat system, the hierarchical structure of the force, the rules against socializing with the community policed, the low pay which was intended to attract only men willing to take orders, the attempt to impose a system of rules which limited the discretion of constables, the splitting of the police into divisions which did not coincide with parish boundaries, and the central rather than local control. Although some of these features were present in the old parish watches, put together they seem designed primarily to ensure a disciplined quasi-military force which rejected notions of communal self-policing. Moreover, while Peel focused on crime and the inefficiency of parochial policing in his speech on the bill, he did add that he 'was confident [the new police] would be able to dispense with the necessity of a military force in London, for the preservation of the tranquillity of the metropolis' (*Parliamentary Debates*, new series, vol. 21, c. 883). This was also clearly no detective force. The stipendiary magistrates retained their officers and, although there was no formal separation of duties, it seems to have been accepted that crime detection would be left to them; indeed, the better pay available to such officers (and the rewards they could earn through detection) attracted the best men away from the Metropolitan Police (Emsley, 1991: 28–9). It was only in 1842 that a handful of Metropolitan Police officers was formed into a detective squad and even in the mid-1860s there were only fifteen detectives. This lack of enthusiasm was doubtless encouraged by the Commissioners' awareness of the popular hatred for the spies used by the government against radicals earlier in the century – a hatred which was underlined by the criticism in 1833 that followed the activities at a political rally of Sergeant Popay, an officer in plain clothes (Select Committee on the Petition of Frederick Young, 1833).

Peel did try to counter the impression that this was a standing army: the officers were dressed in a uniform of top hat and tail coat to distinguish them from soldiers, and they were normally armed only with wooden truncheons. Nevertheless, contemporaries were not so easily put off: 'Down with the Raw Lobsters! No Martial Law! No Standing Armies!'[1] chanted one crowd as police officers protected the king during demonstrations in 1830; a newspaper referred to them as 'these military protectors of our civil liberties'; and David Robinson, a High Tory journalist, called them 'The blue army'. The same charge was made when the new police were later established in the provinces: for instance, the perceived connection between the rural police and the desire to press ahead with the radical reforms of the poor law, which were introduced in 1834, led one commentator to claim that the police were 'in effect another standing army – to make the people submit to all the insults and oppressions which government contemplates forcing upon them' (Ignatieff, 1979: 443; Emsley, 1991: 26; Philips, 1980: 155; Jones, 1983: 174).

Once the Metropolitan Police had been set up, their work also betrayed their main purpose. Although used as an occasional riot squad in London and the provinces, the focus was crime prevention: according to instructions issued to officers in 1829,

> The principal object to be obtained is the prevention of crime. To this great end every effort of the police is to be directed. The security of the person and property will thus be better effected than by the detection and punishment of the offender after he has succeeded in committing the crime.
>
> (Weinberger, 1991: 78)

The prevention of crime was to be achieved by the moralization of the labouring classes: as Chadwick, a supporter of the new police put it, they were 'reformers of the rich [sent] to act against the labouring classes' (Paley, 1989a: 119; Storch, 1975, 1976). They were to target deviant individuals ('trained and hardened profligates') and also deviant communities: according to Rowan, 'we look upon it that we are watching St James's and other places while we are watching St Giles and bad places in general' (Select Committee on the Police, 1834). The police used powers of arrest for suspicion, vagrancy, obstruction, drunkenness and so forth under legislation which shifted the burden of proof to the suspect, such as the Vagrancy Act 1824, the Metropolitan Police Act 1839, the Night Poaching Prevention Act 1862 and the legislation on habitual criminals of 1869 and 1871. These powers also focused attention on the streets and, therefore, on the labouring people who lived, worked and played there (Radzinowicz and Hood, 1986, vol. 5: 231–87; Weiner, 1990: 148–51 and 300–6). Such legislation symbolized the way in which control over important aspects of the debate on crime was placed in the hands of the police. The police could show through the arrest statistics that certain people were dangerous, but, because those arrests depended mainly on subjective assessments by officers of what constituted suspicious behaviour, the size and nature of the problem was largely determined by the police themselves.

Spreading the idea of police reform

The Metropolitan Police were generally given support by various select committees after 1829 (Select Committee on the Police, 1834). Criticism over the handling of a demonstration in Cold Bath Fields in 1833, which led to the death of an officer, and, in the same year, over the behaviour of Popay was deflected by, respectively, blaming the organizers of the meeting and depicting Popay as having 'a mistaken view of his instructions' (Select Committee on Cold Bath Fields, 1833; Select Committee on the Petition of Frederick Young, 1833; Thurston, 1967). Peel seems to have intended the Metropolitan Police to be a model for the rest of the country, and when his party was ousted from power the Whigs showed an interest in police reform. Concerned at the Swing Riots of 1830 and the Reform Bill Riots of 1831, Lord Grey's government drafted, but did not introduce, a scheme which would have enabled local authorities to set up a Police Office with a stipendiary magistrate under the ultimate control of the Home Secretary. The problem was that attempting to cater for the possible objections of local authorities proved difficult, and, in any event, once the Reform Act was passed in 1832 the immediate public order problems receded (Philips and Storch, 1994).

It is wrong to imagine that outside London the eighteenth century was stagnant in terms of police reform. So, for instance, the difficulties of finding suitable magistrates to serve in the new manufacturing districts of the midlands and the north led to rotation offices being opened in Manchester and Birmingham in the 1790s, and across the country parish and town police forces were established or reformed. In some areas there was a confusion of forces: up to 1836 Liverpool had three – a day force under the town council, a night watch under the Commissioners of Watch, Scavengers and Lamps, and a dock police under the Dock Committee (Cockcroft, 1974. Also, Joyce, 1993). Moreover, it was not just urban areas that felt the need for change: in Cheshire a new police was introduced in 1829 (10 Geo. IV, c. 97).

Although Grey's comprehensive bill to remodel police forces was never enacted, there was a clear intention that reform should continue. A number of local authorities took advantage of powers created by the Lighting and Watching Act 1833 (3 & 4 Will, IV, c. 90) to set up or reform day and night patrols (Davey, 1983; Storch, 1989: 231–3; Swift, 1988), and the riots after the introduction of the Poor Law Amendment Act 1834 prompted some authorities in East Anglia to form police forces (Storch, 1989: 236–7). The Municipal Corporations Act 1835 required the creation of a new police force in all incorporated boroughs. This force was placed under a watch committee appointed by the elected town council. As with other reformed police forces of the time, the bulk of officers was recruited from the pre-reform police, and this often gave a significant degree of continuity (Emsley, 1991: 41; Swift, 1988. But Joyce, 1993).

While some of these changes, particularly those under the 1835 act, were bound up in local politics and, therefore, led to opposition from factions of the elite, the fear of radicalism, disorder and crime after 1815 had moved most away from that view. This did not mean that all criticisms vanished, but in future they tended to be dominated by issues of cost and local control rather than by the question of whether a reformed police was needed. County benches did not necessarily resist change or regard central government in the same light as their counterparts had done a century before, but they did remain jealous of their own status and ready to resist anything which might undermine their control over expenditure and the work which officers did (Brundage, 1986; Emsley, 1982, 1991: 38–42; Storch, 1989: 236–52).

In 1836 a royal commission was appointed the title of which provides a clear indication of the intention to push ahead with the creation of new police forces and remove the vestiges of parish policing: 'the Commissioners appointed to inquire as to the best means of establishing an efficient Constabulary Force in the counties of England and Wales'. The Chartist movement of the 1830s and 1840s gave such ideas a great impetus: indeed, the fear of Chartist disorder led to the creation of statutory forces in Birmingham, Bolton and Manchester in 1839 (Emsley, 1991: 41). Edwin Chadwick, the main figure behind the Report of the Royal Commission of 1836–9, favoured a centralized scheme, but the other commissioners on the whole opposed the idea, and those elements of centralization which did find their way into the report, such as a Treasury contribution to new forces and a role for Metropolitan Police officers in appointing and training officers, were in the main not present in the act of 1839 which followed. The Royal Commission emphasized the need for a coordinated response to the problems of professional criminals, who observed no geographical boundaries, and of industrial disorder, which, it was claimed, threatened to overwhelm the limited resources available to local forces. Existing arrangements were regarded as inadequate and, in a passage that reveals the nature of the break with the past which post-Peel policing involved, the Report says:

> To give to private individuals the power of determining whether the law shall be enforced or not, is in effect to give them a *veto* on the acts of the legislature, – and to give them more than the power of pardoning, and abandoning to them the prerogative of mercy.
>
> (Royal Commission, 1839: 99)

The 1839 act (amended in 1840) permitted rather than required the creation of new county police forces, and its adoption was patchy with cost typically the key factor. The experience of the police force at Blofield in Norfolk, which was created by private subscription and then regularized under the Lighting and Watching Act 1833, led local magistrates to press successfully for the adoption of the 1839 act in the expectation that this would spread, and, thereby reduce, the cost to their ratepayers (Storch, 1989: 231–2). On the other hand, Surrey magistrates only established a new police force after the murder of a clergyman by burglars in 1850. Moreover, adoption of the act did not necessarily end debate: in Lancashire in 1842 a majority of magistrates voted for the abolition of their new police force, but this did not amount to the two-thirds required by the act and in the end the force was only reduced in size (Emsley, 1982,

1991: 44–6). A general acceptance of the need for reform existed, but many local authorities did not feel the need to shift away from the parish model and, even after the 1839 act, it was not necessary to do so. The Lighting and Watching Act 1833, the Parish Constables Act 1842 (5 & 6 Vic. c. 109) and the Superintending Constables Act 1850 (13 & 14 Vic, c. 20), all allowed reform without changing the essential flavour and control of the old parish forces (Emsley, 1991: 44–9; Foster, 1985).

Nevertheless, pressure for the abolition of forces based on the parish continued and was increased by the revolutions of 1848 in Europe, Chartism and the growing acceptance of the new police by the media (Emsley, 1991: 62–4). The Home Office also adopted a policy, which it did not always implement, of refusing to send assistance to those counties which had not established new police forces and those boroughs whose forces were regarded as inadequate: during the Rebecca riots in 1843 a request from Cardiganshire was turned down leading the magistrates to adopt the 1839 act shortly afterwards (Radzinowicz, 1948–68, vol. 4: 280–3). In 1853 a select committee criticized those police forces which fell short of the 1839 act, but an attempt to enact compulsory legislation failed because it proposed the amalgamation of small boroughs and counties with their larger neighbours. Eventually, a combination of compromise by the government, and general concern about both the consequences of the winding-down of transportation under the Penal Servitude Act 1853 and the ending of the Crimean War in 1856 enabled the enactment of the County and Borough Police Act 1856 (19 & 20 Vic, c. 69). This obliged local authorities to provide a new police force. The Treasury grant promised to these forces eased their acceptance, and it enabled the government to introduce a system of inspection, which could be used to ensure forces were kept up to strength and to maintain a flow of information to the Home Office that assisted the development of its expertise. However, local authorities were slow to concede control of the work which the police did, and there was no immediate desire on the part of the Home Office to make them (Emsley, 1991: 48–54; Foster 1985: 200). Indeed, it seemed entirely logical that, while there might be a place for greater uniformity, on the whole police forces should reflect local conditions as interpreted by the local ruling elite (Brogden, 1982).

Outside large urban areas like London, the new police forces were often small and recruited officers from the old forces. The focus of their work followed the old pattern of reacting to reports of crime rather than moralizing the poor, and, indeed, while officers in large cities like Liverpool and London were given fairly broad statutory powers which – in spite of the efforts of their superiors – enabled them to exercise discretion, their counterparts in the country were much more constrained (Steedman, 1984: 6, 31–2 and 146–7). Colonel Rowan, in a comment which also points to the objectives of his own force, remarked that, unlike the Metropolitan Police, 'a rural police was rather to prevent crime by detecting offenders than to prevent it by their actual presence in every village' (Emsley, 1991:

43), although, in practice crime and immorality were regarded as so intertwined that dealing with one often meant dealing with the other: so, for instance, Horncastle in Lincolnshire reformed its force under the Lighting and Watching Act 1833 following an outbreak of public drunkenness, gaming and prostitution (Davey, 1983; Emsley, 1991: 36; Swift, 1988).

* * * *

The increased emphasis on the broad goals of efficiency and justice in the criminal justice system, the debates over capital punishment in the late eighteenth century, the concern over radicalism, and the revelations of the criminal statistics of the early nineteenth century meant there was less scope for the private concerns of individual victims and provided the basis for attempts to detach police forces from a narrow geographical base. It is also the case that, while the new police emphasized crime prevention, this was not in terms of deterring potential criminals by the certainty of detection, which had been at the core of John Fielding's work (and had been supported by many who criticized the reliance on the death penalty: Romilly, 1786), rather they looked to the moralization of the poor and the continual harassment of those identified as the least moral sections of the poor – the 'trained and hardened profligates', the people of St Giles, the vagrants and the drunks.

Yet, the private prejudices of local authorities jealous to protect their own control over expenditure and place clear limits on the role of the central state meant that, while police reform did spread throughout the country, the possibility that the constitutional structure of the Metropolitan Police might be used elsewhere was hardly considered in spite of the advantages in terms of efficiency it offered. So, the political power of the City of London enabled it to resist inclusion in the 1829 act, and it is significant that Grey's broader scheme for police reform, devised just a few years after the establishment of the Metropolitan Police, was based around the local magistrates, as were the Municipal Corporations Act 1835 and the County and Borough Police Act 1856. Financial control was seen as crucial to maintaining local prestige and power, but it was also seen as logical that taxes raised locally should be spent in ways that local people (or, at least, a section of them) approved. However, central government was concerned to encourage local authorities to reform their police – not least to reduce calls on the assistance of the army. The alarm caused in the 1830s to 1850s by Chartism, the ending of transportation and the prospect of the demobilization of troops following the Crimean War assisted in pressing the case for reform, and the carrot of Treasury money provided a further incentive. Yet, this did not necessarily presage the end of local autonomy, since it was recognized that a uniform approach to policing was not always the most efficient method and that it was proper to have the police reflect local conditions. So, while the instruments for greater central control were being put in place, there was no inevitability about their being used for that purpose, rather than simply as a means of ensuring efficiency.

Further reading

Evans (1983) provides a good political, social and economic history of the period up to the late nineteenth century, as do the various essays in Thompson (1990); Thompson (1968), among other things, illustrates the strength of radicalism in the late eighteenth and early nineteenth centuries, and Hobsbawm and Rude (1973) provide a fascinating study of the Swing Riots of 1830. Roberts (1969) examines the growth of interventionism by central government from the 1830s. The only general history of crime and criminal justice for this period is Emsley (1996). There are plenty of books on the early history of the new police, but most, like Ascoli (1979) and Critchley (1978), while being informative tend to take a police view and to ignore the perspectives of the policed. Emsley's book (1991) is an excellent corrective to this one-dimensionality, while Palmer (1988) provides a very thorough comparative history of the Irish and English police during this period (see also Radzinowicz, 1948–68, vol. 4).

Note

1. The term 'raw lobster' was one of many used to refer to the police: it came from the similarity between the colour of lobsters before they are boiled and the uniforms of the police.

Chapter 6

Prisons, 1790–1877

The controversy over prison reform

By 1800, while most prosecutions were still initiated by victims and the criminal justice system remained essentially in the hands of local authorities, efforts had begun to secure greater efficiency. The pace of change moved rapidly in the first half of the nineteenth century. The reform of the police and the repeal of the bulk of capital offences were followed by attempts to codify the criminal law, the representation of parties by lawyers had become commonplace, the rules on evidence and procedure were being elaborated and the number of textbooks on criminal law had increased from a trickle in the eighteenth century to a torrent by the 1830s (McGowen, 1983; Radzinowicz and Hood, 1986: 723–40; Weiner, 1990: 57–67). Transportation, which had long attracted criticism, was attacked again by the Molesworth Committee of 1837–8 in terms set by this pursuit of efficiency and uniformity (Select Committee on Transportation, 1837–8). The committee did claim it was expensive to administer and detrimental to the Australian economy, but the core of its attack was that equal treatment of convicts was impossible. This made the punishment not just unpredictable and, therefore, cruel, but also ineffective because it meant that no one knew what to expect and so it failed to deter. The committee also believed that habitual offenders welcomed the opportunity transportation gave to meet up with old friends who had preceded them, and that, while some people did dread the prospect of going to Australia, especially those from rural areas who were thought to be particularly attached to their home country, the increase in emigration would soon remove even their foreboding. The report exemplified the rejection of Paley's notion of deterrence based on discretionary enforcement in favour of the principle that people were only deterred if punishments were certain. However, in spite of the committee's criticisms, not everyone was convinced of the wisdom of abolishing transportation: there was concern at the cost of establishing sufficient new prisons and a general apprehension at the prospect of not sending convicts abroad (Hughes, 1988: 485–580).

Putting the abolition of transportation on the agenda was made possible by the development of prisons in which, it was believed, punishment could be precisely controlled and moral regeneration was possible. The Committee on the State of the Police of the Metropolis (1817a, 1817b, 1818) concentrated on prisons, deploring the way poor management and the lack of classification made them 'schools and academies of vice', but concluding that if they were academies of crime it must be possible for them to become academies of morality. As has been seen, the problem was that, although there was a major bout of prison building at the end of the eighteenth century, the costs involved led many local authorities to disregard new ideas and even to neglect fairly basic sanitary standards. The poor conditions were exacerbated and exposed by the crime wave after the peace of 1815. This put pressure on already overstretched prisons: in 1815 Newgate was 'of all places most horrid', in 1818 Tothill Prison in Westminster was said to be not just inadequate but also 'unbecoming and unseemly', and the Fleet prison for debtors was still dangerously overcrowded in 1825, almost a hundred years after Oglethorpe's damning report. The problems of overcrowding and poor conditions had been exacerbated and exposed by the crime wave which followed the peace of 1815. However, the reform agenda had also been continually kept before the public since the late 1770s by Howard's revisions to his original survey and by those who followed in his wake, such as Lord Loughborough (1793), James Nield (1812), Thomas Buxton (1818), J.J. Gurney and Elizabeth Fry (Gurney, 1819).

Even new prisons were subjected to criticism, and the reformers did not go unchallenged. The house of correction at Petworth, which had been in the vanguard of reform in the 1780s, became overcrowded, and in the 1790s radicals, who had been imprisoned in the Gloucester Penitentiary and in the new Coldbath Fields House of Correction, complained about the use of solitary confinement. Gloucester then suffered from the retirement of Sir George Onesiphorous Paul in 1818 and from the post-war economic depression which made it hard to find productive work for the prisoners. The problems at Cold Bath Fields were worse. It had been built according to the Gloucester model in 1794, but soon afterwards its keeper, Aris, sought to increase his earnings by extortion, cuts in diet and overcrowding. The row which followed had as much to do with party politics as it did with conditions in the prison. An inquiry exonerated the prison in 1800, as prison reformers like Paul and Morton Pitt rallied to its defence, but in 1802 it became the central issue in an election battle for Westminster between Sir Francis Burdett, the radical, and William Mainwairing, who was chair of the Middlesex Quarter Sessions which had responsibility for Cold Bath Fields. Burdett won the election and quickly lost interest in the issue. Nevertheless, other inquiries did follow: in 1818 a select committee said that the level of recidivism indicated 'the experiment of a house of correction has here entirely failed' and blamed the poor system of management.

General criticism of the new prisons was also made by conservatives who pointed to the rise in crime as evidence that they were ineffectual. They were unimpressed by the talk of reforming prisoners, for them the point of the prison was to deter people from becoming criminals by punishing those who did. Writing in the 1820s, the Rev. Sydney Smith doubted that the penitentiaries led to a change of character in prisoners, but, in any case, he argued that people were imprisoned '*principally* for a warning to others', so prisons should be 'engines of punishment, and objects of terror'; places not where people could learn a trade, but where the work they did would be 'monotonous, irksome, and dull':

> the present lenity of jails, the education carried on there – the cheerful assemblage of workmen – the indulgence in diet – the shares of earnings enjoyed by prisoners, are one great cause of the astonishingly rapid increase of commitments.

However, Smith was also scathing in his criticism of unreformed prisons where there was disease and convicts were left unemployed and so able to learn more about crime from other prisoners:

> A return to prison should be contemplated with horror – horror, not excited by the ancient filth, disease, and extortion of jails; but by calm, well-regulated, well-watched austerity – by the gloom and sadness wisely and intentionally thrown over such an abode.
>
> (Harding *et al.*, 1985: 136–8)

The pressure for prison regimes to demonstrate the ability to pursue both moral regeneration and deterrence became more intense. The Society for the Improvement of Prison Discipline advocated the monotonous, unproductive labour of the treadwheel in 1818, and the idea was quickly taken up in county gaols – a move doubtless driven more by the post-war crime panic and by arguments along the lines of those made by Smith, rather than the collapse in the demand for prison labour which had helped to undermine the regime at Gloucester (Harding *et al.*, 1985: 138). The broad effect of all these problems and criticisms was, probably, to slow down the building of new penitentiaries by local authorities (Crawford, 1834: 29; Ignatieff, 1978: 105–7; Innes, 1990b: 117–18; McConville, 1981: 95 and 225; Committee on the State of the Police, 1818).

Nevertheless, a strong belief remained that given the right conditions – in terms of architecture – it was possible to reform prisoners. How this might be achieved led to a debate between those who took the view of the Evangelicals that it required 'an effective missionary engagement' involving a virtually uninterrupted exposure to Christian doctrine, and those like Jeremy Bentham who believed that people acted according to a calculation of the likely pleasure and pain which a course of action might entail, so the pleasure to be derived from crime had to be outweighed by the punishment that followed. Initially, the idea of religious reform was dominant, but it lost ground and by the mid-nineteenth century the control of behaviour through rewards and punishments had been adopted in the form of the progressive stage system, according to which prisoners were rewarded for good and punished for bad behaviour. The decentralized nature of the system meant there was no single method of discipline operating in all prisons, and many regarded the complex schemes for reforming prisoners as not suited to the vast bulk of local prisons where inmates served sentences of days or a few weeks. Moreover, there was the problem of staffing the prisons: there were usually too few officers, no training and money was often tight, so the idea of establishing a particular regime was not uppermost in the minds of most prison staff (DeLacy, 1981, 1986). On the other hand, these sorts of constraints led penologists to design prisons in the nineteenth century so that, with the exception of one or two key people (usually, the governor and the chaplain), they required no individual initiative from officers: the disciplinary system was to be designed into the very structure of the building so that the prison became a machine within which both prisoners and staff were forced into particular modes of behaviour.

For the most part, policy was concerned with male prisoners, but the approach taken to women offenders also changed in the nineteenth century. It had been commonplace in the eighteenth century to see women not as criminals but as the causes of crime. Criminal biographies typically portrayed the young apprentice, like John Sheppard, as seduced by a woman from his work into a life of luxury which could only be supported by crime. The eighteenth-century approach was, therefore, to reclaim those deemed to be prostitutes (a term which was often used to include unmarried women in stable relationships) through institutions such as the Magdalen Hospital and fit them for domestic service or family life (Rawlings, 1992a). However, it was also the case that women were regarded, certainly by the nineteenth century, as normally morally superior to men. This, it was argued, accounted for their lower recorded rates of offending, so female offenders were regarded as unusual and abnormal and, therefore, outside the interest of the policy maker. Such women were mad, or evil, or the helpless product of a defective biological constitution. For many policy makers none of these conditions was regarded as treatable. Nevertheless, the belief that a different approach was needed for dealing with women prisoners from that used for men can be seen in the penal reforms introduced by Elizabeth Fry into Newgate from 1816. She took the view that women could be reformed through work, order, education and religious instruction (Buxton, 1818; Dobash, Dobash and Gutteridge, 1986: 41–56; Gurney, 1819; Zedner, 1991: 117–22). As early as 1818 a select committee called for a separate women's prison in London (Committee on the State of the Police, 1818: 19), although it was not until 1852 that the Directorate of Convict Prisons bought Brixton prison for women convict prisoners, followed by Parkhurst in 1863 and Woking in 1869.

The government-funded prisons: Millbank and Pentonville

The failure of the Penitentiary Act 1779 and the resumption of transportation in 1787 (with first convicts arriving in Australia in 1788: Hughes, 1988) had not led to the complete abandonment of the idea of a government-run, convict prison. Jeremy Bentham's own design for a prison, the Panopticon (1787–91), was accepted by government, but then dropped because, according to Bentham, it was too expensive to run both it and the penal colony in New South Wales (Harding *et al.*, 1985: 126–31 and 156; Semple, 1993). The plan was again considered in 1810 by the Holford Committee, which had been appointed to look at the possibility of reviving the idea of a government penitentiary, but to Bentham's intense annoyance it too rejected his plan. In truth the Panopticon had to some extent become an anachronism by the early nineteenth century. At its core was the eighteenth-century idea of deterrence through theatrical spectacle. Bentham wished to encourage people to visit the Panopticon so that a terrifying display might be constructed in the imaginations of visitors without inflicting harm on the prisoners: 'In a well-composed committee of penal law, I know not of a more essential personage than the manager of a theatre' (Harding *et al.*, 1985: 127 and 126–31; Evans, 1982: 195–235; Foucault, 1980; Crawford 1834: 9n). This approach had been largely rejected in the 1780s and 1790s: punishments had not entirely vanished from public view, but they were increasingly being hidden. The visitors who did go into the new prisons were not the people from the labouring classes who had crowded around the gallows, but the gentry and the middle class at play or foreign penal administrators. In the Holford Committee's view deterrence was secondary to moral regeneration and the latter was to be achieved through isolation, religious instruction and work. The committee did take from the Panopticon (but also from the work of the architect, William Blackburn) the importance of detailed planning in both the building and its internal organization. These ideas informed the construction of the Millbank Penitentiary on a boggy site next to the Thames in London which is now occupied by the Tate Gallery. This prison confirmed the commitment of central government to playing a direct role in the administration and financing of penal policy at home.

The Millbank was not a great success. It opened in 1816 and caught the backlash of criticism about penal reform which came with the post-war crime wave. Although there is plenty of evidence of the harshness of the regime, claims were made that it was too soft, so in 1822–3 the management committee cut the diet and that decision led to the deaths of several prisoners from scurvy. The subsequent inquiry was highly critical of the prison administration, but did little to improve general conditions for the prisoners (Committee of Physicians, 1823; Holford, 1825a, 1825b; Ignatieff, 1978: 9–10, 171–3 and 175–6; McConville, 1981: 111–69). A commitment to the moral reform of prisoners survived the Millbank inquiry, but there remained disagreement over the type of regime which should be adopted: the separate system, in which prisoners were kept in solitary confinement, or the silent system, in which they associated in silence (Forsythe, 1987). Furthermore, the balance between deterrence and rehabilitation shifted according to crime waves and the enthusiasms of administrators and policy makers, and whatever was attempted was subject to examination, and scepticism was fuelled by rising crime statistics. Two of the original prison inspectors appointed by the government under the Prison Act of 1835 (5 & 6 Will. IV, c. 38; see below p. 91), William Crawford and the Rev. Whitworth Russell, were enthusiasts for a separate system with religious instruction, and, although the other inspectors were less convinced of its merits, it is significant that the Rev. Daniel Nihill was promoted from chaplain to governor of Millbank in 1837. However, the severity of the discipline at Millbank led to fears for the sanity of prisoners kept in solitary confinement for long periods. The discipline was relaxed in 1842 as the new model prison at Pentonville opened, and in the following year Millbank became an assessment depot from which prisoners were assigned to other prisons. Some local authorities, already wary about the cost of conversion to a separate system, saw in Millbank's failures confirmation of their fears that this system was both of uncertain benefit and cruel. Apologists, however, blamed the building's design rather than the regime, and, as a result, Pentonville prison was elaborately constructed around the separate regime (McConville, 1981: 160–9 and 175–6; Saunders, 1986; Jebb, 1844; Evans, 1982: 346–67).

Pentonville was also meant to be a model for new local prisons, and the increasing powers acquired by government officials enabled them to ensure its features were incorporated in the plans for new prisons (although persuading local authorities to build remained a problem). Aside from the prison inspectors, whose approval had to be sought before separate cells could be used, under the Prison Act 1839 (2 & 3 Vic., c. 56) the plan of any new prison had to be approved by the Home Secretary and this led to the appointment of Joshua Jebb as an advisor – he acquired the title of Surveyor-General of Prisons in 1844. Jebb and the prison inspectors were able to impose versions of the Pentonville model on about 50 prisons by 1850 (Evans, 1982: 367–87). But some of the problems which had dogged Millbank resurfaced at Pentonville: control, concerns about the mental health of prisoners kept in solitary confinement, and accusations that the prison was too luxurious to act as an effective deterrent. On top of all of this the great champions of the separate system, Crawford and Whitworth Russell, both died in 1847 in circumstances almost worthy of a nineteenth-century novel: Crawford collapsed during a meeting at Pentonville and Whitworth Russell committed suicide in Millbank. The loss of the great promoters of the penitentiary idea undoubtedly played an important part in the speed with which it was abandoned. Pentonville became, like Millbank, a place where convicts were incarcerated before being transported or passed to the new breed of public works prisons (the first of which opened at Portland in 1848) favoured by Jebb where they worked in association (Ignatieff, 1978: 199; McConville, 1981: 193–6 and 440).

The deaths of Crawford and Whitworth Russell also exposed the division among the remaining inspectors over the proper system of discipline and this weakened the inspectorate. By 1863 their numbers had fallen from five to two (McConville, 1981: 177–81 and 215–17; Stockdale, 1976). So it was that in 1850 Jebb, rather than one of the inspectors, was appointed to head the new Directorate of Convict Prisons which controlled the government prisons. During his period in this office (he died in 1863) transportation and the hulks were finally being wound up, although the Home Office retained the power to order a convict to be transported until 1867 (Tomlinson, 1981; Committee on the Hulks, 1847; Branch Johnson, 1970), and the apparently inexorable rise in the criminal statistics continued. So, although Jebb did not dismiss the hope of reformation among the prisoners, he accepted that Pentonville had failed to achieve this, and his main objective became the maintenance of control within the prisons in the face of rising numbers. Rather than seeking to change prisoners' ways of thinking, he formed the more modest goal of trying to force them to conform by imposing a regime of hard labour and military discipline and by a progressive-stages system under which they were rewarded for good behaviour (Clay, 1861; McConville, 1981: 399–407).

The establishment of separate convict prisons for women from 1852 enabled different regimes to be applied to them. The emphasis was on productive work which would give them skills they could use, it was assumed, on release, such as making clothes, washing and cooking; men, on the other hand, were put to unproductive hard labour in the public works prisons. The probationary period before a prisoner could work in association with other prisoners was shorter for women, remission more favourable and supervision on licence less exacting (McConville, 1981: 425–8). On the other hand, before release many women were moved to other institutions and this might greatly extend their initial sentence. Even women who had served their sentence were often pressured into submitting to 'voluntary' incarceration in one of the many institutions run by charitable organizations, such as the Magdalen Hospital or the London Female Penitentiary, in which religion and training in domestic work had a significant role. The argument for extending the incarceration of women in this way was that they were more difficult to reform than men and that, while a man could easily find work labouring, a woman needed domestic skills which took longer to learn (Dobash, Dobash and Gutteridge, 1986: 62–76 and 86–7; Zedner, 1991: 173–216).

Local prisons

Of course, it continued to be the case that, except for the government's convict prisons which broadly took those who were about to be transported and, from the 1840s, those who would previously have been transported, prison administration was largely in the hands of local magistrates, sheriffs and keepers, and they typically remained reluctant to spend too much time or money on prisons. As early as 1793 Lord Loughborough had argued that the state of the prisons was the result not so much of a 'want of GOOD LAWS, as from their INEXECUTION'. Such calls for action were regularly repeated: in 1817 a select committee pressed in vain for the closure of prisons which were too small to enable a proper system of discipline to be introduced (Committee on the State of the Police, 1817b: 328). However, in the early nineteenth century – and particularly from the early 1830s – an increasingly confident central government bureaucracy was being developed which no longer focused almost entirely on foreign affairs and revenue collection, but was beginning to acquire the legal powers, personnel and expertise to undertake a range of tasks in relation to social policy (Roberts, 1969). Moreover, the policy of non-intervention in local affairs seemed less appropriate when the government faced invasion, sedition and revolution, as it believed it did at various times between the French Revolution in 1789 and the climax of the Chartist movement for political reform in 1848. The advantage of central government intervention in social policy was seen as being that it promoted uniformity and efficiency as against the inefficiency, negligence and corruption of some local authorities. Moreover, the fate of new local prisons, such as Gloucester Penitentiary, had demonstrated that relying on the enthusiasm of individuals was not always the best route.

By the early nineteenth century, the precedent of government intervention in prison administration was well established. The Gaol Act 1815 (55 Geo. III, c. 50) tackled the thorny question of prison finance, and its importance cannot be overstated. It abolished fee-taking and provided for the gaolers to be paid a salary determined by the magistrates and paid out of local rates, although there is some evidence that fee-taking did continue (NLW, Radnorshire QS/OB 9, 21 Oct. 1847). Not surprisingly, since the expenditure of ratepayers' funds was involved, this legislation jolted many magistrates' benches into taking a more active interest in the administration of their prisons, and from 1815 prisons are more frequently mentioned in quarter sessions records (Harding et al., 1985: 163; McConville, 1981: 247–8). The Gaol Act 1823 (4 Geo. IV, c. 64) provided the first statement of general principles for local prisons. This act was promoted by Robert Peel, who, as has been seen, on his appointment as Home Secretary in 1822 immediately showed a determination to become actively involved in reorganizing various parts of the criminal justice system and the criminal law. A select committee, which preceded the act, had attempted to accommodate both the reformist agenda of improving the morals of prisoners and the conservative agenda of focusing on prison as an effective deterrent. The problem remained the lack of funds to build adequate local prisons or to adapt the existing buildings to 'a good system of discipline'. This led the select committee to conclude that, in view of the small number of inmates which many local prisons held, it was 'very doubtful whether it would be proper to expend the sum necessary for these purposes' (Select Committee on Prisons, 1822: 4). According to the preamble to the 1823 act, prisons should:

> not only provide for the safe Custody, but shall also tend more effectually to preserve the Health and to improve the Morals of the Prisoners confined therein, and shall insure the proper Measure of Punishment to convicted Offenders.

These aims were to be achieved by 'due Classification, Inspection, regular Labour and Employment, and Religious and Moral Instruction', but solitary confinement was only to be used at night or for discipline. The act required the appointment of visiting justices for the prisons who were to report to the quarter sessions which then reported to the Home Secretary. However, it was all rather vague and loosely drafted: for instance, while facilities for hard labour had to be provided in all prisons, it did not specify the nature of those facilities. Furthermore, it contained no real sanctions for those authorities who chose to ignore its provisions. Nevertheless, it was an important statute which put more pressure on the magistrates to act, provided information (albeit rather defective) to central government, and implicitly confirmed both a hierarchy of expertise and the legitimacy of government involvement (Harding et al., 1985: 143–5 and 163–4; McConville, 1981: 249–50; Select Committee on Prisons, 1822).

Although there had been a move from permissive to mandatory legislation, local authorities were still largely left to interpret and implement the statutes, and this meant the problem of achieving uniformity remained (Weiner, 1990: 103–9). One solution was the appointment of prison inspectors under the Prison Act 1835 (5 & 6 Will. IV, c. 38). The act's full title indicates something of its purpose: 'An Act for effecting greater uniformity of practice in the government of the several prisons in England and Wales; and for appointing Inspectors of Prisons in Great Britain'. This act also increased the Home Secretary's power – and, therefore, the power of the inspectors – by requiring prison rules and diets be submitted for his approval. It has been argued that this 'destroyed the autonomy of the local magistrates; thereafter they merely administered the gaols under Home Office regulation, scrutinized by government inspectors' (Semple, 1993: 310). Certainly the act did give the inspectors a great deal of influence, not least through their ability to expose publicly the defects in the administration of particular local prisons, but, as the Carnarvon Committee was to discover in 1863, the Home Office still lacked both the will to interfere and the appropriate legal mechanism to do so: inspectors could not issue direct orders to justices, and, although many benches followed their advice, others seem to have regarded ignoring it as an important way of asserting their independence from central government (Harding et al., 1985: 145–6; McConville, 1995: 121–2).

As has been mentioned, there was also the problem of the diversity of prisons and prisoners. The small size of many local prisons or their design meant that, in spite of their personal preferences, the best Crawford and Whitworth Russell could hope for was the adoption of the silent system. In addition, theories about reforming prisoners tended to be designed for long-term prisoners, whereas most were only in local prisons for short periods. In any case, for local prison staff the chief concern was typically control, and the magistrates continued to look critically at attempts to introduce expensive systems of discipline (Clay, 1861: 195 and 220–1; Harding *et al.*, 1985: 171–6; Zedner, 1991: 131–72). Even if a local authority became convinced of the need for a new prison, there were other spending priorities and as a result there was often a delay. In Warwickshire it was decided in 1845 that a new prison should be built, but controversy both about that decision and about the design delayed the plans. The decision was eventually confirmed in 1848, but there was no money. In 1852 the issue was revived as a result of pressure from a prison inspector, building work commenced shortly afterwards and the new prison eventually opened in 1861 – a little matter of sixteen years after the initial decision (Saunders, 1986). In Banbury criticisms of the borough prison began at least as early as 1836. Proposals were made for a new building, but nothing happened. Eventually the old prison was closed in 1852, and Banbury contracted with neighbouring authorities to house its prisoners. Once again cost was the key factor, and, in part, Banbury's difficulties were caused both by the unwillingness of the neighbouring Oxfordshire magistrates to help finance a prison and by the opposition to small prisons from the inspectors and from Jebb, the Surveyor-General (DeLacy, 1981, 1986; Renold, 1987: 85–149).

Yet, in spite of all these problems, the increased awareness of conditions in local prisons, which resulted from inspections by the visiting justices and from the publication of the reports of the inspectors, did bring changes and the construction of new prisons. The prisons of the 1850s were quite different from those of the 1770s, and, even though new local prisons were typically built as a result of concerns about the physical conditions rather than out of a desire to implement particular penological theories, the need for approval from the inspectors and the Surveyor-General meant that such theories had a significant impact.

'Hard labour, hard fare, and a hard bed'

In 1856 the troops began returning from the Crimean War, and in the 1850s and 1860s several key features of the eighteenth-century penal system effectively came to an end: transportation, the hulks, and public whipping and hanging.[1] At the same time the Liberals under William Ewart Gladstone were seeking to open up rights of citizenship to a wider section of society by, for instance, the extension of the franchise. But they were also arguing that it was necessary to ensure the fitness of people to exercise those rights by implementing measures of moral improvement, such as education and penal reform. Penal policy replicated the values of economic liberalism, at the core of which was an individual's free will (Garland, 1985). As Weiner has argued,

> We can now see the penal legislation of the 1860s and early 1870s not as a peripheral anomaly, but as an expression of the disciplinary subtext of Gladstonian liberation. It was characteristic of this form of Liberalism to accompany virtually every conferring of benefit with a demand for better behavior.   .
>
> (Weiner, 1990: 152 and 141–55)

Apprehension at the changes in the penal system of the mid-nineteenth century coupled with the fresh perspectives of a new political ideology provided the context within which a more punitive prison discipline was instituted.

As is so often the case, the actual trigger for reform was a crime panic – a spate of violent street robberies in the 1850s and 1860s. The activities of these garotters – so-called after the technique used – seemed to give substance to fears about convicts being released in England (the so-called 'ticket-of-leave men') rather than transported since it was assumed that they were responsible for these crimes. To the dismay of the Home Office, who thought the whole thing to be overblown, newspapers fed, and the police did little to dispel, the panic, and the courts were swept along in their wake (Bartrip, 1981; Davis, 1980; Sindall, 1990). There followed a debate, not just about how convicts should be treated on release, but also about how prisons might be made more effective – and what that meant: if, as people believed, garotting was increasing and was committed by ex-prisoners, then prison was neither reforming nor deterring.

Lord Carnarvon, who was a Hampshire magistrate, undertook a study of these issues and came to the conclusion that reformation was unrealistic, expensive and difficult to assess. Furthermore, he believed a discipline geared towards reformation made prison too comfortable and so undermined its more important and separate objective of deterring other people from committing crimes. He believed that the prison system had to support all other mechanisms of social discipline, such as the workhouse system, and to do this it had to provide a more rigorous and punitive regime than might be encountered in those institutions (McConville, 1981: 22 *et seq.*). These ideas chimed in with the general scepticism about the separate system that had followed the failure of Pentonville, with the more pragmatic approach of Jebb and with the desire for a punitive response to garotting. In 1862 the great social enquirer, Henry Mayhew, attacked the failure of the prisons as judged by rates of recidivism:

> Thus we discover how utterly abortive are all our modes of penal discipline, since the old 'jail-birds,' so far from being either reformed or deterred from

> future offences, are here shown continually to return to the prisons
> throughout the country . . . [I]t is plain . . . that our treatment of criminals
> neither deters nor reforms.
>
> (Mayhew and Binny, 1968: 107)

Carnarvon was able to pursue his ideas when he chaired a House of Lords'
committee on prisons in 1863. The committee adopted Jebb's view of the
essentials of punishment: 'hard labour, hard fare, and a hard bed' (Select
Committee on Gaols, 1863: ix and 125). Religion, which had been at the
core of the Crawford–Whitworth Russell project of reformation, and education were seen as diversions from the punitive nature of imprisonment.
They were to be consigned to those hours when a prisoner was not working, for, while not entirely abandoning the hope that prisoners might
reform, the report stated that the committee:

> do not consider that the moral reformation of the offender holds the
> primary place in the prison system; that mere industrial employment without
> wages is a sufficient punishment for many crimes; that it is in itself morally
> prejudicial to the criminal and useless to society, or that it is desirable to
> abolish both the crank and the treadwheel as soon as possible.
>
> (Harding et al., 1985: 159. But Bowring, 1865)

The Carnarvon Committee did, therefore, share with people like Crawford
and Whitworth Russell the view that criminals were individuals with freedom of choice and the ability to calculate, but differed on how they might
be persuaded to make the 'right' choice. Finally, while the committee did
not favour centralization, it did support greater uniformity between prisons
on the grounds that this was equitable, that it prevented offenders migrat-
ing from an area where the prison regime was harsh to one where it was
soft, and that it was easier to administer (McConville, 1995: 122 and 235).

The Royal Commission on Penal Servitude of 1863 came to similar
conclusions (Royal Commission, 1863), and the Prison Act 1865 (28 &
29 Vic., 126) more or less confirmed this shift towards greater – or, more
accurately, a different form of – severity. The act also tried to meet the
reproach that the Home Office seemed unwilling or unable to do anything about the poor state of many local prisons. In 1859 a leader in *The
Times* (6 Jun. 1859), noting criticisms made of a number of local prisons
in a report by one of the prison inspectors, John Perry, had commented,
'Surely Mr Perry's unsparing exposure of the abuses in these prisons will
be of little use unless the authorities at Whitehall will back his efforts to
improve their condition by immediate interference of the most coercive
character.' The act sought to ensure uniformity by the threat to withdraw
Treasury funding or to close a prison if it failed to meet requirements
laid down in statute or in Home Office rules. Over the next few years the
Home Office did begin to press for changes in those prisons deemed to
be defective, and, while some local authorities were able to prevaricate
for a time, a large number of prisons were closed (Harding et al., 1985:
160, 164 and 192).

Nationalization and the empowerment of Du Cane

This pressure for uniformity and the continued criticism of the regimes in local prisons led many to see nationalization as the logical next step, although the actual trigger for that move came from the Conservative government's promise to reduce local rates. However, the Nationalization Bill of 1876 was met by protests from large deputations of magistrates and their MPs. They welcomed the savings to the rates, but resented the threat to the status of their towns, and, what was even dearer to their hearts, their own prestige, which the loss of a county prison was thought to entail. Those places which had recently erected new prisons at large cost were also understandably annoyed that the government was not going to provide compensation. Yet, opinion was divided: for instance, while Portsmouth magistrates resolved 'to resist [the bill] by all the means in their power', Sussex and Leicestershire justices generally approved of it (*The Times*, 24 Jun., 27 Jun., 1 Jul., 4 Jul., 5 Jul., 12 Jul. 1876; Parker, 1981). As a measure of compromise, magistrates were given a role in the new administration, and the Prison Act became law in 1877 (40 & 41 Vic., c. 21) with the result that 113 local prisons rapidly became 69 (McConville, 1981: 468–82, 1995: 188–93 and 217–32).

Nationalization thrust enormous power into the hands of Edmund Du Cane, a former Royal Engineer, who had been chair of the Directorate of Convict Prisons since 1869 and who in 1877 also became chair of the new Prison Commission, which took over the administration of the local prisons in the following year. Not only did he control all the prisons, but also his decisions were subject to minimal scrutiny. Under the old system debate about local prisons was relatively public, but after nationalization decisions were made within the Directorate/Commission and the Home Office and as a result a general air of secrecy prevailed (Hobhouse and Brockway, 1922: 58–66; McConville, 1995: 236. But, Du Cane, 1885; *The Times*, 27 May 1910). This also meant that Du Cane was largely able to resist any interference from the visiting magistrates (McConville, 1995: 443–508; Forsythe, 1991), and that he could push through his ideas without the need for inquiries or legislation or even discussion.

His approach closely resembled that of the Carnarvon Committee, in that, while he did not entirely dismiss the importance of reformation, he believed that most prisoners were not likely to change, and so he gave priority to deterrence through punishment with education and religion being given limited roles. He also believed in the need to treat all offenders equally:

A sentence of penal servitude is, in its main features, and so far as it concerns the punishment, applied on exactly the same system to every person subjected to it. The previous career and character of the prisoner makes no difference in the punishment to which he is subjected.

(Du Cane (1885) quoted in Garland, 1985: 14)

Hence, McConville's conclusion that, 'The plans were drafted and foundations laid by Carnarvon, but it was Du Cane who built the house', and that Du Cane created 'the most severe system of secondary punishment in English history' (McConville, 1995: 187 and 264–81). McConville has summarized Du Cane's approach:

> do what one can by means of social prevention, especially with the young; if crime has been committed, give special consideration to the young, the impulsive first-time and minor offender, and the mentally deficient; but upon the residue – the ordinary adult offender – it is logically correct, morally justifiable and politically responsible to impose an experience which would deter the prisoner and 'strike terror among possible offenders and show them the stake they will risk.'
>
> (McConville, 1995: 187)

Juveniles

Du Cane did accept the idea that there might be individuals who required special consideration and who should be treated outside the normal prison. That view was not new. The call for the classification of prisoners made by Howard, for instance, was based on the belief that vice was as contagious as gaol fever and that different prisoners had different levels of infection and different degrees of susceptibility. The earliest distinctions made were between adults and juveniles and between men and women.

In the eighteenth century juveniles accused of crime were broadly treated in the same way as adults, athough those under seven – and sometimes, those under fourteen – were exempted from prosecution. If sentenced to imprisonment, children would be put in adult prisons. However, by the mid-eighteenth century attitudes to children were changing. This shift, initially, came as much from compassion combined with a desire to increase the labour force as from a concern about crime. A number of charitable schemes were devised to moralize children rather than to deal with those who had been convicted (Andrew, 1989). Thomas Coram's Foundling Hospital was set up in 1739 as part of a general effort to preserve illegitimate children, both physically and morally, and to 'supply the Government plentifully with useful Hands' (Anon., 1749a: 4; McClure, 1981). The Marine Society, founded in 1756, raised money to send to sea young thieves who, it was believed, had been brought to that lifestyle by parental neglect or encouragement. Initially, it seems that most of the boys volunteered, but by the 1780s the courts were also sending boys to sea through the society (Hanway, 1757a, 1757b; Leslie-Melville, 1934: 113–22; Radzinowicz and Hood, 1986: 133–4). The Female Orphans Asylum (1758) trained orphan girls to become domestic servants, and thereby, it was hoped, prevent them from becoming prostitutes (Leslie-Melville, 1934: 123–6). The Philanthropic Society (1788) aimed to reintroduce outcast boys into society through a vocational training scheme. However, it became an institution to which boys were sent by the courts after a conviction or because their parents were offenders, and, rather than vocational training, such boys were given punitive labour. Much later – in 1830 – the Society for the Suppression of Juvenile Vagrancy was established to train children for emigration (Committee on the State of the Police, 1817b: 332; Radzinowicz and Hood, 1986: 134–5; Hadley, 1990).

Concern about juvenile crime heightened as a result of a rapid rise in juveniles appearing before the London courts between the 1790s and 1820s. It may be that this was not a rise in actual crime but an increase in prosecutions that resulted from the abolition of capital punishment for pickpocketing and shoplifting, which made victims more willing to prosecute juveniles, and from the improvements in policing effected by the reforms of the watch by the parishes, the Middlesex Justices Act 1792 and the spread of prosecution societies (King and Noel, 1993. But, Margery, 1978). Whatever the reason for the increase, contemporaries did not doubt that there was a serious problem of juvenile crime, that this symbolized the moral degradation of the labouring classes as a whole and that the implications for the nation were grave. According to Colquhoun:

> In tracing the progress of those habits which are peculiar to the lower orders of the Community in this great Metropolis, from infancy to the adult state, the cause will be at once discovered, why that *almost universal* profligacy prevails, which, by being productive of so much evil to the unfortunate Individuals as well as the Community at large, cannot be sufficiently deplored.

He claimed that as a result of being constantly taken to alehouses by their mothers children mixed with bad company, and that they were poorly fed, clothed and educated. Those that survived grew up 'under the influence of habits so exceedingly depraved, they are restrained by no principle of morality or religion, (for they know nothing of either), and only wait for opportunities, to plunge into every excess and every crime' (Colquhoun, 1806: 311–14). A select committee in 1817 broadly agreed:

> there are several thousands of Boys in the Metropolis who are daily engaged in the commission of crime; that the causes of this deplorable evil are to be traced to the improper and criminal conduct of parents, – the want of education, – the prevailing habit of gambling in the public streets, which, to the disgrace of our Police, is practised daily with impunity.
> (Committee on the State of the Police, 1817b: 327)[2]

This committee proposed the construction of a juvenile penitentiary. Nothing came of the idea, but in the previous year the magistrates in Warwickshire had begun a juvenile reformatory, which opened in 1818, and around that time the Newgate prison reformer, Elizabeth Fry, opened the Chelsea School of Reform for 'vicious' girls. Both institutions were designed for children who had served a sentence (Radzinowicz and Hood, 1986: 135–6; Saunders, 1986). The first government-funded prison for juveniles was a hulk which opened in 1825, but, like the adult hulks, it came under criticism for its lack of a disciplined regime and was eventually closed in 1843 (Radzinowicz and Hood, 1986: 142–4). In 1838 a special penitentiary was opened at Parkhurst for boys, but it was soon being subjected to the familiar criticism that a regime designed to encourage moral reformation was insufficiently punitive to deter potential offenders, and it was made more severe. Yet, at the same time, the courts took the view that Parkhurst provided the opportunity to reform children before they became mired in crime, and so they sent them when they were very young or when they had committed only very minor offences. By the 1840s Parkhurst was failing, and the younger children and those who seemed likely to reform were being siphoned off to the Philanthropic Society (Radzinowicz and Hood, 1986: 148–55; Weiner, 1990: 51).

The same sort of disagreement as was occurring with regard to the appropriate regime for adults was, therefore, being played out in relation to juveniles, but the pressure to do something about juvenile crime increased in the 1850s and 1860s as concern over adult habitual criminals intensified. It was reasoned that if adult penitentiaries had not worked it became even more important to cut off the supply of habitual criminals by moralizing the young. More emphasis was, therefore, placed on the development of different mechanisms for juveniles so that they could be treated separately from adults and trained to become good citizens (Radzinowicz and Hood, 1986: 161–227; Weiner, 1990: 131–41). The pursuit of this objective led to a move away from the need to prove a criminal offence and towards focusing on treatment in which such proof became less important. Efforts were made to distinguish the trials of juveniles from those of adults and also to speed up the whole process by, for instance, making many property offences triable summarily. There was also a shift away from putting juveniles in prison. This led to the abandonment of Parkhurst as a juvenile penitentiary in 1864 and, in the 1870s, to the development of probation under the supervision of members of the Church of England Temperance Society. But also one form of incarceration tended to be replaced by another. In the 1850s Mary Carpenter wrote approvingly of the Warwickshire juvenile penitentiary and of the Philanthropic Society's institution at Redhill. She set up her first reformatory school in Bristol for criminal children, and later established industrial schools for those thought to be in danger of slipping into crime – although the distinction between the two types of schools began to disappear as early as the 1860s (Weiner, 1990: 137). Her aim was to create institutions which would 'occupy a middle ground between educational and penal establishments' and would engage in 'the early nurture, and the sound religious, moral, and industrial training of the child' (Carpenter, 1851: vi. Also, Humphries, 1981: 209–68). Legislation in the 1850s and 1860s allowed the courts to send children under sixteen to the reformatories and provided some state funding, which in turn enabled government to impose criteria through a certification and inspection system.

Like Colquhoun, it was Carpenter's view that children were not naturally vicious but slipped into crime because of parental neglect:

> the great mass of juvenile delinquency is to be directly and mainly attributed to the low moral condition of the parents, and to their culpable neglect of the early training of their children, or their incapacity to direct it.
>
> (Radzinowicz and Hood, 1986: 165)

A distincion was made between the consequences of unchecked delinquency in boys and girls. Neglected boys, it was believed, were in danger of becoming habitual criminals; girls, on the other hand, were likely to become prostitutes and give birth to illegitimate children who would become a burden on the poor relief system and the criminals or prostitutes of the future. The regimes applied to boys and girls were, therefore, quite different: for instance, in the case of girls the aim was to suppress their sexual inclinations and to train them in domestic skills (Cale, 1993: 214). Inevitably, there was criticism of a system which sought to achieve moral reformation. Carpenter herself was a firm believer in the need for punishment, arguing that a juvenile offender should 'feel the consequences of his conduct', before reformation could be attempted (Weiner, 1990: 116). Nevertheless, it was argued that the regimes she instituted were not a sufficient deterrent. The Home Office was keen to maintain a clear association between crime and punishment. As a result, juvenile offenders were sent to prison for fourteen days (later reduced to ten) before going to a reformatory.

*   *   *   *

During the nineteenth century government became more involved in penal policy. It built experimental prisons at Millbank and Pentonville as architectural realizations of particular penal philosophies. It also intervened in the penal regimes administered by local authorities in their prisons, initially, through permissive legislation, then through mandatory laws, although there was a lack of either the powers or the will to ensure compliance. However, there was a degree of uncertainty underneath all of this. Throughout the first half of the century there was disagreement as to what should be done with prisoners. Should the prison regime seek to reform or punish, and, if reform, should it use the separate or the silent system? What should be done about the small, local prisons where altering the regime was difficult given the condition of the buildings?

What can be said is that, in general terms, from the mid-nineteenth century there was something of a shift in the diagnosis of the problem of crime. Before that time the views of people like Crawford and Whitworth Russell were fairly commonplace, namely, that criminals were rational beings who needed to be taught how to make the 'right' choices. At its core this approach built on a belief in the possibility of social reintegration through moral regeneration. Individuals were to be educated to take responsibility for themselves. Rather than kill or banish criminals, the penitentiary was the place in which they could be brought to their right senses through religion and work. But the difficulties of, and the expense involved in introducing, this system as well as alarm at levels of recidivism, the panic over garotting and, just as damaging, the continual accusations about the luxurious conditions in prison led to a diminution of faith in the effectiveness of the penitentiaries and encouraged a much more limited view of the possibility of reforming prisoners. That in turn led to the punitive regimes advocated by Carnarvon and Du Cane (Forsythe, 1987). In 1858 Thomas Carlyle described prisoners as:

> Miserable distorted blockheads, the generality; ape-faces, imp-faces, angry dog-faces, heavy sullen ox-faces; degraded under-foot perverse creatures, sons of *in*docility, greedy mutinous darkness, and in one word, of stupidity, which is the general mother of such.
>
> (McConville, 1981: 328–9)

The belief became common that criminals were different and were unlikely to change their way of thinking, so that the only solution was to alter their behaviour through a punitive regime which trained them to good habits, even if it did not alter their beliefs, and which, more importantly, acted as a deterrent. At the same time, the greater pessimism about the possibility of improving the morals of adult prisoners encouraged reformers to turn their attention to juveniles, reasoning that the supply of criminals could thereby be cut off.

Further reading

Radzinowicz and Hood (1986) have written an encyclopaedic account of the ideas about crime and criminal justice policy that were being explored in the nineteenth century, while Weiner (1990) identifies themes within such ideas and sets them within their context (see also Garland, 1985). Most historians, however, look at a narrower field. The history of prisons is considered in most detail by McConville (1981, 1995) and Forsythe (1987, 1991. Also De Lacey 1986), while Zedner (1991) is the key text for the study of women in prison in the nineteenth century (see also Dobash, Dobash and Gutteridge, 1986), and Humphries (1981) provides an important insight into the reformatories in the late nineteenth and early twentieth centuries. More thematic and controversial studies of prisons are provided by Foucault (1977) and Ignatieff (1978; see also his auto-critique: Ignatieff, 1983), and the critique by Garland (1985).

Notes

1. Whipping for adults was virtually abolished in 1861, only to be revived shortly afterwards for robbery following a panic over street robberies. Birching of juveniles was retained for a wide range of offences.
2. Colquhoun uses the term 'police' in the original sense of the civil administration in all its aspects.

Chapter 7

The Triumph of the Home Office, 1877–1900

The attack on Du Cane

The different branches of penological theory in the nineteenth century, from Crawford and Whitworth Russell to Carnarvon and Du Cane, all sprouted from the same tree: the idea of individual free will – criminals chose to be criminals. This was also at the core of other aspects of social policy, such as the Poor Law Amendment Act 1834 which allowed poor relief only to those who were willing to enter the workhouse on the reasoning that the indigent's condition was the result of their failure to make the right choices – they refused to work, or married too young, or spent unwisely. Yet, a more sympathetic approach to the poor also emerged around this time, and, in relation to criminals, became dominant in the 1890s.

In 1842, the year that Pentonville opened, Edwin Chadwick produced his *Report on the Sanitary Condition of the Labouring Population of Great Britain* (Home Department, 1842). As secretary to the Royal Commission on the Poor Laws of 1832, Chadwick had been a firm believer in the notion of individual free will and had supported the 1834 act. However, his 1842 report represented an important change in his views in that he concluded there was a link between poverty and illness caused by environmental conditions. In other words, some people were poor not because they had made the wrong choices, but because they were unable to work as a result of insanitary living conditions for which, on the whole, they could not be held responsible. Chadwick argued that the state should intervene through public health legislation to improve the environment in which the poor lived. His change of view seems to have been brought about by a change of methodology: rather than relying on people such as local clergymen to provide the evidence on which he formed his views, as was predominantly the case with the Royal Commission, the data was collected by visits to the homes of the poor. Contemporaries of Chadwick were also showing an interest in the real conditions in which the poor lived.

The novels and non-fiction writing of Charles Dickens (such as, *Bleak House* (1852–3), *Our Mutual Friend* (1864–5) and *Household Words*) are filled with observations about the condition of the poor and the journalist Henry Mayhew began to conduct interviews with the London street people for the *Morning Chronicle* in 1849 (Thompson and Yeo, 1973), publishing *London Labour and the London Poor* a few years later (Mayhew, 1967; Williams, 1981: 237–77). Chadwick, Dickens and Mayhew did not entirely excuse the poor for their condition: the poor in Dickens' novels were subject to the same environmental pressures, but some were good and others bad, and Mayhew subscribed to the idea that prisoners needed to be reformed (Mayhew and Binny, 1968). However, the work of these and other writers was a revelation to the wealthier middle classes and aristocrats who had abandoned the centre of towns, where the poor congregated, for the cleaner air of the suburbs. Mayhew claimed that his inquiries were 'the first attempt to publish the history of a people, from the lips of the people themselves', and in 'supplying information concerning a large body of persons, of whom the public had less knowledge than of the most distant tribes of the earth' (Mayhew, 1967, vol. 1: iii). He juxtaposed the public wealth of London with its hidden poverty:

> The docks of London are to a superficial observer the very focus of metropolitan wealth. The cranes creak with the mass of riches. In the warehouses are stored goods that are as it were ingots of untold gold . . . There are acres upon acres of treasure, more than enough, one would fancy, to stay the cravings of the whole world, and yet you have but to visit the hovels grouped round about all this amazing excess of riches to witness the same amazing excess of poverty. If the incomprehensibility of the wealth rises to sublimity, assuredly the want that co-exists with it is equally incomprehensible and equally sublime.
> (Mayhew, 1967, vol. 3: 308. Also, Beames, 1852; Green, 1995; Mearns, 1883)

These writers addressed the paradox which had worried commentators in the previous century. Then, as has been seen, it was believed that England enjoyed a high degree of liberty because of its prosperity, but this prosperity enabled the poor to indulge in liberty without restraint and that in turn carried the danger of immorality among the labouring poor on whom prosperity depended. To eighteenth-century writers the problem of the coexistence of wealth and poverty was resolved by blaming the poor for their own condition: it was, in brief, the consequence of their idleness and indulgence in immorality. The poor's inability to exercise self-restraint meant others should impose it on them. The problem of who was to do this was regarded as particularly acute in London where the structures of aristocratic authority that existed in the countryside did not operate, so during the eighteenth century the disciplining of the poor was increasingly seen as the task of administrators (the justices of the peace, the overseers of the poor and so forth). The view of nineteenth-century writers like Dickens was that the poor were not necessarily poor out of choice. By juxtaposing extremes of wealth and poverty, he invited people to consider how wealth depended on and engendered poverty, and that, therefore, the rich had a responsibility for the poor. In the later nineteenth century these concerns over the condition of the poor were also prompted by challenges to the industrial and colonial dominance of Britain from, in particular, the USA and Germany and, as will be seen, by a fear that the poor would explode out of their hovels to overrun the rich. However, although the view of the poor was more sophisticated, the solutions offered drew on those developed over the previous couple of centuries in their reliance on intervention by the state.

Environmental conditions were seen as a cause of crime. Chadwick's report was not directly concerned with this issue, nevertheless he saw a link between the conditions in which the poor lived and their immorality. Much later, in 1896, William Douglas Morrison, the chaplain at Wandsworth Prison, wrote that 'the personal, social and economic conditions which generate a criminal disposition and criminal habits of life are fostered to a very large extent by the herding together of the population in a few immense commercial and industrial centres' (Harding *et al.*, 1985: 214). Moreover, as has already been seen (above, Chapter 6), it had long been acknowledged that the surroundings in which children grew up, and, in particular, 'the improper and criminal conduct of parents' (Committee on the State of the Police, 1817b: 127), led to juvenile crime, and, as a consequence, various initiatives from the Marine Society to the reformatories were directed towards protecting children from vicious influences. In the last quarter of the nineteenth century these were supplemented by attempts to regulate the moral environment through action on parental neglect and child protection (see Chapter 8).

The idea that criminals acted by choice was dealt another blow in the latter half of the nineteenth century. There emerged, through the work of positivists such as Lombroso, Ferri and Garofalo, the theory that habitual criminals were born rather than made and that they displayed particular physical characteristics. In Continental Europe such ideas enjoyed widespread popularity, but English commentators seem to have been less convinced and it was not until 1890 that a sustained piece of work was produced by an English writer on the subject, Havelock Ellis' *The Criminal.* While broadly enthusiastic, even he acknowledged the importance of the environment in crime (Ellis, 1890: 24). He also understood that this new theory presented some serious problems:

> If, as now scarcely admits of question, every truly criminal act proceeds from a person who is, temporarily or permanently, in a more or less abnormal condition, the notion of 'punishment' loses much of its foundation. We cannot punish a monstrosity for acting according to its monstrous nature . . . The old conception of punishment was founded on the assumption of the normality of the criminal; he was a normal person who had chosen to act as though he were not a normal person . . . and it was the business of the penologist to apportion the exact amount of retribution due to this

extraordinary offence, with little or no regard to the varying nature of the offender; he was regarded as a constant factor.

(Ellis, 1890: 232)

At the same time it was believed that improvements in public health and better welfare provision meant that the morally unfit were not dying out, as some, who had adapted Darwin's theory of natural selection to humans, would otherwise have expected; instead, they were surviving and reproducing. Suggestions were, therefore, drawn up for the removal of certain categories of the criminal and the indigent poor by, for instance, deportation.

Such theories came up against the notion that offenders should be punished in proportion to the offences of which they have been convicted; indeed, they seemed to many to contravene the whole notion of a criminal trial. In addition, the publication of Dr Charles Goring's critique, *The English Convict*, in 1913 proved devastating. Goring, a member of the prison medical service, claimed that there was no evidence of the existence of 'a criminal type' such as had been claimed by Lombroso. Although his book was undoubtedly flawed and did not amount to the wholesale rejection of positivist theories that some hoped, it was influential: a later edition was even able to boast an introduction by Ruggles-Brise, the chair of the Prison Commission. Nevertheless, the positivist theories did have an impact on policy and legislation (Garland, 1985. But, Radzinowicz and Hood, 1986: 3–35). So, for instance, while the view that offenders should only be punished in proportion to their offences can be seen in the establishment of the Court of Criminal Appeal in 1907 (7 Edw. VII, c. 23) which had the power to review sentences, the radical theories can be found in a shift towards both a more minute classification of deviants (habitual offenders, juvenile offenders, men, women, habitual drunkards, and so on) and the development of treatment programmes under which people were incarcerated for terms that were not solely related to the offence for which they had been tried: for example, the Prevention of Crime Act 1908 which empowered a court to imprison a recidivist to a term beyond that warranted by the offence of which he or she had been convicted; similarly, legislation enabled the incarceration of juveniles and alcoholics for periods which, within broad limits, were determined not by their offences or by the judges but by their response to treatment (see below, Chapter 8).

As has always been the case, criminal justice policy was not formed simply as a result of such debates within criminology and penology. The Du Cane regime came under political attack partly as a result of resentment at the nationalization of the prisons which had been exacerbated by Du Cane's policy of largely excluding local magistrates from the administration (Forsythe, 1991: 23–4). Criticism came also from a number of other sources. There were allegations of cruelty in the convict prisons which were regarded as sufficiently serious to require the setting up of a royal commission in 1878, even though that inquiry dismissed them (Royal Commission 1878–9). Around that time complaints about the prison regime had begun to emerge in the autobiographies of middle-class ex-prisoners. *Five Years' Penal Servitude* (1877) started a flood of such books, and the experiences they described were confirmed by political prisoners such as John Burns of the Social Democratic Federation, who had been in Pentonville, and Irish republicans like Michael Davitt (1885) and O'Donovan Rossa. Pressure groups, including the Howard Association, also joined in the attacks (Forsythe, 1991: 22–3). The English prison system seemed out of step with the views of other nations. As early as 1872, at the first International Prison Congress in London, it had been agreed that 'the moral regeneration of the prisoner should be the primary aim of prison discipline', and 'anything that inflicts unnecessary pain or humiliation should be abolished' (Fox, 1952: 52).

Initially, Du Cane seems to have been largely untouched by these criticisms, but by the early 1890s the pressure was building to head. Morrison, the chaplain at Wandsworth, publicly attacked the prison regime for failing to reform prisoners. More damagingly, the editor of the *Daily Chronicle*, Henry Massingham, mounted a vigorous campaign alleging overcrowding, understaffing, poor discipline, dehumanizing conditions and a lack of productive work; and he turned these allegations into a personal attack on Du Cane. Massingham wrote:

> Our prison system is the worst in the world. It is the least successful. It starves them, it crazes them, it makes brutes of them. It is a mere criminal factory, which pours out of its gates every year an increasing mass of people who will be in and out of the cell for the greater part of their lives.
>
> (McConville, 1995: 707–8)

These attacks drew strength from a struggle for power between Home Office officials and Du Cane, and, in turn, created the opportunity for the officials to step up their criticism of Du Cane. The civil service in general had grown in size and professionalism during the nineteenth century as the state became more interventionist (Pellew, 1982; Roberts, 1969). The permanence of civil servants brought a continuity which politicians did not have and gave them a key role in advising ministers who, in the case of the Home Office, had acquired enormous power under the various Prison Acts. Inquiries were dominated by the evidence of civil servants, particularly since there was an increased dependence on statistics which only government could provide. Civil servants were also able to govern through administrative rule making and the issuing of guidelines and advice, all backed up by inspections and fiscal pressure, rather than having to resort to the public exposure that legislation entailed. Their growing importance changed the balance of power between central and local government, and it also created conflict with semi-autonomous officials like Du Cane who stood outside the government departments.

The nationalization of the prisons had not only increased Du Cane's power, it had also made the Home Secretary responsible to Parliament for their day-to-day administration. This meant that the Criminal Department of the Home Office developed an expertise to rival that of the Prison Commission under Du Cane. Inevitably, this confusion of authority when coupled with Du Cane's strong character and his dislike of interference in his work soured his relationship with Home Office officials. He deepened his isolation by arguing with fellow directors and commissioners, in particular he resented the appointment to the Prison Commission in 1892 of Evelyn Ruggles-Brise, a former Principal Private Secretary to various Home Secretaries. The two men argued almost immediately and, apparently, never spoke again. Ruggles-Brise – admittedly, not an unbiased observer – later recalled Du Cane 'as the embodiment of bureaucratic despotism and arrogance . . . absorbing all matters great and small into his own hands. His word was law' (Fox, 1952: 53).

It is worth noting that at this time, it was not just Du Cane who was under attack from the Home Office, so was Charles Warren, the Commissioner of the Metropolitan Police from 1886 to 1888 (see below pp. 114–17). Both men attempted to assert their independence of government and their right to command their officials without outside interference. In other words, they wished to behave like generals in the field, which was hardly surprising since both had been appointed precisely because of their military background. It must have been intensely annoying for these men to be criticized for adopting the very management styles which had recommended them to ministers in the first place. Nevertheless, it was this which led to conflict with the Home Office (McConville, 1995: 509–648; *Parliamentary Debates*, 3rd series, vol. 330, c. 463, c. 893–4, c. 1342, 1346–7 and 1354–60; *The Times*, 13 Nov. 1888). Warren foolishly, but typically, published an article critical of the Home Secretary's interference and was forced to resign. Du Cane was more cautious and stayed in his post until he retired in 1895, but he became more embittered and isolated.

The bureaucrats' victories were symbolized by the appointments of Ruggles-Brise to succeed Du Cane in 1895 (Forsythe, 1991: 31–44) and of James Monro, a former Assistant Commissioner who had sided with the Home Office against Warren, as Commissioner in 1888. It is important to add a note of caution to this story. To a large extent Warren's defeat was, as will be seen, simply a means of deflecting criticism from the Home Secretary who had appointed him to militarize the police and who wished to avoid the blame both for the brutality of the police in dealing with a demonstration and for the failure of the inquiry into the Whitechapel murders of 1888. Du Cane, on the other hand, did more than merely survive as chair of the Prison Commission from 1877–95, and the impression of the man and his work has come down to us mainly through those, such as Ruggles-Brise, Alexander Paterson and Lionel Fox, who were victors in the struggle and who attacked his ideas by attacking him.

The Gladstone Committee

The bureaucrats' ideological victory with regard to the prisons came initially in the form of criticisms levelled at Du Cane's regime by a committee set up in 1894 and chaired by the Under-Secretary at the Home Office, Herbert Gladstone. This committee reported in 1895 and essentially reversed the approach laid down by Carnarvon thirty years before (Departmental Committee on Prisons, 1895; Harding, 1988; Harding *et al.*, 1985: 215, 237 and 261; McConville, 1995: 554–696; Weiner, 1990: 310–13, 325–8 and 342–4). It carefully demolished each element of the Carnarvon–Du Cane regime by drawing on statistics and the evidence of witnesses.

The problem for Du Cane's critics, as he was quick to point out, was that the decline in the number of prisoners – in spite of a rise in the general population – seemed to support his approach; indeed, the drop of roughly one-third in the average daily number of prisoners between 1878 and 1886–7 had helped to smooth acceptance of the nationalization of the prisons (McConville, 1995: 194–5 and 201–3). The Gladstone Committee, therefore, engaged in a fairly sophisticated critique of these figures, or rather it drew on the analysis helpfully provided by the Home Office. The committee concluded that crime had fallen, not as a result of Du Cane's prison regime, but because of environmental changes and welfare reforms, such as improvements in education, housing and public health. Having explained away the drop in prisoners to its own satisfaction, the committee then turned to attack the prison system on the basis of figures which seemed to indicate a rise in recidivism, the very thing Carnarvon had sought to eradicate:

> In proportion to the spread of education, the increase of wealth, and the extension of social advantages, the retention of a compact mass of habitual criminals in our midst is a growing stain on our civilisation.
>
> (Departmental Committee on Prisons, 1895: 5)

Nationalization had enabled Du Cane to pursue uniformity across the system, but that policy had, in the committee's opinion, led to stagnation, to a reluctance to experiment and to a failure to consider 'the moral condition' of the prisoners. Too many emerged from prison no better – and often a good deal worse – than when they entered. The Liberals' project of social inclusion was failing with these people and they, therefore, remained a threat.

In looking for a new way, the committee took a lead from Lushington, Permanent Under-Secretary at the Home Office and an enemy of Du Cane:

> I regard as unfavourable to reformation the status of a prisoner throughout his whole career; the crushing of self-respect, the starving of all moral instinct he may possess, the absence of all opportunity to do or receive a

kindness, the continual association with none but criminals, and that only as a separate item amongst other items also separate; the forced labour, and the denial of all liberty. I believe the true mode of reforming a man or restoring him to society is exactly in the opposite direction of all these.
(Departmental Committee on Prisons, 1895: 8)

The committee rejected the negativism of Du Cane. It was optimistic about the possibility of reforming the characters of prisoners: 'the great majority of prisoners are ordinary men and women amenable, more or less, to all those influences which affect persons outside.' It, therefore, also largely rejected the idea that criminals were born and were, therefore, essentially irredeemable: 'There are but few prisoners other than those who are in a hopeless state through physical or mental deficiencies who are irreclaimable. Even in the case of habitual criminals there appears to come a time when repeated imprisonments or the gradual awakening of better feelings wean them from habitual crime' (Departmental Committee on Prison, 1895: 13). The committee concluded:

We think that the system should be made more elastic, more capable of being adapted to the special cases of individual prisoners; that prison discipline and treatment should be more effectually designed to maintain, stimulate, or awaken the higher susceptibilities of prisoners, to develop their moral instincts, to train them in orderly and industrial habits, and whenever possible to turn them out of prison better men and women, both physically and mentally, than when they came in.
(Departmental Committee on Prisons, 1895: 8)

The key elements of the Carnarvon–Du Cane regime were attacked. The committee argued that because prisoners were different from each other a uniform discipline led to inequality. Unproductive hard labour, such as the treadwheel, 'keeps the prisoners in a state of mental vacuity, and this we regard as a most undesirable and mischievous result' (Departmental Committee on Prisons, 1895: 19). The committee also rejected the early nineteenth-century idea that separate confinement brought prisoners to reformation through meditation on past crimes. But the silent system, which was used in some male prisons, was condemned as unnatural; it was claimed that there was much value in allowing male prisoners a degree of liberty to talk to one another, as women were already allowed to do. The committee favoured regulated association and productive labour with more emphasis on education, which Carnarvon and Du Cane had regarded as a softening of the punitive nature of the regime. However, in respect of habitual criminals, the committee believed them to be largely indifferent to the risk of relatively short sentences and unaffected by their experiences of prison. For them, therefore, it recommended extended detention. This solution was also put forward for habitual drunkards, who, they conceded, 'are not criminals in the ordinary sense', but whose offending was rooted in their alcoholism and who required a longer course of treatment than the sentence for an offence might provide. This reiterated the conclusions of an earlier report by the Departmental Committee on Inebriates which had proposed that magistrates be allowed to incarcerate habitual drunkards so that they might receive medical treatment and 'be dealt with as patients rather than criminals' (Departmental Committee on Prisons, 1895: 31–2; Harding and Wilkins, 1988; Weiner, 1990: 294–300). The committee also spent a good deal of time on the question of juvenile offenders. The number of juveniles in prison had fallen markedly since the 1870s, but one of the stumbling blocks to a further reduction was that the managers of reformatories tended to refuse admission to those whom they thought it would be difficult to reform, such as repeat offenders (McConville, 1995: 350–61). To cater for these juveniles the committee proposed a government-funded penal reformatory.

The reduced enthusiasm for prisons evident in the Gladstone Committee's recommendations did not affect its support for the institutional treatment of the roots of crime. Incarceration remained, but the committee felt that the more careful classification of offenders would enable them to be placed in institutions which were designed to treat the roots of their offending, as opposed to the Carnarvon–Du Cane idea of applying the same discipline to all. Therefore, the reduction in the prison population was accompanied by an increase in other forms of incarceration (Radzinowicz and Hood, 1986: 618–57). Such ideas also meant that the need for popular participation in the trial process and openness in sentencing became less important. The primary concern was to make decisions about the treatment of individuals rather than to judge whether or not their conduct broke the criminal law: so, more offences were made triable summarily, in particular offences committed by juveniles (Radzinowicz and Hood, 1986: 618–24) and more decisions were placed in the hands of bureaucrats. In line with this idea, many of the Gladstone report's recommendations were implemented by instructions issued to governors by the Home Office, and, although it was necessary to pass the Prison Act 1898, its main objective was to enable the Home Secretary to avoid parliamentary scrutiny in making prison rules (Weiner, 1990: 259–64).

Changes in policing

Sweeping changes in direction of the type instituted by the Gladstone Committee were possible because of the centralization of the prison system. In the police, outside the Metropolitan area, there were difficulties in making such revolutionary changes because local authorities remained in control. Nevertheless, the reliance on Treasury funding did give considerable force to directions issued by the Home Office. Moreover, while some authorities were famously jealous of their power and quick to resist interference, others were weak or indifferent and willing to demur to the

expert advice of the Home Office (Emsley, 1991: 91–3). The police themselves also began to trade on their expertise and professionalism to extend
their claims to autonomy. As against the early years of the new police, when
low pay and autocratic treatment of junior officers led to a high turnover,
the end of the century witnessed the emergence of a corporate identity
with police unionism, newspapers for officers, a national campaign for
pensions and the formation of the Chief Constables' Association in 1893
(Emsley, 1991: 95–103; Steedman, 1984). The police were able to draw
strength both from statistics which showed crime falling after mid-century,
and from continued concern about particularly obstinate problems such
as habitual criminals, whom they were assigned to supervise under legislation in 1869 and 1871. The popularity of the police, at least among the
middle classes, had also grown. The credit for the orderly conduct of
the huge crowds that visited the Great Exhibition in 1851 went largely
to the Metropolitan Police, who were favourably compared with foreign
police and even seen as something of a tourist attraction: 'the quiet and
business-like manner in which, at critical moments, the duties of the Force
have been discharged, has been frequently noticed by foreigners with
surprise and admiration' (*The Times*, 28 Jul. 1866; Custos, 1868: 12).

But a number of problems confronted the police and prompted a shift
in direction, or, at least, a fresh presentation of their work. The Metropolitan Police were dogged by criticism of their methods in dealing with
public order following incidents such as at a public meeting in Cold Bath
Fields in 1833, when PC Culley died during a police charge and an initial
verdict of justifiable homicide was returned by the coroner's jury, and at
the demonstrations over the Sunday Trading Bill in 1855 and the Reform
Bill in 1866. Provincial forces met similar criticism when carrying out such
duties (Emsley, 1991: 68–9; King, 1985). However, their actions were also
praised: *The Times* (28 Jul. 1866, also 25 Jul. 1866; Custos, 1868), for
instance, rejected charges of brutality over the handling of the Reform
Bill demonstration in Hyde Park in 1866 and indeed praised the police
for their restraint in the face of extreme provocation, commenting that
they 'have been throughout far more calm and forbearing than the
police of any country with which we have ever been acquainted'.

The project of crime prevention through the moralization of the poor
by the police had also met with difficulties. In London stipendiary magistrates displayed a wariness about the police arresting people merely on
suspicion and were reluctant to convict on this charge. As a result, the
Metropolitan Police modified their use of such powers (Miller, 1975; Paley,
1989a: 123; Petrow, 1994: 42–5). Employing working-class men as officers
to impose a bourgeois moral order with which they were unfamiliar on
communities with whose traditions and values they were more likely to
sympathize was problematical; indeed, a large number of officers were
sacked by the police forces for drunkenness (Steedman, 1984: 107–8).
There was opposition on the streets to police campaigns aimed at moralization, so that, for instance, although assaults on the police in Manchester

had largely subsided by 1847, they revived in the late 1860s in response to a vigorous moral campaign against prostitutes, vagrants and street leisure activities (Davies, 1985; Jones, 1982: 162–63; Humphries, 1981: 174–208). A lack of officers and the vigour of working-class resistance led to 'no go' areas for police in places like the China district of Merthyr Tydfil, and elsewhere the definition of order enforced was likely to be negotiated with local communities (Jones, 1982; Cohen, 1979). In industrial relations disputes, the response to police intervention depended on your viewpoint: resented by strikers, welcomed by employers and strike breakers. At the same time the working class no more appreciated theft than did the middle class, and as Victorian 'respectability' spread through religion, trade unions, education, stable employment and improved wages, so more working class people sought to distinguish themselves from the street disorder of the 'roughs'.[1] There was, therefore, a tendency for the police to focus on marginalized communities of the unemployed and casual poor, such as the Irish or the people living in poor working-class areas of London such as the Jennings Buildings and the Jago (Davis, 1989; Samuel, 1981; Jones, 1984), and on 'habitual criminals'.

The police recognized that acting as an army of occupation did not achieve much and that a compromise was often necessary for them to be able to operate. Service work was one way of gaining the support of the communities they policed. As early as 1839 the Constabulary Commission had urged the police to undertake such work, for instance, reporting holes in the road and acting as firemen and as inspectors of nuisances (Royal Commission, 1839: 149–59). This also appealed to local authorities who were acquiring a large number of administrative duties and found the police officer a useful means of carrying them out (Steedman, 1984: 159). For their part, while the police recognized the need to extend their involvement in the communities, by the late nineteenth century they were expressing resentment at the number of tasks which were being thrust on them. They particularly disliked work which was time consuming or which made them unpopular, such as acting as poor relief officers or school attendance officers. As early as 1868 one sympathetic writer complained about the sheer number of these extra duties that were laid on Metropolitan Police officers in 82 statutes: 'they relate to the supervision by the Police of a vast multitude of details of more or less importance, connected with vagrancy, public houses, beer houses, sanitary measures, coining, lunatics, street traffic, hackney carriages, and an immense variety of other subjects' (Custos, 1868: 8–9; Emsley, 1991: 82–4; Petrow, 1994: 42–5). Moral policing and administrative regulation came to be regarded as a diversion from what the police came to see as their central tasks of crime fighting and order maintenance, and gradually they were passed on to specialist voluntary and professional agencies and institutions. The role of dealing with what were seen as the roots of crime was treated as a separate task from police work, and that part of the policing of morality which the police retained was becoming simply an aspect of order maintenance, such as the clearing of drunks from the streets. The police were, broadly, concerned with the public sphere, while the private was for the new welfare agencies. They thereby split themselves off from large areas of crime which happened in private space, such as domestic violence.

The importance of crime fighting through detection for the police grew during the nineteenth century. It is true that many forces were too small to have any detective officers and even large ones put more emphasis on uniformed beat officers (Emsley, 1991: 151). However, if nothing else, the crime-fighting role became increasingly significant in terms of the public image of the police. Crime fighting had many attractions for the police since it meant much more carefully targeted operations which focused not on the working class as a whole, but on the 'criminal classes'. The Carnarvon and Gladstone reports both emphasized what they regarded as the problem of a relatively small number of habitual criminals committing a disproportionate amount of crime. The police were seen as having a key role in arresting such people and in supervising them after their release from prison under the Habitual Criminals Act 1869 and the Prevention of Crimes Act 1871 (Custos, 1868: 11; Davies, 1985; Royal Commission, 1863; Sindall, 1990). But of more significance in promoting crime fighting as the defining image of policework was fiction and news reporting. The city was presented in detection fiction as a labyrinth that few could enter, and Dickens revelled in the company of police detectives who could guide him around London. They claimed the ability to decode the city and to separate out its people into the evil and the good by their knowledge and ability to read clues. Dickens listened avidly to the stories told by the detectives because they opened up the secret underbelly of London and he based Bucket in *Bleak House* on one of them, Inspector Charles Frederick Field. But it was Dickens's friend Wilkie Collins who really established the police detective in fiction in his novel *The Moonstone* (1868) – a book which T.S. Eliot called, 'the first, the longest, and the best of modern English detective novels' (Collins, 1966: 7). The model for Collins' detective, Sergeant Cuff, was Inspector Wicher who had been the subject of a series of articles by Dickens in *Household Words*, and whose most famous case involved a child murder in 1860 at Road in Wiltshire, some aspects of which were used by Collins in his story. In the late nineteenth century the emphasis of such fiction was, it is true, thrown onto private detectives, most notably Sherlock Holmes, who made his first appearance in 1887. These stories contained an implicit – often explicit – criticism of the competence of the police as detectives (Reiner, 1992). However, that was not their principal theme, instead they conveyed the importance of detection in ensuring the victory of virtue over sin and in preventing crime by arresting criminals, and in the real world most people saw detection as the work of the police, after all this was how it was presented in newspaper reports of arrests and trials. Whatever the reality of policework, it was crime detection which came to be perceived as the key to policing: within this perspective the police protected society through the prevention of crime and crime was prevented by the efficiency of the police in detecting crime. Yet, it is also worth remarking that the police did not try to deny the tradition of beat patrolling, and in creating a confusion of images in which policework was centrally concerned with protecting the public through detection and also with the unrelated task of wandering about the streets,[2] the police created demands which they have always found impossible to meet.

'Where are the police? Looking after the unemployed'

In London problems with the roles of order maintenance and detection were dramatically exposed in the late 1880s. Disorders involving the unemployed and the police in Trafalgar Square in 1886 and 1887 exceeded anything London had seen for twenty years (Jones, 1984: 281–96; Richter, 1981). The industrial depression of 1884–7 had been longer and had cut deeper into the working class than the previous slumps of 1866 and 1879, and it coincided with an agricultural depression. The assumption that there was only a small and diminishing number of chronically poor casual workers which would be eliminated by continued economic expansion and the efforts of charities was exposed as false by the depression. That message was hammered home by the revelations of, among others, the Rev. Andrew Mearns, a Congregational minister, in *Bitter Cry of Outcast London* (Mearns, 1883) and the Royal Commission on Housing (Royal Commission, 1884–5):

> seething in the very centre of our great cities, concealed by the thinnest
> crust of civilization and decency, is a vast mass of moral corruption, of heart-
> breaking misery and absolute godlessness
>
> (Mearns, 1883: 3–4)

For the middle classes the most alarming consequence of all was the threat to political and social order. The Paris Commune was within recent memory, and G.R. Sims warned:

> This mighty mob of famished, diseased and filthy helots is getting dangerous,
> physically, morally, politically dangerous . . . Its fevers and its filth may spread
> to the homes of the wealthy; its lawless armies may sally forth and give us
> the taste of the lesson the mob has tried to teach now and again in Paris,
> when long years of neglect have done their work.
>
> (Jones, 1984: 224–5)

Disaffection was believed to be spreading to the better-off working people, who were also suffering from poor quality housing and high rents and who were beginning to listen to the arguments of the Social Democratic Federation, a radical, socialist group. Concern about the working people of London was, therefore, prompted not so much by sympathy, or by the 'rediscovery of poverty', or by guilt over neglect and exploitation, but rather by the fear of these people spilling into the West End.

That fear seemed to turn to reality in 1886–7. Following a severe winter a meeting of the unemployed was called in Trafalgar Square in February 1886. The Social Democratic Federation tried to use it as a platform to denounce the government and press for socialist revolution. When the meeting broke up in fights, the Social Democratic Federation led a group towards Hyde Park. As they passed the clubs in Pall Mall they were insulted by members and a riot ensued: property was attacked, shops looted and the wealthy robbed in their coaches. Outcast London had invaded the West End. The police were nowhere to be seen having mistakenly gone to guard Buckingham Palace, which was not in danger. The crowd did return to East London, but panic continued to grip the West End for the next two days, pumped up by police officers who went around telling shopkeepers to prepare for further invasions. The police were heavily criticized both for failing to protect property from the rioters and for spreading alarm. The Commissioner, Sir Edmund Henderson, was sacrificed, and Sir Charles Warren, a well-known war hero and competent amateur archaeologist, was appointed in the expectation that he would bring military discipline to the police's handling of such demonstrations. He soon got his chance as the tension peaked again in the autumn of 1887. Large numbers of the unemployed camped out in Trafalgar Square and St James's Park. Initially seen as objects for pity and assistance, their growing numbers alarmed local property owners. The police called for the help of the cavalry, and together they cleared the area on 13 November – 'Bloody Sunday'. Afterwards, London remained in a state of anxiety with mounted police patrols, soldiers and special constables standing ready. Ironically, in view of Henderson's fate, Warren's handling of the 1887 demonstration brought criticism of his militarism – the *Pall Mall Gazette* called him 'this soldier in jackboots' (Ascoli, 1979: 160) – and the Home Secretary, Henry Matthews, was all too willing to join in these attacks to deflect criticism from himself. The opportunity to sacrifice another commissioner soon arrived because on top of the 'Bloody Sunday' incident came accusations that the crime-fighting role of the police had been neglected as Warren pursued the task of order maintenance, for which, of course, he had been appointed.

Criticism of the detective branch of the Metropolitan Police peaked in the 1880s, but had been building up for some time. In 1860 there had been disquiet over its involvement in the investigation of the murder at Road (Barrister-at-Law, 1860), and in 1867 there was censure of the police response to Irish republican attacks: in that year the Fenians blew up part of Clerkenwell Prison, and the Prime Minister, the Earl of Derby, wrote to Disraeli, the Chancellor of the Exchequer, claiming that the police had advanced warning, 'It is really lamentable that the peace of the Metropolis . . . should depend on a body of police who, as detectives, are manifestly incompetent' (Richter, 1981). Two years later the detectives were reorganized, but a corruption scandal in 1877 decimated their ranks and their reputation. Howard Vincent was appointed to repair the damage. He both restructured and expanded the detective branch, so that by the middle of the 1880s there were some 800 officers in the Criminal Investigation Department (Petrow, 1993; Thurmond Smith, 1985). James Monro was then appointed in 1884 as Assistant Commissioner with responsibility for the detectives, but, as a result of Warren's appointment and his concentration on the military effectiveness of the Metropolitan Police, Monro complained of under-staffing and resigned in 1888.

Monro left his office on 31 August 1888. His replacement, James Anderson, was ill and so, rather than taking over, he left for Switzerland on sick leave. On the evening of Monro's departure Mary (Polly) Nicols was murdered. So the hunt for the Whitechapel murderer (later dubbed by a journalist, 'Jack the Ripper') began without a senior officer in charge of the detectives. As well as Polly Nicols, between 31 August and 9 November 1888 in and around Whitechapel Annie Chapman, Elizabeth Stride, Kate Eddowes and Mary Kelly were all murdered and mutilated. They were probably all victims of one murderer who may also have killed Emma Smith on 6 April 1888, Martha Tabram on 7 August 1888, Alice McKenzie on 16 July 1889 and Frances Cole on 13 February 1891, and may have been responsible for knife attacks on other women who survived: Annie Millwood on 25 February 1888 and Ada Wilson on the night of 27–28 March (Sugden, 1995; Walkowitz, 1992).

In general terms, there had been growing optimism about declining levels of crime and support for the police's record, and there is good reason to suppose that the police did have a real impact on crime (Gatrell, 1980; Jones, 1982: 117–43), but there remained a difference between crime in bulk as recorded in the criminal statistics, and the individual, brutal crime, which was the stuff of newspaper reports – the murder at Road, the Fenian bombings and the Whitechapel murders. There is no contradiction between, on the one hand, people believing that the police are worthwhile, even essential in the fight against crime, and, on the other, thinking that they are incompetent for failing to arrest an individual murderer.

For many in the East End, however, the murders confirmed a general feeling that the police were not providing adequate protection against crime. There was a climate of fear in Whitechapel fuelled by the impotence of the detectives: 'in a great city like London, the streets of which are continually patrolled by police, a woman can be foully and horribly killed almost next to the citizens peacefully sleeping in their beds, without a trace or clue being left of the villain who did the deed' (Sugden, 1995: 19). *The Times* (13 Sept. 1888) commented, 'it is now beginning to be admitted that the detectives are once more at fault'. The detective who was unable to identify the criminal had no value, and this failure challenged the promise of protection through detection. Local feeling can

be gauged by the rapid formation of vigilance committees: one was established after Tabram's murder to patrol the streets, and others appeared
after Nichols was murdered. The chair of the Mile End Vigilance Committee pressed the Home Secretary: 'The present series of murders is
absolutely unique in the annals of crime . . . and all ordinary means of
detection have failed' (Sugden, 1995: 2). A committee of leading business
people was driven to offer a reward of £100 because 'in spite of murders
being committed in our midst our police force is inadequate to discover
the author or authors of the late atrocities', and this was followed a month
later by a petition to the Home Secretary signed by about 200 traders.
The Whitechapel District Board of Works added its voice by asking Warren
to deploy more police officers (Sugden, 1995: 19; *The Times*, 3 Sept., 12
Sept., 19 Oct. 1888). The radicals took the opportunity to hit back at
the police for their behaviour at the Trafalgar Square demonstrations: at
a meeting of the unemployed in Hyde Park in October 1888 a placard
read, 'The Whitechapel Murders. Where are the Police? Looking after
the Unemployed!' (Sugden, 1995: 134–5 and 286).

Warren went to great lengths to defend himself and his force against
each accusation. He did show a willingness to follow up all sorts of ideas
for solving the crime. But the bizzare nature of some of these – such as
the decision to photograph the eyes of one victim in the hope that an
impression of the murderer might be discovered imprinted on them –
smacked of desperation and brought ridicule on the force from an
unsympathetic Press which resented the lack of cooperation from the
police: 'However much or little they know, the police devote themselves
energetically to the task of preventing other people from knowing anything', one journalist angrily reported (Sugden, 1995: 4, 70–1 and 135;
The Times, Sept.–Nov. 1888 *passim*). Warren pointed out that he had sent
large numbers of officers into Whitechapel to patrol and to carry out
house-to-house inquiries, but the fact remained that he had neglected
the detectives in favour of boosting the force's ability to deal with public
order problems. There was also Monro's resignation and the absence of
Anderson. Finally, the emphasis of Warren's regime was reflected in the
absence of the word 'crime' from his annual reports (Ascoli, 1979: 158).

As has been mentioned, in addition to these problems, Warren also
quarrelled with officials in the Home Office and the Home Secretary,
Henry Matthews. Monro's resignation was part of a larger dispute that
Warren was having with Matthews over the control of the Metropolitan
Police. Warren believed that as Commissioner he should have command
of all officers, and that, while the Home Secretary had the power to dis-
approve of rules and regulations made by the Commissioner, he could
not give orders to police officers or issue circulars – a view which Matthews
vigorously challenged. This argument blew up over Warren's resentment
at Monro's direct contact with the Home Office. He threatened to resign
and so Monro was forced out, but he joined the Home Office where he
advised civil servants on matters concerning the CID and held meetings

with Anderson and the principal detective inspectors (*Parliamentary Debates*, 3rd series, vol. 130, c. 463, c. 893–4, c. 1342, 1346–7 and 1357–60; *The Times*, 13 Nov. 1888). The discord between Warren and Matthews went back to Warren's handling of the Trafalgar Square disturbances, although it seems likely that he would have ridden that storm but for the exposure of the weaknesses in the detective branch during the inquiries into the 1888 murders. In the end Warren was forced to resign over an article he had written in *Murray's Magazine*, not – it was said – because the article was critical of the Home Office, but because he had published it without the permission of the Home Secretary. The response that Warren had written similar articles before without the Home Office making any complaint was brushed aside by Matthews who told the Commons that he was unaware of these, even though some had appeared in *The Times*. As one commentator put it, the article 'was merely the accident which determined a resignation sooner or later inevitable' (*The Times*, 13 Nov. 1888; *Parliamentary Debates*, vol. 130, c. 1354–6). The removal of Warren enabled the Home Office to appoint James Monro as commissioner, and, although he too fell out with the Home Office, he, together with the next two commissioners, worked to strengthen the detective force.[3]

*   *   *   *

Even as late as the report on the poor laws of 1832, the problems of rural society were still significant in determining the direction of social policy, but within a generation, and certainly by the 1870s, attention was firmly on the town – and, more often than not, on London. The difficulties which London faced were exacerbated by the fragmentation of its government: power resided with a huge number of parishes and local boards of guardians (who were responsible for the administration of the poor law), all fiercely jealous of their powers. The inefficiency of these authorities had led Peel to circumvent them when he established the Metropolitan Police, but their existence remained an obstruction to any coherent solution to the alienation caused by the existence of extreme poverty in the midst of extreme wealth, so that when the problems of the East End were exposed the response was, at first, to contain the problem there and to protect the West End. Warren failed to achieve this and was, therefore, sacrificed, although the problem had already gone beyond attempts to treat it as a policing issue.

At the same time, criminal justice policy had become the subject for wrangling between different parts of the administration. Civil servants in the Home Office were developing their expertise and were increasingly keen to expand their power by challenging the old structures of authority, represented by Du Cane and Warren. The significance of this shift in authority was signalled by the removal of Warren and the appointment of Monro, by the setting up of the Gladstone Committee, and by Du Cane's retirement and his replacement by Ruggles-Brise. Decision-making on penal policy and on the Metropolitan Police became increasingly private, bureaucratized, centralized and de-politicized. This trend was furthered by a move towards dealing with poverty and crime through treatment rather than punishment, which placed greater emphasis on the need for careful classification by experts working in private.

Further reading

The works of Henry Mayhew are enormously useful in understanding the mid-Victorian view of the poor discussed in this chapter (Thompson and Yeo, 1973; Mayhew, 1967). The essays on the detectives by Dickens in *Household Words*, and the detective fiction of Wilkie Collins and, of course, of Conan Doyle are worth revisiting for what they do (and do not) say about the police and the expectations which the Victorians had of them. Steedman (1984) has written a lengthy study of the Victorian provincial police, and, of course, Emsley (1991) should also be consulted. Gatrell (1980) provides a detailed examination of the evidence on the decline in crime in the late nineteenth and early twentieth centuries. The standard study of prisons in the period is by McConville (1995), although those of a weak constitution are advised not to ask the price. The Whitechapel Murders of 1888 have attracted the worst sort of writer, but Sugden (1995), while concerned with the same murder-tourism as the others, is more thorough in his use of newspapers and records; the best book on the events surrounding the murders is by Walkowitz (1992). Richter (1981) describes the disorders of the period, most particularly the Trafalgar Square demonstrations, but it is to Steadman Jones (1984) that historians should go first for a study of 'outcast London', although his work should be read alongside Green's (1995) fine book.

Notes

1. This distnction defined Mayhew's work in that he studied 'the street folk' who, unlike the 'respectable' working people, led lives which were quite outside the experience of his middle-class readers.

2. To a large extent the idea of patrolling often seemed as much concerned with disciplining police officers as with moralizing the poor: constables were expected to patrol at a certain pace and could be surprised at any point by superior officers.

3. Charles Warren features as the reactionary general in William Morris's *News from Nowhere*. After leaving the Metropolitan Police, he returned to military duty in China and South Africa, and later worked with the Boy Scouts. He died in 1927 (Boos, 1982: 73).

Chapter 8

Building the New Jerusalem, 1890–1950

'Socialism in the arms of Individualism'

By the end of the nineteenth century the main threats to British industrial and imperial dominance were believed to be international competition and a working class which was morally and physically unfit. It had been accepted that government intervention – through, for instance, public health legislation – was necessary to secure a healthy environment, and, by the early twentieth century, that had been extended to providing assistance to individuals through education, medical treatment, housing provision, pensions and unemployment benefit. However, the research of Charles Booth, begun in 1886 (completed 1903) and published in seventeen volumes as *Life and Labour of the People in London*, had revealed a greater extent of poverty than had been suspected with some 30 per cent of the working class living below the poverty line. The depth of 'the problem of poverty in the midst of wealth' (Pfautz, 1967: 24) led Booth to conclude that, unless action was taken to alleviate the plight of the poor, socialism would take a firm grip and the capitalist system would be doomed. He proposed the creation of a more inclusive society through a programme of what he called 'Socialism in the arms of Individualism', adding that,

> In taking charge of the lives of the incapable, State Socialism finds its proper work, and by doing it completely would relieve us of a serious danger.
> The Individualist system breaks down as things are, and is invaded on every side by Socialistic innovations, but its hardy doctrines would have a far better chance in a society purged of those who cannot stand alone. Though interference on the part of the State with the lives of a small fraction of the population would make it possible, ultimately, to dispense with any socialistic interference in the lives of all the rest.

> (Pfautz, 1967: 30–1)

In 1895 A.J. Balfour, the Conservative politician who later became Prime Minister, argued that, 'Social legislation, as I conceive it, is not merely to be distinguished from Socialist legislation but it is its most direct opposite and its most effective antidote' (Fraser, 1973: 129). This attitude prompted a flood of inquiries by royal commissions, select committees and departmental committees (including the Gladstone Committee), and of legislation and voluntary initiatives around the turn of the century. These laid the foundations for the construction of the welfare state which really got underway in the decade before the First World War.

There remained the problem of those who were believed to be irredeemable. As Booth's remarks indicate, for him the aim of social inclusion did not extend to them, and he proposed that they be moved to labour colonies. The eugenics movement, on the other hand, explored methods by which their fertility might be reduced so that they might simply die out (Garland, 1985), and the Gladstone Committee recommended in 1895 giving extended sentences to habitual criminals. The new welfare state maintained moral distinctions which legitimized discrimination and intrusion: the undeserving should be punished and the deserving assisted. So, for instance, the Royal Commission on the Poor Laws (Royal Commission, 1909) argued that, while there should be no return to the punitive principles of the Poor Law Amendment Act 1834, 'The causes of distress are not only economic and industrial; in their origin and character they are largely moral' (Matthews, 1986). The Liberal administration, which was elected in 1906, constructed its welfare provisions on these distinctions by seeking to rescue only the deserving from the poor relief system: so, Lloyd George's old age pension of 1908 was not available to those who 'habitually failed' to work or to save, or to criminals for ten years after their release (Hay, 1977). The broad aim was to identify and normalize 'all those legal citizens (or prospective legal citizens) who lack the normative capacity to participate and exercise their new-found rights responsibly'. They either became normalized or were segregated off (Garland, 1985: 249).

The Gladstone Committee classified offenders so that only the worst would go to prison, while the rest would be channelled into specialized treatment programmes (Radzinowicz and Hood, 1986: 618–57). The blame for the failure of the prison was no longer placed on architectural defects or poor quality staff, instead the prison itself was seen as the problem (Garland, 1985: 60). It was too broad brush in its treatment of offenders. Habitual criminals, habitual drunkards, mentally disordered offenders, first offenders, young prisoners, women, women with infants, remand prisoners and debtors were all believed to require distinct methods of treatment in special institutions (Harding et al., 1985: 205–35). As has been seen, the policy of removing juveniles from adult prisons can be traced back to the early nineteenth century, but it was refreshed by the establishment of the reformatory and industrial schools and then the Borstal system, which was given statutory recognition in 1908 (see below p. 125). The Probation of Offenders Act 1907 formalized a system of probation which had been introduced from the 1870s as voluntary schemes to keep people out of prison by the Police Court Mission of the Church of England Temperance Society, the Church Army, the Salvation Army and the St Giles's Christian Mission (see also the Probation of First Offenders Act 1887), and it came to play an increasingly important part in reducing rates of incarceration (Bochell, 1976; McWilliams, 1983, 1985; Radzinowicz and Hood, 1986: 633–47). The Administration of Criminal Justice Act 1914 aimed to divert fine defaulters from prison. The Inebriates Act 1898 enabled a court to commit an offender to an inebriate reformatory for up to three years if an offence was committed while under the influence of drink or if an offender admitted to being, or was found by the jury to be, an habitual drunkard. However, as early as 1908 a departmental committee found that this was little used because magistrates were unaware of their powers or unwilling to use them, and because the term 'habitual drunkard' caused problems of definition; at the same time, when the powers were used, the tendency was to commit for the full three years which was found to be too long where the individual was amenable to treatment. By 1921 all fifteen state reformatories had been closed, and the main response to drunkenness shifted to licensing and the control of the opening hours of public houses (Harding *et al.*, 1985: 252–4; Harding and Wilkins, 1988; Zedner, 1991: 220–63). The Mental Deficiency Act 1913 sought to remove mentally ill people from the prisons and place them into special hospitals, such as Rampton, built in 1910, and Moss Side, opened in 1919 (Broadmoor dated back to 1863), but there were problems over diagnosis and the availability of places (Zedner, 1991: 264–96). In the case of habitual criminals, the Gladstone Committee had rather limited aims. It focused on professional criminals who, it suggested, should be given an extended sentence over and above that which the instant offence warranted: 'As loss of liberty would to them prove eventually the chief deterrent, so by their being removed from the opportunity of doing wrong the community would gain.' When Herbert Gladstone became Home Secretary this proposal was enacted in the Prevention of Crime Act 1908, under which someone who had three convictions after the age of sixteen and had persistently led a dishonest life could be declared by a jury to be an 'habitual criminal', and, if the protection of the public required it, the judge could add five to ten years to the sentence. A special prison was constructed at Camp Hill on the Isle of Wight in which the regime was more relaxed: prisoners were allowed to earn money, smoke and read newspapers (Departmental Committee on Prisons, 1895: 31; Harding *et al.*, 1985: 237–8). However, the sentence did not prove very successful: it contravened the principle that a sentence should be proportionate to the offence committed and it became difficult to get juries to declare someone an 'habitual criminal'. Furthermore, while it was claimed that almost all those in convict prisons were habitual criminals (Thomson, 1925), a committee of inquiry in 1932 (Departmental Committee, 1932) found that only a few prisoners were actually detained under the act and, in an unusually perceptive comment, remarked that most of these were 'of the type whose previous convictions testify as much to their clumsiness as to their persistence in crime'.

The fairly rapid failure of some of the policies that emerged from the Gladstone Committee did not undermine the significance of its move from a broadly undiscriminating and punitive approach to offending to one based on classification and treatment. However, even at its peak between the two World Wars, this new approach never had a clear field. There remained powerful support for a punitive strategy and, as a result, policies were often compromised or lost. Nevertheless, the period up to the 1950s was predominantly an optimistic one with policy makers believing that it was possible to change individual behaviour through state intervention.

The march of the liberal progressives

The 'liberal progressives' (Bailey, 1987), who pressed these new ideas, drew on the philosophy propounded by T.H. Green at Oxford in the 1870s, and they took key offices in the bureaucracy: for instance, C.E.B. Russell and Arthur Norris, who each served as chief inspector of reformatory and industrial schools either side of the First World War, Sydney Harris, head of the Children's Branch at the Home Office from 1919 to 1934, and Alexander Paterson, who was at the Prison Commission from 1922. In many ways Green and his followers harked back to the motivation that had driven John Howard and Elizabeth Fry, namely, that spiritual fulfilment was possible only through a practical philanthropy which involved missionary work among the poor: Norris, Russell and Paterson had all been active in youth club work, and their interest in social policy stemmed both from a genuine concern for the sufferings of the poor and from a belief, similar to Booth's, that action was needed to maintain Britain's place in the world and to prevent 'systematic socialism'. Paterson wrote in 1912 that, 'No country that has joined the struggle for supremacy can allow the finest human material to grow stiff and idle for lack of help and understanding' (Bailey, 1987: 8–9). They regarded the degraded physical and moral state of the poor as the other side of economic success, and believed, therefore, that society had a duty to protect and to educate. This view sat alongside, rather than replaced, the individualism which lay at the core of liberalism because, like Booth, the liberal progressives believed in a form of state intervention which would enable individuals to take responsibility for themselves. For them there was no difficulty in accepting that a penal policy based on reformation might lead to sentences disproportionate to the crime. Indeed, the whole point was to move the focus away from the crime and place it on the offender, so that the cause of their offending might be treated: according to Paterson, 'The exact period which he should spend in prison should not be determined entirely by the gravity of his offence, but by his fitness for the resumption of social life' (Ruck, 1951: 66). In the extreme case of an habitual offender who was 'never likely to be a useful citizen, then a completely indeterminate sentence is the only safeguard' (Ruck, 1951: 66). Such ideas came up against, and often had to yield to, the belief that punishment should be proportionate and imposed only on those who had committed a crime, and this was based on the proposition that the criminal acted voluntarily and was morally responsible for her or his action. However, there was some nibbling at this by defining various offenders as 'defective' – physically, mentally or morally – and by redefining punishment as treatment or care (Forsythe, 1991: 9–17; Garland, 1985; Harding, 1988).

In spite of the significance of the changes introduced after the Gladstone Committee by the Prison Commission under Ruggles-Brise, criticisms came from those liberal progressives who thought the Commission was insufficiently radical and who caricatured Ruggles-Brise as little more than a disciple of Du Cane. An anonymous writer was driven by these attacks to write an unprecedented series of ten articles on prisons in defence of the Commission for *The Times* in 1910 (*The Times*, 27 May, 30 May, 1 Jun., 3 Jun., 4 Jun., 10 Jun., 15 Jun., 21 Jun., 27 Jun., 4 Jul. 1910. But see Tighe Hopkins in *The Times*, 10 Jun. 1910). To some extent, Ruggles-Brise felt obliged to move slowly because of fears about how the public might react to sudden, radical changes in prison discipline (Forsythe, 1991: 35–40). But it was all too slow for the liberal progressives. To them it seemed that Ruggles-Brise had largely ignored the spirit of the Gladstone Committee's recommendations, and remarks, such as those he made in a speech to the International Prison Congress at Washington in 1910, appeared to confirm his conservatism: 'In Europe we place the constituent elements of punishment in the following order: retributory, deterrent, and reformatory'. Similarly, in 1912 the Prison Commission declared, 'Our constant effort is to hold the balance between what is necessary as punishment . . . from a penal and deterrent point of view, and what can be conceded consistently with this, in the way of humanising and reforming influences' (Fox, 1952: 63; Ruggles-Brise, 1921). To liberal progressives, who took the view that reformation or, as it was called, 'training for citizenship' (Fox, 1934: 41) should come first for all prisoners, such statements seemed to imply a system little different from that of the Du Cane regime and to ignore the Gladstone principle that prison 'should have as its primary and concurrent objects, deterrence and reformation' (Departmental Committee on Prisons, 1895: 8 and 18–19). Moreover, they attacked the view of Du Cane and Ruggles-Brise that a punitive prison regime acted as a deterrent, arguing that deterrence was best achieved by certainty of detection, not by the construction of a harsh prison regime (Fox, 1934: 31; 1952: 12–13).

The liberal progressives subscribed to the doubts which Lushington, Permanent Under-Secretary at the Home Office, had expressed to the Gladstone Committee about the value of incarceration in changing the character of prisoners, and, indeed, he was frequently quoted by them right up to the 1950s. Sydney and Beatrice Webb wrote in 1922,

> We suspect that it passes the wit of man to contrive a prison which shall not be gravely injurious to the minds of the vast majority of the prisoners, if not also to their bodies. So far as can be seen at present the most practical and the most hopeful of 'prison reforms' is to keep people out of prison altogether!
>
> (Webb, 1922: 248. Also, Departmental Committee on Prisons, 1895: 8; *The Times*, 31 Jul. 1925)

The doubts of the Gladstone Committee about prisons had been magnified by the experiences of suffragettes before the First World War, whose plight led to attention being focused on women prisoners for the first time since Elizabeth Fry (Blagg and Wilson, 1912; Lytton, 1914. But see, Robinson, 1862), and of conscientious objectors imprisoned during the war. In 1919 an inquiry was set up under the auspices of the Labour Party and the encouragement of the Webbs. The report, *English Prisons To-Day*, was edited by Hobhouse, an academic-turned-journalist, and Brockway, who had been imprisoned as a conscientious objector. Published in 1922, the year after Ruggles-Brise had retired from the Prison Commission, it was a long and crushing attack on his work. The authors criticized the secrecy of the Prison Commission, its lack of accountability and its imposition of a single regime in all prisons, but more importantly they castigated, 'The persistence in the principles of prison treatment of retributory and deterrent factors, to the exclusion of truly preventive and educational principles' (Hobhouse and Brockway, 1922: 85).

It will hardly come as a surprise to find that neither the Gladstone committee nor the liberal progressives devoted much of their attention to women offenders; even though it was claimed in 1912 that there was more recidivism among women than men (Blagg and Wilson, 1912: 13), the main problem continued to be seen as offending by men. The discussion of adult and young women offenders did acquire a scientific tone from the late nineteenth century, but in essence little had changed since the eighteenth century and the evil influence which Elizabeth Lyon supposedly had on John Sheppard: the problem in terms of crime was seen as mainly the irresistible influence for evil which independent and sexually active (the two were assumed to be synonymous) women were supposed to have over men. Yet, whereas before the early twentieth century there was little agreement as to how women offenders should be treated, work on psychology and psychiatry seemed to many to offer a solution: it was claimed that the involvement of women in crime was the result of emotional disturbances which could be treated therapeutically, and as late as the 1970s a regime at Holloway prison in London was designed around the delivery of such treatment (Burt, 1931; Dobash, Dobash and Gutteridge, 1986).[1]

Paterson and juvenile offenders

Although Maurice Waller succeeded Ruggles-Brise as chair of the Prison Commission, it was Paterson who became its key figure during the inter-war period. His view was that, 'Men come to prison as a punishment not *for* punishment' (Ruck, 1951: 23). To him the aim of the penal system was to protect society and this could be achieved either by life imprisonment, which was not acceptable to public opinion, 'or [the prison] must bring such influence to bear upon him while in custody that he will, on the day of his discharge, be an honest, hard-working and self-controlled man, fit for freedom, and no longer an enemy of society' (Ruck, 1951: 24). The problem in achieving the latter goal was not whether it was possible – in most cases Paterson believed it was – but that it required a regime carefully suited to the individual offender. This was a difficult proposition since he agreed with Cyril Burt, the psychologist, who wrote that, 'Crime is assignable to no single universal source, nor yet to two or three: it springs from a wide variety, and usually from a multiplicity, of alternative and converging influences.' Indeed, Burt identified 'more than 170 distinct conditions' associated with criminality (Burt, 1931: 599–608). Classification was, therefore, a key feature of Paterson's approach and, indeed, he argued – unsuccessfully – for 'an Examination Centre' where people could be assessed before trial by psychiatrists, psychologists and social inquirers, so that the court could send offenders to the appropriate institution (Ruck, 1951: 27 and 45–54). The training regime was to be built around controlled association and the constructive use of the prisoners' time: Paterson rejected the idea that solitude would bring a criminal to reform on the ground that, 'He is not naturally introspective' (Ruck, 1951: 78). Anyway, he reasoned that taking individuals out of the company of others was hardly suited to enabling them to reintegrate into society on release (Ruck, 1951: 76–81). Paterson criticized the progressive stage system, which had been in use since the 1840s and had been so highly regarded by Jebb, on the grounds that it was complex, cumbersome and open to inequities. Instead, he favoured the American system by which prisoners were given privileges on first entering, rather than having to earn them, and these were only lost by bad behaviour or a slackening of effort (Ruck, 1951: 86–90).

Initially, Paterson's main responsibility at the Prison Commission was the Borstal system (Hood, 1965: 103–32), which Ruggles-Brise had played the key role in setting up. The need for a more skilled labour force to compete with other nations, the declining birth rate, the long-standing concern to regulate the moral environment in which children grew up, and both the fall in demand for child labour and the steady rise of opposition to it, all led to a greater emphasis on the protection and discipline of young people from the 1880s. This found expression in child protection initiatives, such as the campaign against child prostitution led by W.T.

Stead of the *Pall Mall Gazette*, the establishment of the National Society for the Prevention of Cruelty to Children and Barnardo's Homes, and legislation which raised the age of consent to sixteen and gave the police greater powers in relation to children (Walkowitz, 1992). At the same time, around the turn of the century, it was believed that a new youth culture was emerging which was alienated from, and a threat to, mainstream society (Pearson, 1983). That sense of alienation and threat were encapsulated in books such as Arthur Morrison's *A Child of the Jago* and Clarence Rook's *The Hooligan Nights*. Rook wrote of the youth 'Alf' that, 'Regular employment, at a fixed wage, does not attract . . . It does not give him the necessary margin of leisure, and the necessary margin of chance gains' (Rook, 1979: 19). This stood in direct contrast to the belief in the importance of a disciplined, fully employed, vigorous and hard-working mass of people able to work and to fight (Weiner, 1990: 358–65).

It was against this background that the Gladstone Committee criticized the imprisonment of young people, and that criticism led to an experiment at Bedford Prison in 1900, which moved the next year to Borstal (Rochester) Prison in Kent and received statutory approval in the Prevention of Crime Act of 1908 (Hood, 1965). Reformatories were still under private control, and, although they received part of their funding from the state, they relied on donations which were dwindling by the turn of the century. This led to overcrowding, poor quality training and high recidivism: as one commentator put it, they had a 'bad effect on the health, the discipline, and the general tone of the inmates' (Holmes, 1902: 9). However, Gladstone focused on the view that reformatories were not sufficiently severe and prisons were too severe for certain types of juvenile offenders. The committee, therefore, saw the need for an institution which sat between the reformatory and the prison, combining 'penal and coercive sides' with a system of training and work 'qualified generally to exercise the best and healthiest kind of moral influence' (Departmental Committee on Prisons, 1895: 30). The aim was to prevent young people becoming habitual offenders by removing them from prison (a policy with which Du Cane agreed) and placing them in special institutions – the Borstals. Ruggles-Brise took great pride in his achievement in establishing the Borstal system, and later recalled that its genesis lay in a visit he made to a convict prison,

> I was struck . . . by the number of young convicts whom I found there, and my researches into the history of the older convicts revealed the fact that most of them owed a life of crime to the fact that they had been sent to penal servitude in their early years. It was to meet this great evil, and to find an alternative to penal servitude for the dangerous criminal between 16 and 21 that we started the Borstal system.
>
> (Bailey, 1987: 188–9)

The Prevention of Crime Act 1908 was fairly vague in that it allowed (within very broad limits) an open-ended sentence so as to enable a programme of treatment to be suited to an individual offender in a way which could be determined by an administrator rather than by the sentencing judge. The act spoke of placing inmates in 'detention for such term and under such instruction and discipline as appears most conducive to his reformation and the repression of crime'. Although, in practice, the regime applied to juveniles in Borstals seems to have been fairly undiscriminating (all were assumed to need broadly the same treatment). The act gave administrators, in general, and Ruggles-Brise, in particular, a fairly free hand to devise what they regarded as an appropriate regime. He favoured one which included vocational, physical, moral and religious training, but he also emphasized – and this was where the liberal progressives took issue with him – that the Borstal should punish young offenders with bad records:

> It is a fundamental principle of English prison administration, which, it is hoped, will never be departed from, and which is in no way contravened in a Borstal institution, that prison life must be deterrent – a punishment first of all for the crime or misdemeanour that has been committed.
>
> (*The Times*, 4 Jun. 1910; Hood, 1965: 95–103)

He dismissed the views of those who wanted greater emphasis on training, arguing that they were 'places of detention under "penal" discipline of grown lads and young men – many with bad records of crime' (Bailey, 1987: 191, also 186–92). Unsurprisingly, the plight of girls who were convicted of offences was largely ignored: the only female Borstal was a former inebriate reformatory in Aylesbury where the regime was unimaginative, consisting of training in domestic tasks (Bailey, 1987: 227–55).

Problems emerged fairly quickly (Forsythe, 1991: 50–3). The courts failed to send to Borstal those whom Ruggles-Brise believed were most suited to its discipline, and most of the staff were not adequately trained to operate a regime which tried to combine punitive and reformatory discipline. More fundamentally, Russell, as chief inspector, voiced his opposition to the emphasis on punitive discipline before the First World War, and that was also the essence of the criticism in the chapter on Borstals in *English Prisons Today*, which was probably written by Paterson (Bailey, 1987: 195–6). Ruggles-Brise believed that military training was an important way of reforming these young people, whereas Paterson claimed it merely encouraged outward conformity which broke down once they were released. He argued that what was needed was a system which ensured the internalization of a new value system: 'It is self-discipline that the Borstal boy needs most, and the army (and prison) system of mechanical obedience entirely fails to engender it' (Bailey, 1987: 196, also 186–96). His idea was to provide a moral framework within which youthful vigour and self discipline would be encouraged: 'The task is not to break or knead him into shape, but to stimulate some power within to regulate conduct aright, to insinuate a preference for the good and the clean, to make him want to use his life well, so that he himself and not others will save him from waste' (Ruck, 1951: 97). The criticism did unfairly caricature the Borstal system under Ruggles-Brise – it had, for instance, moved more towards education by the time he retired in 1921 (Forsythe, 1991: 53–8) – but gave an indication of the priorities of the post-war breed of liberal-progressive bureaucrats.

Liberal progressives, rejecting the notion of innate evil, believed that juvenile offenders were 'the product of social impairment', and that, 'The elements of a boyish crime are a desire for something, the opportunity to obtain it with probable impunity, the lack of self-control to restrain him' (Bailey, 1987: 243 and 10). Cyril Burt, writing in 1924, also emphasized the role played by the psychological environment: 'the typical delinquent is a child with a dull, uneducated mind, struggling to control an emotional and impulsive temperament, both housed in a weak, afflicted body, and living with a demoralized family in an impoverished home' (Bailey, 1987: 14). None of this precluded the acknowledgement of the role of poverty in the aetiology of crime because English psychology encompassed the view that the mind developed through interaction with the environment. So, for instance, Burt believed that, while hereditary factors were important, the main causes of crime were environmental – a view with which Paterson agreed (Bailey, 1987 15–16; Burt, 1931: 599–608; Ruck, 1951: 30–44). As had long been the case, much emphasis was placed on the question of parental control, particularly during the First World War when the absence of fathers at the Front and of women at work was blamed for a sharp rise in juvenile crime (Smith, 1990; Weinberger, 1993). But while the identification of the role of the family in juvenile crime was not new, the solution offered by the liberal progressives was. The approach taken by the Marine Society in the eighteenth century and by Mary Carpenter in her reformatory and industrial schools in the nineteenth had been to remove children from families which were regarded as providing a poor moral education. The liberal progressives did continue this approach, but also explored the possibility of giving assistance so that the child might remain at home. This sort of thinking both legitimized state intervention in the family and, during the First World War, sent a clear message to mothers about their post-war role. If, as was believed, juvenile offending was linked to parental neglect, it seemed logical to treat it as a child protection issue rather than a criminal justice one. The focus, it was argued, should be on the welfare of the child rather than on the offence: 'The problem of delinquency in the young must be envisaged as but one inseparable portion of the larger enterprise for child welfare.' The offence should, therefore, be seen as of secondary significance: merely a trigger which alerted the authorities to a problem. Although such ideas were not entirely new, they were extended and developed through the Children Act 1908 and the Children and Young Persons Act 1933. However, this theoretical assimilation of child neglect and juvenile offending was often less evident in practice (Bailey, 1987: 69–114). For instance, the 1933 act replaced reformatories and industrial schools with approved schools, and in theory children were assigned to a particular school simply on the basis of age and of an assessment as to the type of training they required, but in practice a distinction was normally made by using the schools for offenders while neglected children were treated in the community.

There was opposition to many of these changes, and it drew particular strength from the rise in the number of juvenile offenders after the Children and Young Persons Act 1933. The liberal progressives argued that the act reduced the stigma of a court appearance for juveniles by shifting the emphasis from punishment to welfare, and that this had encouraged victims and the police to bring more prosecutions. Critics, however, were convinced that the increase was due to a lack of parental discipline which was being encouraged by the lenient treatment of offenders. So, while the liberal progressives wanted the state to provide juveniles with a secure environment (either at home or in an institution) and training through which they could improve their self-control, their critics argued that the state's role was to supply the punitive discipline which was lacking at home and which they believed was at the root of the problem. These critics did achieve a number of significant victories. For example, the House of Lords removed a clause from the Children and Young Persons Bill which would have abolished whipping for juveniles, and the Departmental Committee on the Treatment of Young Offenders (1927), which was so influential in the framing of that bill, disappointed Paterson's expectations by not recommending the abolition of imprisonment for people under 21 (Bailey, 1987: 107–9, 117–46 and 221–3).

As well as criticism from politicians to the changes being pressed by the liberal progressives, there was the pragmatic opposition or simple neglect of their policies within institutions because staff lacked the training or inclination to do more than act as custodians (Harding *et al.*, 1985: 220–1). The other stumbling blocks were the Treasury and the courts. The Treasury has rarely been keen to spend the large amounts of money that new penal schemes tend to require, and there was a reluctance to fund new Borstals when the drop in the prison population meant there were empty prisons which could be converted. Even then the Borstals could not cope with the rise in the number of juvenile offenders during the inter-war years, and this meant that young offenders were held in prison for longer periods while they waited for a place – further frustrating Paterson's aim of abolishing imprisonment for juveniles. In 1931 the Treasury also opposed state observation homes where children could be assessed before being dealt with by magistrates' courts, since it was feared that it might lead to pressure from local authorities for the funding of other parts of their responsibility (Bailey, 1987: 227–9, 62, 88 and 90). The second difficulty lay in the attitude of the courts. Although the magistracy supplied many significant reformers, there were plenty of magistrates who believed in punishment as a deterrent and were unconvinced by programmes designed to rehabilitate. Many magistrates' courts failed to implement fully the requirements in the Children Act 1908 for the differential treatment of juveniles in court, and the informal origins of probation meant there were great variations in the support given to it by magistrates before the First World War (Bailey, 1987: 36–47, 178–86 and 225–6; McWilliams, 1983, 1985).

The Criminal Justice Act 1948

The liberal progressives' agenda was in the ascendancy in the 1920s and 1930s, and by the late 1930s they were moving towards major reform in the shape of the Criminal Justice Bill 1938. The Conservative Home Secretary, Sir Samuel Hoare, who had been appointed the year before, was a descendant of Elizabeth Fry, whose example he wished to emulate. With that degree of exaggeration so beloved of all politicians, he declared himself

> struck by an anomaly. On the one hand, penal reform had, compared with other social reforms, made little or no advance in 50 years. On the other hand, a mass of invaluable material had been accumulated by practical experience and expert inquiries for creating an up-to-date and efficient prison system.
>
> (Bailey, 1987: 255)

He claimed that the 1938 bill would 'sweep away the remnants' of the Victorian penal system and would properly show 'the outward and visible signs of the new outlook upon the problems of crime and delinquency' (Playfair, 1971: 177). Unfortunately, the outbreak of the Second World War in 1939 meant those reforms had to wait for another ten years.

The war did bring a rise in recorded crime if the period immediately after the war is compared with that which preceded it (Smithies, 1982). But this was believed to be the consequence of the disruptive effect of modern warfare on the civilian population, which would pass as life went back to normal, and it was, therefore, not viewed with any great alarm. However, the war had opened up the possibilities of a more interventionist-style of government to deal with, among other things, rationing scarce resources, conscription, civil defence and the relocation of children away from areas that were likely to be bombed. This provided a model for the possibilities open to a post-war government in tackling the social problems which had scarred the inter-war years and fitted in well with the liberal-progressive programme.

Learning from the failure of the Lloyd George government in the First World War to prepare for the peace, the wartime government commissioned from William Beveridge a plan which was published in 1944 as *Social Insurance and Allied Services.* Poverty, he believed, was due to idleness, disease, ignorance, squalor and want: idleness would be tackled principally through a planned economy which delivered full employment as envisaged by the economist Maynard Keynes; disease through the creation of the National Health Service; ignorance through a reformed education system; squalor through improved housing; and want through benefits for those who were temporarily unemployed, widows, the sick, the elderly and families with children. In 1944 Jowitt, speaking for the government, welcomed Beveridge's all-embracing approach to social problems:

> Social security can only be achieved by many and diverse methods . . . economic justice, political justice, justice everywhere, full employment, organisation of the health services, maintenance of a stable price level, a satisfactory housing policy.
>
> (*Commons Debates*, vol. 404, c. 984)

It was also assumed that the eradication of poverty and ignorance would reduce crime.

The liberal-progressive project fitted in well with the remodelled welfare state. Ideas from the 1938 bill re-emerged in the Criminal Justice Act 1948, which the chair of the Prison Commission, Lionel Fox (1952: 66), regarded as the culmination of the work begun in 1895. Later commentators have been less enthusiastic: Professor Morris (1989: 77) dismissed it as 'little more than a penological dinosaur, obsolete in its conceptions and largely unadaptable to the changing world of post-war Britain'. This is to read history backwards, which, while not the deviant activity some make it out to be, can lead to unfair criticisms. It is hardly surprising that there was a willingness to accept the optimism of the pre-war liberal progressives. There was general confidence about the future in 1945, and, in any case, the penal reforms of the inter-war period seemed to have worked since, although the prison population had risen during the war, the trend during the century had been one of falling numbers, and the Borstal system appeared to have succeeded in terms of reducing both the adult prison population and recidivism amongst ex-Borstal inmates (Bailey, 1987: 214–15). In these circumstances there seemed no need for a full-scale inquiry or change in direction.

The 1948 act abolished penal servitude, hard labour and the somewhat complicated divisions of imprisonment without hard labour which had grown up. In their place it introduced a single sentence of imprisonment for adults, with the exception of habitual offenders, for whom a new sentence of preventive detention was introduced, and of those sentenced to 'corrective training', which was a 'kind of junior preventive detention' or a senior Borstal training for those aged 21–30 (Harding *et al.*, 1985: 210–12 and 239).[2] The successes of the Borstal system during the inter-war period led to its extension under the 1948 act as part of the aim of removing all young offenders from prison. But the consequence of increasing the number sent to Borstals was to reduce their success which had, to a degree, relied on the ability to select inmates (Hood, 1965). Attendance centres were also set up by the act. These built on experiments, undertaken by various magistrates and supported by Paterson and the Howard League under which young offenders were not incarcerated but were required to give up parts of their leisure time (McClintock, Walker and Savill, 1961). The act also introduced detention centres. These represented something of a triumph for the liberal progressives' opponents, and may have been the price paid for the abolition of whipping by the act. Young male offenders could be sent to detention centres for a short term of punitive discipline: according to the Home Secretary, Chuter Ede, they were intended 'to give a short but sharp reminder that [the offender] is getting into ways that will inevitably lead him into disaster' (Dunlop and McCabe, 1965: 1). The anomaly of such punitive institutions existing within a system geared towards rehabilitation perhaps explains the sloth displayed by the Prison Commission in opening centres and their policy of organizing the regimes so as to provide an element of training. However, the punitive aims of the detention centres and the declining reputation of the Borstals were to make the centres popular with the courts (Dunlop and McCabe, 1965; Hood, 1965: 73–4).

* * * *

On the whole, between the 1890s and the 1940s there was a shift from punishment to rehabilitation or training, which moved attention away from the crime and focused it on the individual. As a consequence, there was an emphasis on diverting offenders away from prisons, which had failed to reform prisoners and were associated with the discredited Du Cane regime. The simultaneous expansion of welfare programmes blurred the distinctions between criminals and those in need of protection or training, particularly when it came to children. Casting this approach not as punishment, but as apolitical, scientific and caring treatment which was good for the individual and for society meant that a broader definition of those in need of treatment than was provided by the criminal law could be imported, and that rigorous standards of proof, protection of the individual's rights and accountability became less important. A more intrusive and omnipresent form of intervention by state and voluntary agencies was legitimized which no longer rested simply on the proof of criminality (Smith, 1990: 129–31). However, the idea that the liberal progressives swept all before them can be taken too far. Aside from the detention centres, the move to abolish capital punishment was defeated (see, Chapter 9), the goal of removing all juveniles from prison was never fulfilled, and there was stubborn resistance to the elimination of distinctions between offenders and non-offenders and to the undermining of the principle that punishment should follow, and be proportionate to, an offence. Moreover, the characterization of the liberal progressive regimes as in some way more humane depends on one's viewpoint. For instance, the idea that different people required different periods of training tended towards more open-ended sentencing in which a release date was dependent on an administrative rather than a judicial decision and was, therefore, less open to scrutiny. It is also worth noting that the most serious prison riot for at least 70 years occurred in the inter-war period at Dartmoor in 1932 and was violently suppressed by armed officers (Adams, 1992: 104–69; Fitzgerald, 1977: 121–9; Priestley, 1989: 104–13).

The police: 'efficient, trustworthy and versatile'

Many of the concerns which shaped penal policy also influenced policing. However, there were important differences in the impact which these had. The liberal progressives were able to make substantial headway with their agenda in the realm of penal policy because the penal system was centralized, and this placed an enormous amount of power in the hands of a relatively small group of like-minded individuals. Centralization also meant that their exercise of this power was rarely exposed to the glare of publicity. The police, on the other hand, were decentralized and lacked clarity about their objectives and methods. They talked in broad terms of trying to prevent crime and maintain order, but how these goals were to be achieved was less clear. There were limitations of funding and the recognition that there had to be compromise with the communities being policed. Moreover, the police were often seen by local authorities and central government as a convenient body of civil servants who could be entrusted with a range of tasks which were only loosely (if at all) linked to their core objectives.

As has been seen, the role of the police in the moralization of the working class had not disappeared by the end of the nineteenth century, but moral campaigns tended to be directed towards more narrowly defined goals, often as the result of pressure from interest groups or the obsession of a chief officer: so, for instance, there were crusades against prostitution prompted by the sexual purity movement of the 1880s, and action against street betting around the turn of the century (Brogden, 1982; Dixon, 1980; Walkowitz, 1992). The origins of the women police lay in concerns about the morals of young women for whom the First World War had provided a degree of financial and social independence (Bland, 1985; Levine, 1994). The direction of policing, as of social policy generally, was also influenced by the decline of Britain's industrial and imperial strength. One important consequence of this was the development of political policing. There had always been a reluctance to engage in this sort of activity, as evidenced by the Popay case in 1833, and this was not really reversed until an outbreak of Irish republican violence in the 1860s. The incompetence displayed by the Metropolitan Police at that time led to the strengthening of the detectives, and then the establishment of the Special Irish Branch – which became simply the Special Branch – (Porter, 1987). Special Branch maintained a covert existence, partly because of the nature of its work and partly because it was believed that there would be opposition to secret policing. It survived because of a combination of the fear of a revival of Fenian violence, the growth of the Social Democratic Federation, the anarchist outrages in the 1890s – such as the bombing incident in 1894 featured in Joseph Conrad's *The Secret Agent* (1907) – and, particularly after the assassination of Tsar Alexander II in 1881, the pressure from foreign governments annoyed that Britain's open-door policy on immigration made it a haven for their terrorists (Porter, 1985). The concern that foreigners were importing socialism fed into worries about the weakening of the British working class which went back to the 1830s and which were really brought home by revelations about the poor physical state of recruits in the Boer War (1899–1902). That the police were an important part of the response to such issues also seemed amply justified by various incidents, particularly the murder of four police officers by anarchists in London in 1909 and 1910, and the lengthy siege of houses in Sydney Street which ensued and which was famously overseen by Winston Churchill, the Liberal Home Secretary (Rumbelow, 1988). Paranoia about foreigners accelerated in the run up to and during the First World War – reaching fever pitch over the rumour that there were thousands of German spies in the country posing as waiters. After the war the familiar concerns about the consequences of demobilization were given added bite by the Russian Revolution of 1917, and by unemployment, the rise of the Labour party and anger at the failure of Lloyd George's government to implement promised social reforms. The role of political policing expanded to involve not just the Special Branch but also MI5, and it prospered by emphasizing a subversive threat in the 1920s and 1930s, which seemed to many to be proved genuine by the General Strike of 1926 and by the emergence of radical groups on the Left, such as the National Unemployed Workers Movement, and on the Right, such as the British Union of Fascists (Emsley, 1991: 136–40).

The police also played an increasingly significant part in industrial disputes – a role which the 1839 Constabulary Commissioners' Report saw as justifying reform of the police (Royal Commission, 1839: 68–88). By the late nineteenth century trade unions had struggled for, and gained, both the right to exist and certain exemptions from civil actions, but the law also gave the police a broad discretion to proscribe behaviour connected to industrial disputes through their power to arrest for obstruction of the highway or breach of the peace. Police reaction to strikes and to strike breaking did vary, however, those chief constables who responded with vigour were generally able to call on the backing of the Home Office and so face down any criticism from local police authorities, as happened in south Wales during the strikes of the 1920s. The army did continue to play an occasional role in the policing of industrial disputes well into the inter-war years, although the ability of the local authorities to use soldiers had been restricted by government after the early nineteenth century (Emsley, 1991: 115–17 and 137–8; Morgan, 1987; Weinberger, 1991).

By the 1920s the importance of the police to the government was clear, as one civil servant in the Police Division of the Home Office later put it, that period 'established the [Police] Service in what was virtually a new, and certainly important, role as an executive Force, efficient, trustworthy and versatile, and ready at a call to guide, assist or restrain the civil population in a wide variety of ways' (Sir Arthur Dixon, quoted in Emsley, 1991: 138). In spite of criticism from the radical press, this was the view which was also held by the bulk of newspapers and, it seems reasonable to suppose, by the bulk of their middle-class readers, many of whom rallied behind the police during the General Strike of 1926 just as their great-grandfathers had done during the great Chartist meetings of 1848. That popularity among the middle classes had undoubtedly been increased by the defeat of police trade unionists in the police strikes in 1918 and 1919. This had led to the setting up of the supposedly apolitical Police Federation to represent junior officers, and to the denial of the right to strike in the Police Act 1919. The police were regarded as outside the melee of party politics, and governments were unwilling to risk policies that might imply criticism: so, for example, the first Labour government in 1923 dashed hopes that it would reinstate police officers sacked for going on strike. The apogee was the report of the Royal Commission on Police Powers and Procedure in 1929. It had been set up as the result of two rare complaints by members of the middle class that police officers had abused their powers. The police were vindicated and the incidents blamed on individual officers (Royal Commission, 1929: 98–109). The commission rejected the idea that officers routinely abused their positions by assuming broad extra-legal powers, and it did so in a statement which, although an anachronism at the time it was made, has been repeated many times since as if by that act of repetition it was made true:

> The Police of this country have never been recognised, either in law or by tradition, as a force distinct from the general body of citizens. Despite the imposition of many extraneous duties on the Police by legislation and administrative action, the principle remains that a Policeman, in the view of the common law, is only 'a person paid to perform, as a matter of duty, acts which if he were so minded he might have done voluntarily.' Indeed, a Policeman possesses few powers not enjoyed by the ordinary citizen, and public opinion, expressed in Parliament and elsewhere, has shown great jealousy of any attempts to give increased authority to the Police. This attitude is due, we believe, not to any distrust of the Police as a body, but to an instinctive feeling that, as a matter of principle, they should have as few powers as possible which are not possessed by the ordinary citizen, and that their authority should rest on the broad basis of the consent and active co-operation of all law-abiding people.
> (Royal Commission, 1929: 6; Emsley, 1991: 142–7; Gatrell, 1990: 272–5)

There were, however, some expressions of dissatisfaction with the police and their behaviour. Moreover, even as the love affair between the police and the middle class was blossoming, it was also facing its greatest challenge in the shape of the motor car. The car was seen by the police as a target for thieves and a means of committing crime (Mannheim, 1940: 115–17), and it led officers into confrontational situations with middle-class drivers. The problem got so bad that in 1928 the Home Secretary felt obliged to ask officers to act with caution when dealing with drivers – as opposed, one surmises, to acting with the more casual regard to rights and rules that was the norm for street encounters with pedestrian, working-class people (Emsley 1993).

The decentralized nature of policing continued to make the relationship between chief officers and their respective police authorities crucial, but also difficult to summarize. In broad terms, however, in the nineteenth-century watch committees, which were in charge of borough forces, met frequently and, while they listened to the advice of the chief officer, they regarded him as a servant; in the counties, on the other hand, the police committees met only infrequently (usually, quarterly) and inevitably this meant that the chief officer was more autonomous (Brogden, 1982; Emsley, 1991: 87–91). Police autonomy received powerful backing from a string of judicial pronouncements beginning in the late nineteenth century which declared the police officer to be more like a servant of the Crown than a servant of the police authority and, therefore, hampered the ability of the police authorities to intervene in the decisions of chief constables. In one case a court ordered that a chief constable's use of officers from another force to police a strike had to be paid for by his police authority even though it did not approve this action (Lustgarten, 1986). The Home Office also supported greater autonomy for chief officers and would typic-ally favour them above their police authorities, partly perhaps because of its natural suspicion of local government and partly because loosening these connections increased the influence of the Home Office itself. Chief officers also established links with one another, and government encour-aged this, especially during the First World War and the industrial unrest of the 1920s and 1930s. The Home Office further increased its power by acquiring expertise (a special department devoted to the police was set up after the Police Strike) and by assuming the role of a proponent of good practice through directives sent to chief officers. However, as with the penal system, the Treasury was not wholly in favour of greater central-ization, so, for instance, it resisted the idea, floated between the wars, of a centralized training system for police officers. For their part, the watch committees and chief officers in charge of small borough forces resisted suggestions from government that they might amalgamate with larger county forces, even though, as the Departmental Committee on Detective Work (1940) argued, their inefficiency undermined the image of modern policing: 'from the point of view of the detection of crime there can be no doubt that the existence of so many small forces introduces a serious element of difficulty and complication' (Emsley, 1991: 163). The Second World War did lead to temporary mergers to cover gaps in policing and to improve collaboration, and, perceiving this to have been a success, the government pushed through the Police Act 1946 which allowed compulsory amalgamations by the Home Office, but the power was little used (see Chapter 9).

* * * *

Cohesion, social inclusion and coordination were key features of social policy in the nineteenth century. The influence of central government became palpable and, while local authorities remained powerful, even in policing with its strong element of localism there were significant centripetal tendencies and also bonds of shared professional identity with officers from other forces which undermined the influence of the local police authorities. The expansion of public administration in the twentieth century was built on the belief that the central state was the most efficient instrument for the resolution of social problems. Social policy was colonized by professional bureaucrats who were confident that their expertise made them uniquely able to resolve problems, and who, although constrained by spending limits, were otherwise subject to fairly minimal levels of accountability. The view that the detection of offenders and their treatment were apolitical and even scientific matters meant that, while there was some case for inspection and auditing, there was little need for democratic accountability.

Further reading

General histories for this period abound: a good starting point is Thompson (1990) and on the welfare state see Thane (1996). Sadly, while primary materials in the form of newspapers and parliamentary debates are a little more widely available than for the nineteenth century, reports of official inquiries and government publications are more difficult to obtain because the Irish University Press's reprints of key reports do not go beyond the nineteenth century. This may be one reason why the historiography on crime and criminal justice is relatively thin on the ground for this period. The liberal progressives did believe in presenting their own case, and many of their books, although out of print, are fairly easy to obtain (Ruggles-Brise, 1921; Hobhouse and Brockway, 1922; L. Fox, 1934, 1952), but, not surprisingly, they present only one side of the picture. Garland (1985) and Weiner (1990) are essential works on penal policy in the late Victorian and Edwardian periods (but see Forsythe, 1995), but there are few thorough studies for the post-First World War period with the exception of Bailey (1987), who examines the development of the liberal-progressive project with respect to juvenile offenders, and Hood's (1965) history of Borstals, which has not entirely been supplanted by Bailey, particularly since it takes the story up through the troubled period of the 1950s and 1960s. The police are a little better served by their historians. As well as the books by Emsley (1991), Critchley (1978) and Ascoli (1979) and the essay by Gatrell (1990), there has been work on the policing of industrial disputes in the twentieth century by Morgan (1987) and Weinberger (1991), although they differ on certain key issues, such as the role of the Home Office, and there is also Porter's (1987) book on the development of political policing.

Notes

1. Another such regime was established at Cornton Vale in Scotland at this time (Carlen, 1983).

2. Preventive detention and corrective training were to prove as unsuccessful and as little used as their predecessors had been (Advisory Council on the Treatment of Offenders, 1963). Both were abolished by the Criminal Justice Act 1967 which introduced the extended term of imprisonment, but that also was little used (West, 1963; Harding *et al.*, 1985: 238–40; Taylor, 1960–1. See, Cross, 1971).

Chapter 9

An End to Optimism, 1950–1997

The weakening of the liberal-progressive programme

As has been mentioned, figures from either side of the Second World War suggested that there had been a rapid increase in crime: as early as 1944 *Police Review* had claimed that there was 'substantial evidence of a serious increase in crime in many parts of the country' (Smithies, 1982: 188). The average daily prison population rose from a pre-war figure of around 10–11,000 to 19,700 in 1947, which the Prison Commission called a 'reversion to conditions which have not been seen for some 40 years' (*The Times*, 6 Aug. 1948). However, it was generally believed that once the dislocation of the war had passed, the crime statistics would begin to fall (*The Times*, 23 Jan. and 3 Jun. 1948). So, even though the levels stayed high into the late 1940s, the optimism which had driven policy in the inter-war period remained: a leader in *The Times* (7 Feb. 1948) commented, 'The Government need not fear that there is any considerable body of opinion left demanding the cat, oakum and the broad arrow.' Then the figures seemed to peak in 1948 (Smithies, 1982: 201).

The liberal progressives remained strong: Paterson's acolytes, such as Sir Lionel Fox (1942–60) and then Arthur Petersen, were in control at the Prison Commission,[1] and their philosophy dominated the content of the Criminal Justice Act 1948. Their influence can be seen right into the 1960s in the recommendations of a committee headed by Lord Longford which moulded the penal policy of the Labour government of 1964 to 1970 (Labour Party Study Group on Crime and the Penal System 1964). The Children and Young Persons Act 1969 followed Longford's suggestion (which itself built on the Children and Young Persons Act 1933) that children who had committed offences should not normally be treated differently from those deemed to be in need of care or control, that the primary concern should be the welfare of the child, and that the emphasis should be on helping the child and the family rather than on the legal process. Longford's original proposals had been watered down following criticism that in trying to decriminalize juvenile justice and focus on welfare issues, they undermined the child's rights to a fair hearing (Home Office 1965b; Bottoms, 1974).

Longford also supported the abolition of capital punishment. This had been part of the Criminal Justice Bill in 1948, although the clause was lost in the House of Lords. A royal commission was appointed (1949–53), but abolition lay outside its terms of reference. In the end it was a series of highly-publicized cases which created the groundswell of opinion against capital punishment, although it is arguable that the controversy surrounding these cases reflected not so much a revulsion against hanging as a feeling that too many mistakes were being made (Hale, 1961, 1963). There had been disquiet before the war over cases such as the hanging of Edith Thompson in 1923 for encouraging Frederick Bywater to murder her husband. The principal reason for her conviction seems to have been her alleged adultery with Bywater: as one contemporary writer, who was hardly sympathetic to her, put it, 'her execution . . . although technically justifiable on legal grounds, was, in the considered judgment of sober public opinion, as essentially unjust as it was expedient' (Young, 1923: xxx). A select committee did recommend temporary abolition in 1930, but nothing came of this. After the war, a nineteen-year-old, Derek Bentley, was hanged in 1953 for the murder of a police officer which was committed by a boy called Craig, who was not hanged because of his age, and which was carried out while Bentley was being held by another officer. The case prompted protests: about 200 MPs led by Nye Bevan, a leading Labour politician, petitioned the Conservative Home Secretary, and on the night before the execution a crowd gathered at the Houses of Parliament chanting 'Bentley must not die' (*The Times*, 28 Jan., 29 Jan. 1953). In another case the conviction of the confessed serial-killer John Christie seemed good evidence that Timothy Evans, who had been hanged in 1950 for the murder of his wife and baby, was innocent: not only had he been convicted principally on Christie's evidence, but Christie now admitted murdering Mrs Evans, although he denied killing the baby. However, an inquiry held just one week before Christie was hanged decided that Evans had been rightly convicted of both murders. Then, in 1955 the hanging of Ruth Ellis (Goodman and Pringle, 1974) for the murder of her lover led to an international uproar, and seems to have prompted the film *Yield to the Night* (1956) which powerfully dramatized some of the abolitionist arguments. Other controversial cases followed, such as the hanging of James Hanratty for a murder committed on the A6 near Cannock Chase in 1962 (Blom-Cooper, 1963), ensuring that the arguments over capital punishment continued. Eventually, in 1965 it was, for all practical purposes, abolished (Christoph, 1962; Morris, 1989: 77–85).

Alongside these changes in the criminal justice system, there was some liberalization of the criminal law in the 1960s: for instance, the Suicide Act 1961, which abolished a range of criminal offences connected with suicide attempts; and the legalization of homosexual acts between consenting adults in private (Sexual Offences Act 1967) and of abortion under certain conditions (Abortion Act 1967). However, the sixties was not simply a period of sudden and unremitting liberalization. First, such measures typically had a long history: the campaign to abolish capital punishment went back two hundred years, and the Wolfenden Committee had made recommendations about the law on homosexuality in 1957 following a number of scandals and also criticism of police practice in the early 1950s (Departmental Committee on Homosexual Offences, 1957; Wildeblood, 1955). Second, the sixties also saw measures which substantially toughened the criminal law, such as the extension of the criminalization of drug use under legislation in 1964, 1965 and 1967 (Newburn, 1991), and the use of the criminal law to underpin restrictive immigration laws from 1962 (Layton-Henry, 1984; Rawlings, 1985b).

In spite of the strength of the liberal-progressive agenda in the 1960s, problems had been building up since the mid-1950s. The expectation that as the dislocation of the war receded so crime would diminish was disappointed. Crime figures, which had fallen back after 1948, began rising again in the mid-1950s (Smithies, 1982: 201), and in 1960 the Inspectors of Constabulary reported that crime had increased so much that it was in danger of getting beyond the control of the police (*The Times*, 28 Jul. 1960; McClintock and Avison, 1968). In addition, research into criminology and criminal justice was producing some disturbing results. The lack of such research had concerned some liberal progressives who saw it as a means of ensuring more precision in the classification of offenders and in the application of training techniques (Home Office, 1959). The Criminal Justice Act 1948 (section 77) allowed the Home Secretary to provide funding, but, at first, this power was used sparingly to support individual projects. It was only in 1957 that the Home Office opened its Research Unit, and, at the same time, the Institute of Criminology was established at Cambridge, although its funding came from other sources (Butler, 1974; Lodge, 1974). Hopes that criminologists would underwrite and strengthen the liberal-progressive project were quickly dashed (Bottoms and Stevenson, 1992: 20–3; Hood, 1965: 83–9). For instance, the rehabilitation of juveniles through incarceration was challenged, partly, as a result of rising crime, but also because of a study by Mannheim and Wilkins (1955), which had been started with a Home Office grant. This, of course, threw doubt on the effectiveness of long periods of custody in the Borstals, which had been the jewel in the crown of the Paterson era. As well as negative research, the organization of prison regimes around the idea of allowing prisoners to associate, which was an important part of 'training for citizenship', was undermined by a build-up of newspaper reports about bullying and by the Prison Officers' Association expressions of concern about the threat which such regimes posed to the safety of its members.

But there were also more fundamental difficulties facing the liberal-progressive project. Both Labour and Conservative post-war governments were committed to the programme of social reconstruction begun by the

Beveridge report which was meant to eradicate deprivation and, thereby, crime (Priestley, 1989: 175). The signs seemed encouraging. Rowntree, who had drawn an alarming picture of the extent of poverty at the beginning of the century, declared in 1951 that, with some minor provisos, the problem of poverty had been solved by changes in welfare provision and by the policy of full employment (Rowntree and Lavers, 1951). The economy appeared healthy, famously leading the Prime Minister, Harold Macmillan, to claim in 1957 that, 'most of our people have never had it so good', although at the same time warning that such prosperity was in danger from, among other things, inflation (*The Times*, 22 Jul. 1957). All of which led to the question, if poverty was virtually defeated, why was crime rising rapidly?

> The facts speak for themselves. During the decade 1949–1959, the national wealth has risen by over a quarter and average earnings have gone up in real value by 35 per cent. In the same period crimes reported to the police have increased by 45 per cent and there are two and a half times as many reported crimes of violence as there were ten years ago. This is a distressing accompaniment to the benefits of the welfare state, the virtual elimination from our society of poverty and widespread unemployment, the increased leisure now enjoyed by all classes and the educational opportunities open to all.
>
> (Royal Commission, 1960: 4)

It was only in the early 1960s that it became clear the problem of poverty had not been resolved (Abel-Smith and Townsend, 1965), but by that time the economy was in trouble, faced, among other things, by competition from revived and technologically more advanced manufacturers in Germany and Japan. Then, in the 1970s oil price rises bit into the industrial base even further. As a result, unemployment and welfare expenditure began to rise at a time when there was pressure to abandon the tax-and-spend approach of the post-war period and to cut back on public expenditure. These failures of the post-war state were initially papered over by blaming foreign bankers (the 'gnomes of Zurich', as one Labour minister called them) and the uncompetitive practices of trade unions. Eventually, the welfare state came under attack. To some extent its problems were put down to scroungers and fraudulent claimants (Committee on Abuse of Social Security Benefits, 1973), but soon they came to be seen as exemplifying the whole ethos of unchecked liberality which was regarded as pervading the welfare state. There was, it was argued, a failure to police resources or to inculcate proper moral values in those whom it assisted. This legitimized the shift from the immediate post-war idea of a caring welfare state, which helped the poor, to that of a disciplinary state, which regarded the poor as feckless and criminal (Hall, *et al.*, 1978). Moreover, those on the political Left, who professed sympathy for the poor, attacked the interventionism of welfare agencies in the lives of claimants and the general failure of the welfare state to redistribute wealth from the rich to the poor. But in the atmosphere of fiscal restraint which became dominant by the mid-1970s, it was the opinion of the New Right which became more influential during the 1970s. They argued that the welfare state sapped the moral fibre of individuals and saw in this the explanation both for rising welfare expenditure and for increases in crime. By providing for every eventuality from childbirth through unemployment and sickness to retirement, the welfare state was said to have made people unwilling – even unable – to look after themselves financially, or to exercise control over their own behaviour and that of their children:

> The moral fibre of our people has been weakened. The state which does for its citizens what they can do for themselves is an evil state; and a state which removes all choice and responsibility from its people and makes them like broiler hens will create the irresponsible society. In such an irresponsible society no-one cares, no-one saves, no-one bothers – why should they when the state spends all its energies taking money from the energetic, successful and thrifty to give to the idle, the failures and the feckless?
>
> (Boyson, 1971: 5)

The greater affluence of the young and attitudes to child rearing which scorned discipline were said to have made young people more independent, hedonistic and socially destructive: teenagers had more money and more freedom and were open to a broader range of what were considered to be corrupting influences – television, film, comics and Rock 'n' Roll. The stories of cinemas being wrecked in 1956 during the showing of the film *Rock around the Clock* featuring Bill Haley and the Comets brought all of these issues together, as in the 1960s did the battles between Mods and Rockers on the beaches of the south coast and images of 'Swinging London', and in the next decades hippies, skinheads, punks and ravers (Cohen, 1972; Newburn, 1997; Pearson, 1983: 17–24). Ethnic minorities were also targets for blame. They had long suffered from racism and racist violence, but little notice was taken of this, and even when in the 1960s the Labour government professed a desire to eradicate racism, it coupled legislation on racial discrimination with tighter control of immigration, which in effect depicted Black people as the root of the problem rather than racists (Layton-Henry, 1984; Rawlings, 1985b). Although heavy sentences were handed out to some of those involved in attacks on Black people in Notting Hill in 1958, it was generally assumed that such violence was unusual. Instead, the focus was on the immigration status of ethnic minorities and their alleged propensity for various types of crime – from pimping by the Maltese population of London in the 1950s to mugging by Afro-Caribbeans in the 1970s, 1980s and 1990s.

Pessimism in penal policy, 1955–1979

Rises in crime figures and in the prison population and pressure on public expenditure strengthened opposition to the liberal-progressive project. The link between crime and the economic structure had been weakened by claims that poverty had been eradicated. Instead, it became common-place to claim that crime was due not to poverty, but to a lack of self discipline which the policies of the welfare state and the liberal progress-ives encouraged. The solution was to move towards more punitive forms of discipline which would make good the failings of institutions, such as the welfare state, the family and the school.

By the 1960s prison policy was changing markedly from the liberal-progressive agenda. The Prison Rules of 1964 did continue to emphasize rehabilitation: 'the purpose of the training and treatment of convicted prisoners shall be to encourage and assist them to lead a good and use-ful life'. But, although this had been moved up from rule 6 in 1949 to rule 1, events were overtaking it. As well as a rise in the general prison population, the abolition of capital punishment and its replacement by a mandatory life sentence for murder increased the number of long-term prisoners (Smith, 1979). Furthermore, the judges were handing out very long sentences in a handful of well-publicized cases: in the 1960s George Blake was sentenced to 42 years for spying, the Great Train Robbers to 30 years, and members of the Kray and Richardson gangs, which had operated various rackets in London, also received long terms. The pub-licity these trials and sentences received created the impression that such prisoners were more numerous than was actually the case. At the same time the ability of the prison to hold them securely was brought into question by a number of escapes. In 1964–5 two of the Great Train Rob-bers, Charles Wilson and Ronnie Biggs escaped (Biggs, 1981); they were followed the next year by George Blake (Bourke, 1970; Randle and Pottle, 1989), Frank Mitchell, a violent offender with links to the Krays and the Richardsons, and thirteen prisoners who had been on a coach taking them to Parkhurst prison. The government appointed Lord Mountbatten to conduct an inquiry, but limited him to 'make recommendations for the improvement of prison security'. He proposed the classification of each prisoner according to an assessment based not on training requirements, but on the likelihood of an escape and the threat to the public which that might pose (Mountbatten of Burma, 1966). A follow-up report con-ducted by a committee under Professor Leon Radzinowicz rejected Mountbatten's idea of placing all those prisoners who were regarded as posing the greatest danger in a single prison – something which would have involved a large cost and was, therefore, not entirely welcomed by the government – and, instead, proposed that they be dispersed around the system (Advisory Council on the Penal System, 1968. But see Cohen, 1974). The implementation of this idea led to tighter security at many prisons even though they held only a minority of high category prisoners. The Mountbatten and Radzinowicz reports exemplified a shift away from the liberal-progressive position in which security had a lower priority: Paterson wrote, 'The prison record that shows no escapes and no assaults is too often counted a record of success. It is the record of many receptions but few returns that is the triumph of a good prison administration' (Ruck,

1951: 29. But Hood, 1965: 77–9). But Mountbatten and Radzinowicz cannot be seen as the source of this shift, that lay in the perception that the liberal progressives' ideas had failed.

As the general prison population doubled between 1945 and the mid-1960s, the problem of overcrowding became serious. Although as early as 1950 the Franklin Committee (Home Office, 1950) had warned that prisons were overcrowded, the government was confident that the numbers imprisoned would fall and the problem would thereby be resolved: as late as 1954 a minister declared that 'the prison population has fallen substantially below the peak, and the trend, I am glad to say, is still a downward one' (*Commons Debates*, vol. 535 (1954–5), c. 1101). His confidence was misplaced. The prison population climbed. By the late 1950s many prisoners were crammed three to a one-person cell for long periods, the buildings were decaying, and there was a lack of adequate sanitation (*Commons Debates*, vol. 597 (1958–9), c. 504–7). Even before 1939 the liberal progressives had complained about the lack of funding for new buildings which would be suited to the implementation of their training regimes. The Treasury (like all funding authorities right back to the eighteenth century) baulked at the high expenditure involved and so more often than not new accommodation was created by converting buildings (Fox, 1952: 188; Ruck, 1951: 75; *The Times*, 6 Aug. 1948). As the prisons filled up after the war, so the priority became simply housing prisoners and, inevitably, this meant the liberal-progressive project was further marginalized. There was some new building underway in the mid-1950s, but mostly it was a case of re-opening old prisons, extending existing ones, converting country houses and ex-armed service establishments, and ignoring the basic requirements of the prisoners (*Commons Debates*, vol. 535 (1954–5), c. 1100–1; Harding *et al.*, 1985: 198–9; Home Office, 1959). The objective of training for citizenship was still given lip-service, but increasingly the concern was simply to provide sufficient accommodation, prevent escapes and stay within Treasury spending limits.

However, as well as stretching the capacity of the prisons, a bewildering range of non-custodial penalties was adopted (Bottoms, 1981; Hood, 1974a; Vass, 1990). Although such an approach fitted in with the views of many liberal progressives and with research such as the Mannheim and Wilkins (1955) study about the destructive impact of imprisonment, the adoption of non-custodial penalties from the 1960s was prompted more by prison overcrowding and its cost to the Treasury. As a result, potentially innovative ideas such as community service (Advisory Council on the Penal System, 1970; Criminal Justice Act 1972) tended to be under-resourced. There was also the problem of persuading the courts to use such penalties instead of sending people to prison. Attempts were made to compel the use of non-custodial sentences (see, for instance, Criminal Justice Acts 1961 and 1967),[2] but these often failed. Indeed, these alternative penalties often merely increased the number of prisoners. For instance, under the Criminal Justice Act 1967 in certain cases where someone had been sentenced to a term of imprisonment, the court was required to suspend that sentence for a period of time, and the offender would only go to prison if he or she reoffended within that period (Home Office, 1965a). However, the suspended sentence was often used by courts in cases which would previously have resulted in a non-custodial sentence, such as a probation order. This meant that if the individual did reoffend he or she might go to prison for an offence that would not have been regarded as warranting such a sentence (Ancel, 1971; Bottoms, 1981; Committee of Inquiry, 1979; Sparks, 1971).

By 1969, although efforts to create more alternatives to custody continued, government seemed resigned to a continued increase in the prison population, and the White Paper, *People in Prison*, published in that year, revealed how much the objectives of imprisonment had narrowed:

> First, it is the task of the service . . . to hold those committed to custody and to provide conditions for their detention which are currently acceptable to society. Second . . . there is an obligation on the service to do all that may be possible within the currency of the sentence 'to encourage and assist them to lead a good and useful life'.
>
> (Home Office, 1969: 7)

The idea of 'humane containment' was elevated above that of rehabilitation (Home Office, 1969: 7–9), and as one prescient commentator put it at the time:

> *People in Prison* may . . . mark the end, in England, of the whole penological era which began with the publication of the Gladstone report in 1895. A major objective of penal policy during that time . . . has been to keep as many offenders as possible out of prison. But it is possible, even likely, that this objective is no longer realistic.
>
> (Richard Sparks in Morris, 1989: 135)

In the late 1970s the Home Office declared, 'there is no evidence that the prison system does or can exert . . . a positive reformative influence' (Committee of Inquiry 1979: 63). Of course, there was nothing new in this. Lushington had said as much on the Home Office's behalf in his evidence to the Gladstone Committee in 1895, and it was also the view of the liberal progressives, however, they had sought to establish other institutions in which inmates could be reformed, such as the Borstals. By the late 1970s the belief had virtually vanished that any institution was likely to be effective in these terms. As a consequence there was a good deal of confusion about what their purpose was. Nevertheless, the idea of moving away from having prisons at the core of the penal system was never contemplated, not least because governments saw them as a means of signalling to voters that they were 'tough on crime', and also because prisons were regarded as providing the sanction which would underpin and make effective non-custodial sentences. In these circumstances, there was little concern about overcrowding, insanitary conditions and uninspiring regimes (Stern, 1993).

Governments either seemed indifferent to such conditions or feared that improving them would be seen as cossetting criminals. The prisons would simply have to cope, and what went on inside them was of secondary concern.

The conditions in prisons were only highlighted when dissatisfaction among staff and prisoners began to erupt into protests. Poor pay, under-staffing, the impact of overcrowded prisons on working conditions and the emphasis on security caused discontent among prison officers which was manifested from the 1970s in acrimonious industrial disputes. These actions increased the suffering for prisoners, who, in addition to over-crowding and poor sanitation, were often locked up for long periods, particularly if there was a staff shortage or an industrial dispute. There were a number of riots at different prisons, the most serious of which were at Parkhurst in 1969, Hull in 1976 and Gartree in 1972 and 1978 (Evans, 1980: 83–93; King and Elliott, 1977). These problems became increasingly pressing for the Labour government (1974–9) as it drew towards a General Election in the late 1970s. As will be seen, the govern-ment was also under attack because of rising crime and growing police dissatisfaction, so it was regarded as important to dampen down the prob-lems in the prisons and to this end the Home Secretary asked Mr Justice May to undertake an inquiry (Evans, 1980: 94–109).

May criticized the 'over-hopeful – sometimes merely fashionable – expectations of non-custodial disposals' which had, he felt, led to the under-resourcing of the prisons. He also detected the restraining hand of the Treasury. Indeed, in evidence the Treasury admitted cutting capital expenditure 'mainly as a consequence of decisions taken in the period 1974–76 to reduce total public expenditure', which had meant that increased spending on staff had been paid for by reducing the funds available for improving conditions for prisoners (Committee of Inquiry, 1979: 59, 14 and 16). The Home Office reiterated its view that 'there is no evidence that any particular regime . . . is more effective than any other in reducing the probability of . . . reoffending' (Committee of Inquiry, 1979: 27). This, of course, left some fundamental problems. If 'training for citizenship' was unrealistic, what was to be done with prisoners? May wanted 'custody which is both secure and yet positive', by which he meant that, as well as preventing escapes, the prisons 'must also so far as possible be hopeful and purposive communities and not be allowed to degenerate into mere uncaring institutions dulled by their own unima-ginative and unenterprising routines' (Committee of Inquiry, 1979: 72). But what exactly this meant was unclear, beyond merely maintaining the mental and physical well-being of the prisoners (whatever that meant). Certain key questions were not within May's ambit, most obviously, in view of its long history of failure (in reforming prisoners, in reducing recidiv-ism, in cutting crime), what was the purpose of the prison? Moreover, the political context meant that once again the value of looking at the whole of the penal system, rather than just one part, was ignored. Nevertheless,

May did make some useful contributions, the most significant of which was the recommendation that a Chief Inspector of Prisons be appointed who would be formally independent of the Prison Department and whose reports would be published. This proposal was implemented by the Criminal Justice Act 1982, creating a thorn in the side of Home Secretaries in the 1980s and 1990s as successive chief inspectors kept the subject of prison conditions in the public eye.

Paradoxically, in the 1970s, although the liberal-progressive cause was on the wane, a therapeutic regime was being established at Holloway prison in London (and at a new prison, Cornton Vale, in Scotland: Carlen, 1983; Dobash, Dobash and Gutteridge, 1986). It was constructed around the belief that, while offending by men was to be discouraged, it was not abnormal, whereas offending by women was evidence of mental instability. This invited the conclusion that they might be 'cured' of their offending by therapy. Barely any research had been done before the regime was established to prove any of this, or even to test the best methods of treatment: as Dobash, Dobash and Gutteridge (1986: 133) put it, the design of the new regime was based on policy papers that were 'at best unclear and at worst meaningless'. In practice, the regime did not mean that the prison became like a hospital. In fact, it created a more intense imprisonment: 'under the name of therapy, it is seen as important to be 'nice', as opposed to not being bad, and women may be disciplined for failing to do something good rather than for actively doing something wrong' (Dobash, Dobash and Gutteridge 1986: 158). Futhermore, security remained a key issue and the regimes were staffed by prison officers.

Penal policy, 1979–1997

While in opposition the Conservatives had attacked the Labour government (1974–9) over rising crime and the problems within the criminal justice system (see, Chapter 10) and on entering office (1979–97) they pledged to be tough on crime by, among other things, locking up more people for longer terms. A succession of Home Secretaries promised to increase sentences served by violent offenders, including those serving life terms, and significantly not only were proposals from the Advisory Council on the Penal System (1978) on maximum penalties ignored, but the Council, which had (rightly or wrongly) been associated with a liberal penal policy, was itself abolished.

Nevertheless, the crime statistics and the prison population continued to rise and to outstrip the ability of the prisons to cope. Overcrowding became so acute that sentenced prisoners were held in police cells – most of which were barely suitable for holding people overnight. At the same time, prison conditions became increasingly a matter of public debate as a result of the reports of Her Majesty's Chief Inspectors of Prisons and as the judiciary rapidly expanded the rights of prisoners, prompted by decisions of the European Court of Human Rights (Maguire, Vagg and Morgan, 1985: 19–78). In addition, research exposed the abuse suffered by women prisoners (Carlen, 1983; Dobash, Dobash and Gutteridge, 1986) and racism within prisons (Genders and Player, 1989). Staff discontent rumbled on. Then a riot erupted at Strangeways prison in Manchester in 1990, settling down into a stand-off that continued for 25 days. It sparked off what was later described as 'the worst series of prison riots in the history of the British penal system' (Woolf and Tumim, 1991) which focused public attention on the prisons, albeit for a relatively brief period (Scraton, Sim and Skidmore, 1991).

The government fended off allegations about overcrowding and the loss of control within prisons by appointing Lord Woolf to conduct an inquiry (Adams, 1992; Coyle, 1994; King and McDermott, 1995; Woolf and Tumim, 1991). Woolf was in favour of prisoners serving their time in a constructive way in the hope that this might reduce the likelihood of their reoffending. He recommended that the prison system be constructed around three basic objectives: first, the need for security which would protect the public by preventing escapes; second, the need to control dangerous and potentially disruptive prisoners; third, the need for prisoners to be treated fairly by, for instance, creating a Prison Ombudsman. He felt that there had been too much emphasis on security and too little on justice for prisoners, that there had been a failure of management and leadership within the prison service, and that junior prison staff were undervalued. Woolf was also keen to connect the prison to the community in various ways in the hope that this would end the dislocation and alienation which, he believed, perpetuated crime.

The government did accept the Woolf Report, but refused additional resources to fund its recommendations, and, as a result, many were ignored, partially implemented or put off for as long as 25 years (Home Office, 1991). Although the ideas were hardly radical and many within the prison service were sympathetic towards them, they were out of line with the even more punitive approach which was emerging from the Home Office in the early 1990s. For instance, 1990 saw not just the start of the Woolf inquiry, but also a speech by David Waddington, the Home Secretary, to the Conservative Party Conference in which he declared his support for capital punishment, tougher penalties for violent offenders and the principle that 'life imprisonment in the worst cases will mean life'. He also announced his intention to alter the parole system, under which prisoners were released early, so that serious offenders would stay in prison for longer. His response to Strangeways was to announce increases in the penalties for riot and escape (this became the Prison Security Act 1992).

Yet, the need to hold down public expenditure remained, and the cost of a large prison population did lead the government throughout the 1980s and 1990s to seek to divert people from custody. However, the question of cost was usually not explicitly raised. In 1988 the government published its White Paper, *Punishment, Custody and the Community* (Home Office, 1988) which argued that, while serious violent offenders should be imprisoned, for other offenders, such as thieves and burglars, prison 'reduces their responsibility; they are not required to face up to what they have done and to the effect on their victim or to make any recompense to the victim or the public'. Offending was the result of individuals making wrong choices, so stopping re-offending required them to be taught 'self-discipline and motivation' through 'punishment in the community'. This would combine punishment, programmes to reduce re-offending, reparation to the community and, if possible, compensation to the victim. The Criminal Justice Act 1991 renewed attempts to curb the discretion of sentencers: the core of this act was, according to one minister, 'to avoid putting people in custody unnecessarily' (Earl Ferrers, *Commons Debates*, vol. 528, 1502). While seeking to increase sentences for serious offenders, it aimed to reduce the use of prison for minor offences. Sentencers were instructed that the penalty imposed should reflect the gravity of the offence and should not be increased in order to achieve rehabilitation or a deterrent effect, although a longer sentence could be imposed for violent or sexual offences to protect the public. The most controversial aspect of the act was that it specifically precluded a sentencer from considering the offender's previous convictions or any failure to respond to previous sentences. In addition, the act introduced the unit fine system by which fines were linked not just to the seriousness of the offence, but also to the disposable income of the offender. Finally, the act sought to impress on the public and the courts that alternatives to custody were not 'soft options', both in order to demonstrate that encouraging their use did not contradict the government's intention of being tough on crime and because of the long-standing difficulty of convincing courts to use these penalties in place of imprisonment (Home Office, 1990). Non-custodial sentences were rearticulated around notions of control and punishment rather than rehabilitation.[3] The probation service was given a key role in implementing this new approach, much to the annoyance of many within the profession who saw it as directly contrary to their original purpose of turning people away from offending (Newburn, 1995: 92–107).

The act proved to be highly controversial. Soon after it came into force newspapers attacked unit fines: ignoring the act's objective of trying to achieve equality of impact, they focused entirely on the disparity in the level of fines imposed on different offenders for similar offences. The act was also criticized by the media and by sentencers for the restrictions it placed on the courts' ability to take into account previous offences since this led to people with long records receiving what were regarded as light sentences. More generally, the focus on diverting offenders from custody tended to prove unpopular among the Conservative Party membership, and Home Secretaries who built more prisons were always likely to receive a warmer welcome from the Party Conference than those who showed concern about financial prudence or the plight of prisoners.

The government was stung into rapid action. At a time when the Labour opposition was enjoying a good deal of success in pressing its own credentials as the party of law-and-order, the Conservative government was undoubtedly concerned about accusations that it was being too soft on offenders. It seemed unwilling or unable to defend the act and within eight months of it coming into force had introduced amending legislation. The Criminal Justice Act 1993 abolished the unit fine system, and instructed sentencers that, when considering the seriousness of an offence, they were permitted to take into account previous convictions, the failure to respond to previous sentences and if the offence was committed while the offender was on bail. Clearly the likely effect of these amendments was to increase the prison population still further, particularly when coupled with the government's general endorsement of a more punitive attitude around this time (Cavadino and Dignan, 1997; Harding and Koffman, 1995: 119–62; Vass, 1990).

In October 1993, Michael Howard, who became Home Secretary in that year, announced his 27-point plan to the Conservative Party's Annual Conference. He was prompted by various events: an IRA bomb in Bishopsgate at the heart of London's financial district; the murder of the toddler James Bulger in Bootle by two young boys; and various media panics over a range of topics from juvenile crime to the behaviour of 'New Age' travellers. But he was also anxious to try and wrest control of the debate from Labour. He implemented various changes which emphasized a more punitive approach, from particular administrative decisions such as increasing the length of time which the killers of James Bulger should be incarcerated following a campaign by his family and certain newspapers, to legislation, such as the Criminal Justice and Public Order Act 1994 and the Crime (Sentences) Act 1997, both of which increased prison sentences for certain categories of offender and, thereby, were likely to swell the prison population: the 1997 act, for instance, made life sentences mandatory for someone who committed a second serious sexual or violent offence, a third offence of trafficking Class A drugs was to be punished with a minimum sentence of seven years, and a third offence of domestic burglary with a minimum of three years (Ashworth, 1997; Home Office, 1996; Windlesham, 1996).

So, prisons remained at the core of the government's policy, and, in spite of problems over expenditure, it embarked on prison building programmes: as early as 1983, at the same time as trying to cut back on police spending (see Chapter 10), the government announced the construction of 16 new prisons (King and McDermott, 1995: 302). In addition, the Criminal Justice Act 1991 established the power to contract out the management of existing prisons to private firms and to allow them to build and run new prisons: in 1992 the Wolds, a remand centre run by a security company, Group 4, was opened. Reviving the private sector's involvement was undoubtedly controversial, but even critics of the prison system were divided on its merits: some refused to contemplate the state relinquishing its monopoly over punishment, while others argued that the state's failure to provide even decent conditions for prisoners meant that serious consideration needed to be given to this new approach (Ryan and Ward, 1989; Taylor and Pease, 1989). To develop the policy on privatization and to introduce management styles from business, the government took the prison service out of the Home Office and put it into the hands of an executive agency in 1993, the Prison Service Agency. This meant that, while the Home Secretary laid down broad objectives, the running of the prisons was, in theory, left to the Director-General (King and McDermott, 1995; Stern, 1993: 269–78). The government's belief that public administration should be run like a business led to the appointment of Derek Lewis as Director-General because, rather than in spite, of his lack of previous experience of the prison service. He was to receive a startlingly rapid education in the difference between the public and private sectors.

There were improvements in prison conditions by the early 1990s, but any embarassment about a high prison population had virtually disappeared. Woolf's dismay at the way in which prisons were being used as a weapon in electoral politics and his plea for 'not more ministerial interference – but less' (King and McDermott, 1995: 327) was ignored, as was the view of a previous Home Secretary, David Waddington, who, in spite of a generally robust attitude to punishment, had called prison 'an expensive way of making bad people worse'. First, as has been seen, Waddington's successor, Kenneth Clarke, reversed the 1991 act and raised various maximum sentences in the Criminal Justice Act 1993, and then Michael Howard told the Conservative Party Conference in 1993 'We shall no longer judge the success of our system of justice by a fall in our prison population . . . Let us be clear. Prison works.' (Newburn, 1995: 123). So, for the first time a high – and increasing – number of prisoners, instead of being evidence of failure (that is, as showing rising crime), was presented as proof of the government's determination to protect the public by taking criminals out of circulation and of its success in achieving that goal. The prisons were, therefore, even more important to the government and, as a result, Howard proved reluctant to relinquish to the Director-General his power to intervene in their administration. Eventually, a conflict with Derek Lewis ensued which ended with his dismissal in October 1995 following an unfavourable report on prison security (Morgan, 1996). Moreover, around this time Judge Stephen Tumim, HM Chief Inspector of Prisons, who had been a constant critic of the conditions in prisons, did not have his contract renewed.

Juvenile offenders

The growing tide of pessimism in penal policy can also be seen in relation to young offenders. As has been seen, the Mannheim and Wilkins

(1955) study had cast serious doubts on the ability of the Borstal system to rehabilitate offenders, there were also the fairly gloomy prouncements in the White Paper, *Penal Practice in a Changing Society* (Home Office, 1959; Hood, 1965; Lowson, 1970), and a negative assessment of the value of probation work in a study by Davies (1969). As the Borstals lost their purpose so their regimes came more closely to resemble those of the prisons. Things were no better in approved schools where recidivism was high and there were allegations of brutality leading to inquiries in 1959 and 1967. Although the schools were replaced by community homes under the Children and Young Persons Act 1969, a reluctance by these homes to take the more delinquent juveniles meant they were dumped into Borstals and detention centres (Harding *et al.*, 1985: 245). The air of pessmism was also reflected in the fact that large parts of the Children and Young Persons Act 1969, which had been a signficant expression of liberal-progressive optimism, were not implemented by either the Conservative government of 1970–4 or the Labour administration (1974–9) which followed it (Newburn, 1997: 640–3). Those parts that were implemented tended to suffer from inadequate levels of finance and staffing. The idea in the 1969 Act of assimilating the treatment of those who offended and those in need of care or control was compromised, even reversed. By the late 1970s it was clear that the solution to juvenile crime was regarded as being a more punitive regime which, it was claimed, would deter. In October 1979 an experiment was announced to test a 'short, sharp, shock' discipline at detention centres. It seems to have been forgotten that this had been tried when the centres were established under the Criminal Justice Act 1948 and had proved unsuccessful (Dunlop and McCabe, 1965). History repeated itself (Thornton *et al.*, 1984). Nevertheless, this punitive approach led to the replacement of Borstal training by youth custody with sentences linked, not to the rehabilitation of the offender, but to the gravity of the offence (Criminal Justice Act 1982).[4]

There was a dramatic fall in the 1980s in the number of juvenile offenders and of those between the ages of 14 and 16 who were receiving custodial sentences during the 1980s. Interestingly, this seems not to have been the result of legislation, but of changing practice among enforcement agencies, more specifically the increased use of the caution by the police (Allen, 1991; Newburn, 1995: 128–45; Newburn, 1997: 643–51). In any event, the downturn did nothing to halt the demonization of youth, for, although the Children Act 1989 and the Criminal Justice Act 1991 laid an emphasis on the welfare of the child, their enactment coincided with an upturn in concern about young people in newspapers and among politicians and police officers who continued to see in juvenile offending a metaphor for broader social problems. In the wake of the murder of James Bulger, government and opposition sought to outbid one another in their enthusiasm for punitive responses for dealing with this 'crime wave'. The Criminal Justice and Public Order Act 1994 introduced more severe sentences for all offenders, but, in particular, it created the secure training order for 12 to 14-year-olds, which lasts between six months and two years with at least half of the sentence served in detention and the rest under supervision.

*   *   *   *

For the first 25 years after the Second World War the liberal-progressive project seemed to dominate penal policy. But as early as the mid-1950s it was under attack as a result of statistics which seemed to indicate that crime was increasing rapidly and of research which questioned the efficacy of the methods employed by the liberal progressives. By the 1970s the Right were arguing for more punitive discipline to make up for the morally crippling effect of the welfare state, and the Left saw the welfare state not as benevolent but as part of a pervasive disciplinary system (Finlayson, 1994). The cost and apparent failure of the welfare state brought a pessimistic attitude to social policy which justified – in some people's view, required – a reduction in expenditure. This pessimism also affected criminal justice policy. The expectation that a combination of rehabilitation for offenders and social and economic policies would cut off the causes of offending had not been fulfilled. The optimism of the first half of the twentieth century gave way to a loss of direction summed up in 1966 when the Royal Commission on the Penal System, which had been established two years before, wound itself up without reaching any conclusions because it had found its task impossible. So, although as late as 1980 one commentator thought the rehabilitative ideal 'a remarkably lively corpse' (Pease, 1980: 149), by the 1990s it was definitely beginning to smell. It became common to argue that 'nothing works', and that the most the state could do was to protect society by taking people out of circulation. This encouraged neglect, underfunding and, among people working within the penal system, frustration that their work was undervalued (Coyle, 1994). However, by the early 1990s the idea that prison did not work and that this was clear from the increase in the number of prisoners was being turned on its head, as politicians claimed that prison did work by protecting the public from those who were locked up. Government and opposition politicians vied to show strength and willingness to make 'hard choices' in all areas of policy from the prison to the pound. This meant that penal policy which could be demonstrated to be hard on offenders, whether or not it was successful in cutting offending, came to be regarded as an important means of demonstrating a political party's ability to govern.

Further reading

See the end of Chapter 10.

Notes

1. The Commission was abolished in 1963 (Criminal Justice Act 1961) and management of the prisons brought within the Home Office (Evans, 1980: 110–13).

2. Mandatory sentencing was sometimes introduced primarily for other objectives, such as reducing the disparity between different magistrates' courts in the suspension of a driving licence following a drink-driving conviction.

3. This had been suggested as early as 1974 by the Advisory Council on the Penal System (1974).

4. Both youth custody and detention centres were replaced by young offender institutions under the Criminal Justice Act 1988.

Chapter 10

The Thin Blue Line

The police, 1945–1979

The police were always able to fit in with both the liberal-progressive and the punitive approaches to crime control, so the shift from one to the other made little difference to them. In theory at least, they deterred potential offenders by their presence and were crucial in identifying offenders who could then be handed over to the penal authorities to be dealt with in accordance with the current fashion. The chief problem in the period up to the 1980s was not whether the police were essential to controlling crime – it was assumed that they were – but the difficulty of recruiting an adequate number of officers.

The police were strongly defended by the first Labour Home Secretary after the Second World War, Chuter Ede, who said in 1945, 'The civilian police force of this country is an object of universal admiration . . . and undoubtedly some of the more recent phases of their activities [in war-time] have given them an even higher standing with the ordinary citizen than they ever had before' (Bottoms and Stevenson, 1992: 7). They were 'the foundations of law and order' (*The Times*, 13 Feb. 1948). However, the loss of 2,700 officers whose retirements had been frozen by the war, as well as low pay and low general levels of unemployment presented difficulties in recruiting. Attempts to improve pay in the late 1940s largely failed to alter the situation, and in 1954 the Home Secretary reported that the Metropolitan Police was almost 20 per cent under strength (*Commons Debates*, vol. 523 (1954–5) w.a. 224). Technology did something to alleviate the shortage as police forces bought more cars and fitted them with radios, but many forces were too small, or too conservative, or disapproved of car patrols on the grounds that they undermined the relationship between the police and the public (*The Times*, 18 Nov. 1960). Furthermore, improved communications and, in particular, the adoption of the '999' service gradually led to an increased demand from the public.

The rise in reported crime continued into the 1960s without a significant improvement in recruitment levels. Many forces sought to improve their efficiency by adopting the unit beat system in which a force's area was divided up into beats patrolled by a combination of officers on foot and in cars backed up by improved radio communications (Bottoms and Stevenson, 1992: 28–32; Emsley, 1991: 149–52; Jones, 1990–1). There was also concern about the functioning of small police forces: larger forces, it was believed, would be more efficient, cheaper and better equipped. The idea of getting rid of small forces through amalgamations had been suggested regularly since the 1930s, but the political will was not there. Even after the Police Act 1946 allowed the Home Secretary to order mergers, it was the general rule that nothing would be done against the wishes of police authorities, and since most were opposed almost nothing was done: 'Local authorities are naturally jealous of their independence, and the view has been taken, I think rightly, that their police forces should not be amalgamated against their wishes unless these is a clear case for doing so on the grounds of public interest' (*Lords Debates* (1958–9), c. 36. Also, *Commons Debates* (1958–9), c. 755–78).

As well as staffing problems and rising crime, the police found themselves regularly in confrontation with their natural source of support, the middle classes: the black market, which had emerged in the war as a response to shortages of goods and in which a wide spectrum of society took part, continued as rationing dragged on into the 1950s; the volume of motor traffic increased rapidly, so did motoring law and so did the possible flashpoints with middle-class drivers; and from the late 1950s sections of the middle class took to the streets to protest about a range of issues such as nuclear weapons, apartheid in South Africa, the Vietnam War, road building and live animal exports.

It was against this general background that the Royal Commission on the Police (1960–2) was set up, although the trigger was a series of scandals and squabbles in the late 1950s: accusations of corruption in the Brighton and the Worcester forces, disputes in Cardiganshire and Nottinghamshire between the chief constables and their police authorities, and various allegations that officers abused their powers. In 1958 the Metropolitan Police Commissioner expressed concern that public support was draining away, which he put down to an 'increasingly critical outlook by a more widely and highly educated public' (Ward and Benn, 1987). Most immediately, there had been fierce criticism in Parliament of the Home Secretary for paying £300 damages to settle an action brought against a police officer for an alleged assault (*Commons Debates*, vol. 613 (1958–9), c. 1239–1303; Oliver, 1997: 3–21; Reiner, 1992).

The Royal Commission was appointed to examine the constitutional relationship between the chief constable, the police authority and the Home Secretary, and also police disciplinary procedures, pay and the amalgamation of forces. There were two reports in 1960 and 1962. While historians have dwelt far more on the second report, which dealt with the constitutional issues and with complaints against the police, at the time the most immediate problem remained recruitment and, therefore, police pay. This issue had exercised the Conservative Party Conference in 1960, and the Home Secretary, R.A. Butler, had promised action (*The Times*, 13 Oct., 15 Oct., 18 Nov. 1960). The Royal Commission was, therefore, encouraged by the Prime Minister, Harold Macmillan, to produce a rapid report on pay (*Commons Debates*, vol. 615 (1959–60), c. 1452–3), which it did. The report asserted that 'the main weapon in the war against crime must always be the police' and that 'it is the uniformed man on the beat who provides the most effective deterrent to crime' (Royal Commission, 1960: 6, 21). Moreover, on the basis of a rather skewed interpretation of an opinion poll, it denied that confidence in the police was ebbing away. The solution to crime was believed to be more police officers, and, it was reasoned, people would only be attracted into the service by better pay. To this end the report, therefore, made a number of recommendations, although in the long term problems of poor recruitment and retention remained until resolved in the late 1970s by a combination of increased unemployment and a huge pay award.

The second report favoured a reshaping of the existing constitutional relationships (Royal Commission, 1962). It led to the Police Act 1964 which placed the Home Office in the dominant position in relation to both the local police authorities and the chief constables (Jefferson and Grimshaw, 1984; Reiner, 1991: 22). Under the act the police authority had 'to secure the maintenance of an adequate and efficient police force'; the police were, however, placed 'under the direction and control of the chief constable'; and the whole was subject to the Home Secretary who had various powers which were to be used in a manner 'best calculated to promote the efficiency of the police'. The vagueness of the act, the continued willingness of the courts to support the autonomy of the police, and the tendency of the Home Office to sympathize with chief officers have relegated the local police authority to the position of the weakest partner in this relationship. The most powerful player is the Home Office, although it has tended to rely not on this fact but on its close contact with chief officers so as to establish policies based on consensus (Reiner, 1991). The Home Office's position was enhanced further by the Local Government Act 1985. This abolished the metropolitan county councils and allowed the Home Secretary to decide the budget and staffing levels of the metropolitan forces, which account for roughly half of the police strength in England and Wales (Reiner, 1991: 24–36). In the wake of all these developments in statute, case law and practice since 1964, Robert Reiner has concluded:

> In the operational sphere the chief constable is clearly said to reign supreme. However, in the administrative and regulative functions of maintaining, providing, and equipping the police, ascertaining their requirements, and monitoring their efficiency, the role of local police authorities is entirely subordinate to and overdetermined by, central government.
>
> (Reiner, 1991: 28)

The Police Act 1964 created a new complaints process, although this continued to be run by the police themselves and was, therefore, criticized as breaching principles of natural justice. The act also increased the Home Secretary's powers to amalgamate forces. Unlike his predecessors, Roy Jenkins, who became Home Secretary in the new Labour Government in 1964, was not afraid to use his powers, slashing the number of forces in England and Wales from 117 to 49 in 1966 (this fell to 41 after the Local Government Act 1972: Emsley, 1991: 174).

Although in the background to the setting up of the Royal Commission there had been allegations about police misbehaviour, the report did not properly address this issue, nor did such allegations cease with the implementation of the Police Act. In the early 1960s there were inquiries into the Sheffield 'rhino whip' affair, which found that detectives had assaulted suspects in order to extract confessions, and into the behaviour of Detective Sergeant Challenor of the Metropolitan Police, who retired on grounds of ill health following claims that he had abused suspects and planted evidence (Grigg, 1965). The Metropolitan Police faced accusations about corrupt practices among detectives in the late 1960s, and in the 1970s the Drugs and the Obscene Publications Squads were under investigation. Robert Mark was appointed Commissioner in 1972 and promised action, but, while there was a clear-out of officers, no major public inquiry into the police was undertaken (Cox, Shirley and Short, 1977). It was argued that there was nothing fundamentally wrong and that any impropriety was the result of the actions of individual officers who would be rooted out. Nevertheless, serious allegations of corrupt police behaviour coupled with concerns about the way these have been handled have continued to surface throughout the country right up to the present day: before it was wound up, the Metropolitan Police's Special Patrol Group was regularly criticized for alleged use of heavy-handed tactics and some even accused them of involvement in the death of Blair Peach in Southall in 1979 during a clash between fascists and anti-racists; members of the Metropolitan Police's Robbery Squad were subject to investigation; a number of murder convictions secured by various forces were overturned in the 1980s and 1990s in circumstances which placed serious doubt on the conduct of police inquiries (for instance, the Guildford Four, the Birmingham Six, the Maguires and Judith Ward, who had all been convicted of terrorist crimes; Stefan Kiszko, who had been convicted of murder, as had the Cardiff Three; and the Tottenham Three, who had been convicted of murdering a police officer during a riot); the Greater Manchester Police were criticized for their handling of a student demonstration; and the West Midlands Serious Crime Squad was disbanded after serious doubts were raised about working practices. Equally as damaging were allegations that the police were not taking seriously certain types of offence, such as sexual assault, domestic violence and racist attacks (Rose, 1996).

The occasional inquiries that were held were narrowly focused. The Royal Commission on Criminal Procedure was appointed in 1977 by the Labour government following criticisms of the investigation of the murder of Maxwell Confait (Price and Caplan, 1977), but its report (Royal

Commission, 1981) assumed that the problem of abusive practices among detectives was caused by defective procedural rules and that altering those rules would change the behaviour. It did lead to the establishment of an independent element in the overseeing of police complaints, but investigation remained in the hands of the police (see the Police and Criminal Evidence Act 1984). A decade later the Royal Commission on the Criminal Justice System was appointed in 1991 in the wake of the various serious miscarriages of justice which had surfaced in the late 1980s and early 1990s. But its encouragingly broad title gives a rather inflated impression of the inquiry since its central question, which was to look at the effectiveness of the justice system in convicting the guilty and acquitting the innocent (this had also been identified by the previous commission as its main concern), was limited by the requirement that the commission have 'regard to the efficient use of resources'. It too became principally an examination of rules and procedures, and did not grasp broader issues of accountability or police practice (Royal Commission, 1993).

Although both royal commissions grew out of miscarriages of justice, by the time they produced their reports the political climate had changed. The objective of safeguarding the innocent was sidelined by rising crime figures. These were taken as showing that the key problem was that too many of the guilty were escaping. The 1981 report had been commissioned by the Labour government and, as will be seen, by the time it appeared Conservative ministers were more keen to show a commitment to crime control measures than to criticize the police; although having said that, it is true that the Police and Criminal Evidence Act 1984, which was the legislative outcome of the report, was attacked by the police for being too protective of suspects and thereby hampering their work. The 1993 report emerged at a time when the government neither wished to push vast extra resources into the police nor be seen as critical of them. As has been mentioned, Howard's 27-point plan, announced in 1993, focused more on punishment. The commission's report was largely forgotten, although it did lead to the creation of the Criminal Cases Review Commission (Criminal Appeals Act 1995). This is an independent body charged with the task of reviewing alleged miscarriages of justice and, in appropriate cases, referring cases to the Court of Appeal. It was such a referral that led to Derek Bentley's conviction for murder being quashed in 1998 (see above, page 140).

The police after 1979

Up until the early 1980s the police were largely able to ride out criticisms as governments assumed both that rising crime required more police officers and that their commitment to law and order could be demonstrated by pumping greater resources into the police and recruiting more officers (Easton and Rawlings, 1996; Rawlings, 1991, 1992b). The police were pushed into the limelight, which they welcomed at first: the Police Federation, for instance, saw the opportunity to press issues such as pay, and chief officers were delighted to find that the media were seeking out their opinions on a wide range of subjects. But increased expenditure and attention brought with them expectations of lower crime and, as these failed to be met, the police were exposed to critical scrutiny.

In the run up to the 1979 General Election the Conservative opposition criticized the Labour government over increases in recorded crime and conflated this issue with economic decline, and launched attacks on trade unions and the support which some Labour ministers had given to strikers: 'the vandals on the picket lines and the muggers in our streets have got the same confused message – "we want our demands met or else" and "get out of the way give us your handbag"' (Margaret Thatcher, when Leader of the Opposition, in Brake and Hale, 1992). The Conservatives promised to 'spend more on fighting crime even while we economize elsewhere' (Rawlings, 1991; Downes and Morgan, 1997). The Police Federation, which had clashed with the Labour government over pay in 1976, ran advertisements in the national press calling for the parties to address problems of law and order, and, while the Federation did not specifically endorse the Conservatives, the advertisements coincided with a major speech by Margaret Thatcher on law and order (Clarke and Taylor, 1980). For its part the Labour government seemed devoid of ideas and unable to respond effectively. The crime statistics had, indeed, been rising, recruitment to the police remained a problem and the penal system was in turmoil. The government's only answer was to mollify the police by setting up the Edmund Davies inquiry into pay in 1977 (Ascoli, 1979: 340–2), just as in the following year it tried to quieten discontent in the prisons through the May inquiry.

After the election in May 1979 the new Conservative government under Thatcher immediately sought to show clear water between itself and the previous government on law and order by implementing in full the pay award recommended by Edmund Davies (Home Office, 1978). Throughout the early 1980s ministers were keen to show their support for the police, and often did so in terms linked to spending: the Prime Minister, Margaret Thatcher, told the Party Conference in 1985, 'The government will continue steadfastly to back the police. If they need more men, more equipment, they shall have them' (*Police Review*, 23 May 1985). They also provided new statutory powers, such as those contained in the Police and Criminal Evidence Act 1984 and the Public Order Act 1986, and the Home Office displayed its willingness to back those chief constables who were criticized by their police authorities (Loveday, 1986; Reiner, 1991: 24–36; Spencer, 1985). Not unnaturally, such support gave the police greater confidence to attack their opponents and even to criticize aspects of government policy: the Crown Prosecution Service, set up as a result of the Royal Commission report of 1981,[1] was a particular target, as were the constraints on the exercise of police powers contained in the Police and Criminal Evidence Act 1984. Some chief officers were encouraged to go to extremes which tended to backfire. For instance, during a row with his police authority in 1982, the chief constable of Greater Manchester, James Anderton, announced:

> A quiet revolution is taking place around us and the prize is political power to be wielded against the most cherished elements of the establishment, including the monarchy. It is as much the duty of the police to guard against this as it is to guard against crime. I sense and see in our midst an enemy more dangerous, insidious, and ruthless than any faced since the Second World War. I firmly believe there is a long-term political strategy to destroy the proven structure of the police and turn them into an exclusive agency of a one-party state. I am also convinced that the British police service is now a prime target for subversion and demoralization.
>
> (Hain, 1984: 37; Rawlings, 1985a: 83–4)

Anderton came in for a good deal of criticism and many in the police sought to distance themselves from the tone of such remarks, but his image of the police as the thin blue line of protection was repeated, albeit in more measured terms, by colleagues. It was also reflected in, and reinforced by, contemporary fictional representations of the police in the 1970s and early 1980s as struggling against a combination of violent crime and legal obstacles, such as the British television series *The Sweeney* and a wave of films from America, most notably those featuring Clint Eastwood as 'Dirty Harry', whose nickname adequately described his approach to policing.

However, within the lifetime of that first Thatcher administration (1979–83) its policy of reducing crime by higher spending on criminal justice ran into two main problems. The first was that achieving reductions in taxation it had promised by cutting public expenditure had been more difficult than expected, not least because rising unemployment had increased spending on welfare benefits. The government, therefore, broadened its scrutiny of public spending, and the police, which had previously been insulated, looked a likely target because the Edmund Davies award had increased their pay more rapidly than other public sector workers and because high unemployment made recruiting officers less of a difficulty. The second problem was that crime had continued to rise and detection rates fall, and that picture appeared worse with the publication by the Home Office of the British Crime Surveys, which revealed that large amounts of crime were never reported to the police and so did not appear in the statistics (Hough and Mayhew, 1983).[2]

As the government approached the 1983 General Election ministers recognized they were vulnerable on the issues of public expenditure and rising crime. They began to move their position by arguing that criminal justice policy had less impact on crime than had previously been claimed. This both enabled the government to subject the police to tighter financial controls and excused the lack of progress on crime rates. Douglas Hurd, when Home Secretary, later summed up this view by saying, 'The truth is that, however many laws we change, however much equipment we provide, however many police officers we put on the streets, these measures will not alone turn back the rise in crime' (*Police*, Jun. 1986). Although this approach was somewhat at odds with the prison building programme announced in 1983, it did fit in with the general premise of Thatcherism that government intervention tended to create problems rather than solve them[3] and that individuals should be expected to look after themselves, their children, their property and their community: 'Combating crime', Thatcher herself declared, 'is everybody's business, everybody's responsibility. It cannot be left solely to the police' (*The Times*, 26 May 1988). Crime prevention no longer simply meant government or its agents stepping in to moralize the poor or to detect crime; at its core was individual responsibility. Individuals not only chose to be criminals, they also chose to be victims by not taking measures to protect themselves (for instance, women going out alone at night) and their property (not locking up a car or a home) (Stanko, 1990). In 1985 a leading Conservative, Norman Tebbit, linked all of this to the government's policy of broadening the ownership of property, including houses and shares, by saying that the general problems facing the inner cities could be solved not by more government spending but by 'bringing back personal responsibility (through ownership), security (through law and order) and stability (through strengthening a sense of personal obligation, most notably within families)' (Brake and Hale, 1992: 14; Taylor, 1987). As has been seen, the family had always been seen as crucial in controlling the behaviour of children, but, while the liberal progressives had tended to see families which failed to fulfil this role as requiring assistance so that they could meet their responsibilities,[4] now families were simply blamed.

Ministers were careful not to go too far and claim that the police made no difference, but this was the implication of their new approach and it laid the police open to the type of scrutiny to which the rest of the public sector had been subjected – although it is worth noting the comment of Howard Davies, former head of the Audit Commission, who, in summing up the 1980s, said that 'Of all the public services the police were the least affected by the Thatcher revolution' (McLaughlin and Murji, 1993: 95). In 1983 the Home Office issued a circular (114/1983) to chief officers which said that, 'the constraints on public expenditure . . . make it impossible to continue with the sort of expansion which has occurred in recent years', and that the police 'should make the most effective use of the substantial resources now available to it'. A steady drizzle of circulars followed which pursued the same theme and which were backed up by inspections and audits.

Chief officers and the Police Federation complained loudly that 'we are a public service and not simply subject to market forces' (*The Independent*, 8 Aug. 1988). On the other hand, a new breed of chief officer emerged in the 1980s who had studied at university, often to higher degree level, was articulate and willing to engage in academic as well as popular debate, was atuned to the language of managerialism and was alive to the advantages which acquiring a status analogous to that of a managing director might bring in terms of greater control and autonomy. Even so, money remained a key issue: as one senior officer argued, while 'the measurement of cost is likely to be relevant . . . it is not an end in itself, it is a constituent part of a wider understanding of what the community expects from the police' (Butler, 1992: 42).

The police could hardly deny the evidence of the statistics, although they claimed their work had been made more difficult by the additional procedures laid down in the Police and Criminal Evidence Act 1984 to safeguard suspects and by what they saw as the incompetence of the Crown Prosecution Service – nicknamed the 'Criminal Protection Service' (Kinsey, Lea and Young, 1986: 30–4; Rawlings, 1991; Saunders and Young, 1994). The police faced accusations that they either ignored or lacked sensitivity in handling certain types of crime: this was most starkly revealed by a television documentary on the Thames Valley Police which showed the brutal interrogation of a woman who had reported being raped (also Hall, 1985), but also emerged in claims that the police were not taking complaints about domestic and racist violence seriously.

The police were also criticized over the performance of their other historical role of order maintenance. There were serious problems (including two deaths) in the handling of demonstrations in London's Red Lion Square, in 1974, Lewisham in 1977 and Southall in 1979. In the 1980s there was rioting against the police in several inner city areas, most notably in St Paul's, Bristol in 1980, Brixton in London and Toxteth in Liverpool in 1981, and a few years later in Handsworth in Birmingham and Tottenham in London, where a police officer, Keith Blakelock, was murdered. The immediate reaction of the police was to buy more defensive and offensive equipment and to improve riot control tactics (Cashmore and McLaughlin, 1991; Jefferson and Grimshaw, 1984; Joshua, Wallace and Booth, 1983; Kettle and Hodges, 1982; Mainwaring-White, 1983; Northam, 1988; Rawlings, 1985a; Scarman, 1975; Unofficial Committee of Enquiry, 1980).[5] The police also argued, against much of the evidence, that the inner-city rioters were either criminals and did not represent the views of the majority, or, in so far as they represented critical opinion, that the protests were a reaction not against the police but against racism, unemployment and government neglect. In his inquiry into the Brixton riot, Lord Scarman (1981) largely confined himself to censuring a few inexperienced officers. He rejected the notion that there was institutionalized racism in the police. However, the report infuriated the police by arguing that they were out of touch with the community and lacked accountability to those whom they claimed to be serving. This was a serious allegation, after all the assumption had long been that the police acted with the consent of the community (Royal Commission, 1839: 12–13). The

Metropolitan Police attacked the report and the notion that the Black community in Brixton was law-abiding by, among other things, producing statistics which purported to show that Black people were responsible for a large proportion of violent street crime (Greater London Council, 1982; Sim, 1982).

Yet, it was hard for officers to reject Scarman's backing for community policing, in which, as the name suggests, the police rebuilt relationships with the community. Indeed, several senior officers around the country were enthusiasts for this idea. Not least of its attractions was that community policing offered the prospect of further weakening the influence of the police authorities by building links directly with communities on agendas set by the police themselves (Rawlings, 1985a). In some areas important progress was, indeed, made as the police struggled both to demonstrate greater sensitivity to the needs of victims and to meet the criticism that they failed to take some crimes seriously. The paradox was that, at the same time as community policing schemes were promising a more intensive and open relationship with the police, concerns about national and international crime (terrorism, drug trafficking, money laundering) were leading to the creation of specialized units and of links between forces (domestic and foreign) which were concealed and had no direct connection with, or accountability to, any identifiable community. Furthermore, senior officers seem to have found it a struggle to convince juniors of the value of community policing since it generally seemed to focus on what appeared to be trivial issues raised by community groups, such as broken pavements and defective street lights.

In the event, community policing schemes often failed to meet the expectations of protection and broad involvement in policing which had been built up and, inevitably, this had negative consequences for the police. The commonly-held belief that protection required both fast response to calls for assistance from the public and officers walking the beat and that, therefore, these should be at the core of community policing was typically not met – the resources were simply not available. This perceived shortfall in protection coupled with the police and the politicians' determination to keep the issue of crime at the forefront of the public's mind (for, as has been seen, different reasons), and the message of Home Office campaigns on crime prevention from the mid-1980s that people had to protect themselves and their property, doubtless encouraged not just more locks, bolts and alarms and more journeys driving children to and from school, but also the use of more private security patrols by shopping malls, local authorities and even groups of householders (Johnston, 1991, 1992), and may have lent legitimacy to the activities of vigilantes.

Recent public opinion surveys seemed to support the idea that confidence in the police had fallen since the 1950s (Emsley, 1991: 177 and 181). Moreover, the shortfall between the public's expectations of the police and the police's ability to meet them seemed to be illustrated by a regular dribble of cases. For instance, the grief of the family and friends of Stephen

Lawrence, a Black student, murdered by racists as he waited for a bus in London, was deepened by the inept police investigation. After several years of senior officers supporting those detectives who handled the case, a public inquiry in 1998 eventually drew an apology from an assistant commissioner in the Metropolitan Police. At the other end of the spectrum there was the case of Sydney Cooke. In 1998 Cooke was released from prison after serving nine years for the manslaughter of a fourteen-year-old boy. Because of the expectation that he would be attacked as a paedophile, he was persuaded to go into voluntary custody at a police station in the West Country. Rumours quickly circulated about where he was staying – even that he had been seen queuing in a Burger King restaurant because staff in police canteens would not prepare food for him. Demonstrations were held outside police stations in Yeovil, Bristol, Bridgewater and Minehead, and one of these exploded into a riot during which the police were stoned and petrol bombs thrown. In a reversal of the expectations that ideas such as community policing had built up, the police in both the Lawrence and Cooke cases were seen as protecting the offender and not the potential victims, and therefore, as acting against the best interests of the communities. Although in the Cooke case the police were in an invidious position – should they require him to leave the police station and so allow him to disappear or be attacked – this made little difference to the impression that the police were acting against the interests of the community. Such examples might be multiplied: the reluctance to investigate domestic violence (both the beating of women by their partners and the abuse of children), sexual violence (rape and so forth) and violence against gays. There was a sort of double jeopardy for the victims of such crimes. The view that they were not 'real crimes' encouraged the prosecution of those who, having nowhere else to turn for protection, took action themselves: the imprisonment in the 1980s of Emma Humphries and Sara Thornton for killing abusive partners are just two out of dozens of examples (Nadel, 1993). From the mid-1980s the police did begin to acknowledge their deficiencies and to advertise their enthusiasm for investigating such offences, although statements by senior officers and media campaigns do not necessarily change attitudes among junior officers. The police also tried to give community policing a harder edge through a strategy known as zero tolerance (although, as with community policing generally, it also goes under a number of other names). This represents something of a move back to the programmes of moralization so beloved of the Victorian pioneers of policing. Police respond to community concerns about a particular area by lowering their tolerance of illegal behaviour and thereby, it is hoped, drive out petty and serious offenders and improve the quality of life for residents.

From the Conservative government's point of view, the imposition of financial restraint on the police held obvious dangers since it threatened its image as being tough on crime. To a large extent the failures of the Labour opposition meant that it did not have to try very hard, at least until the late 1980s when successive Shadow Home Secretaries began to make headway. Nevertheless, ministers expressed their full support for the police at every opportunity. The chilly reception accorded to successive Home Secretaries by delegates at Police Federation conferences encouraged them to demonstrate that support by the cheaper alternative of giving the police more legal powers through, for instance, the Police and Criminal Evidence Act of 1984 and the Public Order Act of 1986. This was not wholly successful since, as has been seen, the police were critical of the impact of the 1984 act and also of the Crown Prosecution Service. For a time in the mid-eighties, however, the question of expenditure was pushed into the background by another of the government's priorities: the trade unions. During the Miners' Strike of 1984–5, junior officers were often earning large amounts in overtime and the Home Office supported chief constables against those police authorities which both resented the high level of expenditure involved in policing the strike and expressed alarm at the removal of officers from ordinary duties. This false dawn seems merely to have increased police resentment at government policy once normality returned. The mutual admiration that can be found in abundance in ministerial speeches and in the pages of *Police* and *Police Review* did not survive the strike. Officers found that they, rather than the government, were on the receiving end of much of the criticism for the strategies employed and began to complain at being used 'by the Coal Board to do their dirty work' (*Police Review*, 24 May 1985. Also Rawlings, 1992b). The price of confrontational policing had never been clearer, and it made the continued pursuit of value for money rankle even more. By 1990 a senior officer was claiming that 'within the service there is a depressing lack of confidence in the ability of central government to recognize and provide for the need and efficiency of the service', and in the following year it was reported that a Scotland Yard 'think tank' had expressed 'undisguised pessimism' about the future if the Conservatives were to win the impending General Election – which, when it came in 1992, they duly did – (Newing, 1990; *The Observer*, 16 Jun. 1991).

The pressure on public expenditure and the desire for tax cuts ensured that the pattern continued into the Conservative governments of John Major in the early 1990s. In 1993 a White Paper, *Police Reform: A Police Service for the Twenty-First Century*, was published in which the government expressed its commitment to law and order, but added,

> While the police service has grown in strength and efficiency, levels of crime have also risen significantly. Crime, and with it the fear of crime, has increased in absolute terms and in terms of its sophistication. The police service alone cannot tackle the problem of crime. They need the active support and involvement of the communities whom they serve.

The police were congratulated for providing 'an excellent service in response to increasing demands', but criticized for only spending half their time 'fighting crime' and not having 'clear priorities' (Home Office,

1993a: 1). The White Paper emphasized the importance of a 'partnership' between the police and the community, and proposed important changes to the constitutional structure established in the Police Act 1964 (Jones and Newburn, 1997). Yet, although the impact of these changes was clearly going to be enormous, discussion was dominated not by the White Paper (which, in an altered form that diluted the more extreme centralist tendencies of the original proposals, became the Police and Magistrates Court Act 1994), but by proposals contained in the Sheehy Report, *Inquiry into Police Responsibilities and Rewards* (Home Office, 1993b). This was another stab at police pay, but, unlike previous efforts, it was at bottom an attempt to reduce pay costs.

The doubling of recorded crime since 1979, the decline in detection rates and the long list of miscarriages of justice which were blamed, primarily, on the police made some feel that the early 1990s was an ideal time to probe the police pay and spending issues more aggressively: as a member of the Sheehy committee put it 'the time is ripe for taking on the boys and girls in blue' (*Guardian*, 2 Jul. 1993). Of course, this was a strategy fraught with danger for a government which still wanted to be seen as supporting the police. By the time the Sheehy report came out Kenneth Clarke, who had initiated the inquiry, had been replaced as Home Secretary by Michael Howard. He decided his priority was to counter the attacks being made on the government's law and order policy by successive Labour Shadow Home Secretaries, Roy Hattersley and Tony Blair, and that this required calming police anger rather than inflaming it. Howard had to head off the wave of police protests which greeted the Sheehy report, but still meet the government's overall objective of reducing expenditure. So, while many of the Sheehy proposals were dropped, others were repackaged as management tools which gave greater control to senior officers. By this means Howard obtained a broad degree of support from the chief constables and isolated the Police Federation – its wholesale rejection of the report appeared unreasonable, particularly when other areas of public service had been suffering severe cutbacks for fifteen years or more (Easton and Rawlings, 1996).

But the government was on the back foot. The Labour opposition began to reorganize from the mid-1980s and by the early 1990s was determinedly trying to establish itself as the party of law and order. Work by criminologists on the Left, such as the Islington Crime Survey (Jones, MacLean and Young, 1986) and the book, *What's To Be Done About Law and Order?*, shifted from the agenda of the liberal progressives, in which the focus was on the offender, and, deriving inspiration from victimology and feminist criminology, 'started from the premise of taking people's fears of crime seriously' (Jones, MacLean and Young, 1986: 3). The Labour party moved away from the criticism of the police that had been commonplace during the Miners' Strike and regrouped around the new agenda, although in practice its approach often resembled that of the Conservatives when in opposition in the late 1970s: so, for instance, Blair's promise that

Labour would be 'tough on crime and tough on the causes of crime' (Downes and Morgan, 1997: 100) came largely to emphasize the former and did so in terms of more police officers and longer prison sentences. The degree to which Labour succeeded in capturing the high ground was illustrated by the levels of enthusiasm with which delegates to the Police Federation's annual conference in 1990 greeted the Home Secretary and his Labour Shadow: while David Waddington, the Home Secretary, was endured in silence, Roy Hattersley drew a standing ovation (Rawlings, 1992b: 21). As has been seen, Michael Howard fought back, but, although he tried to squash the row over Sheehy, constraints on expenditure meant that he was not able to return to policies that would have improved support from the police, and his strategy of increasing punishment never had the same bite.

Postcript: the 1997 General Election

Howard's 'toughness' on crime did not save his government, which was heavily defeated in the 1997 General Election, albeit largely on quite different issues. However, his general approach lived on in the policies of Labour's Home Secretary, Jack Straw. Indeed, in spite of the fierce attacks by Labour on the Conservatives in the 1990s, it was often difficult to separate them. In 1993, as Shadow Home Secretary, Tony Blair declared the Bulger murder to be 'a hammer-blow against the sleeping conscience of the country' (*Independent on Sunday*, 14 Apr. 1996), and pressed forward with a demonstration of Labour's 'tough' law and order policy which was to match that of the Conservatives. In the long run up to the 1997 Election the Labour Party furiously tried to establish that it would make a strong government in terms of both the economy and crime, and so reacted angrily when in 1996 Michael Hesletine, the Deputy Prime Minister, said, 'Labour today is saying it wants to be tough on crime, but it votes against all the things the Conservatives have done to achieve one of the fastest falling crime rates we have seen in this country for many years. Labour traditionally is on the side of the villain, whereas the Tories are on the side of the victim' (*The Times*, 29 Jan. 1996). The fear of what the impact of being seen as 'soft on crime' might be on the party's chances at the 1997 General Election meant that Labour in opposition (and later in government) did not really challenge Conservative policies on crime, it simply tried to outbid them. When Howard announced that those convicted of a second violent offence would automatically be sentenced to life and that certain categories of repeat offenders would receive a minimum sentence, the most effective criticism came not from the opposition, but from the judges, including the Lord Chief Justice, Lord Taylor, and the former Conservative Lord Chancellor, Lord Hailsham. Lord Ackner, a former Law Lord, astutely observed, 'Mr Howard is playing politics with the administration of justice. He is saying to the Opposition: "Look how tough we are on crime. You are not as tough as we are" and thereby hoping to achieve political advantage' (*The Times*, 1 Feb. 1996). But Labour were anxious not to fall into Howard's trap and oppose his policies, and on being appointed as Home Secretary after Labour's election victory in May 1997, Straw immediately set about demonstrating how much tougher he was than Howard. Within the ten days of the election he had announced a Crime and Disorder Bill. He aimed to continue the recriminalization of juvenile justice by removing various obstacles in the way of punishing children, such as the legal presumption that children under 14 years do not know the difference between right and wrong. He also wanted to extend provisions for reparation and community work penalties to offenders aged between 10 and 16. The rationale for all of this was fairly clear, as one of Straw's officials put it: 'Punishment for kids is all pretty ineffective at the moment. We want to make it clear that being sent to court will be no soft option . . . These reparation orders will be all about making the punishment fit the crime' (*The Sunday Times*, 11 May 1997). When an experiment in dealing with juvenile crime by confronting the offender and her or his parents with the victim seemed to be proving successful in reducing rates of offending in Aylesbury, it was significant that, while Straw welcomed the idea, he was keen to emphasize that this was 'not a soft option' (Straw, 1997. Also, Downes and Morgan, 1997).

∗   ∗   ∗   ∗

The police continued to occupy a key position in government policy on law and order in the period after 1945. Within crime fiction and much of the political debate the police have long represented the forces of order, and the police, not the penal institutions, have been seen as at the core of the criminal justice system. But, in practice, since the failure of the moralization project in the nineteenth century, the police have had imprecise goals and standards by which to judge their work. As a result, when government turned its attention to cutting public expenditure in the 1980s, the police found it difficult to justify continued high levels of funding. They also struggled to connect with the authority of popular consent through community policing. Such connections were not part of the police tradition, which emerged as a means of controlling, not cooperating with, those communities regarded as deviant; the cooperation of those seen as not deviant was regarded as largely irrelevant to crime detection. Moreover, the police were unable – and, among junior ranks at least, often largely unwilling – to deliver the level of service required by communities.

More broadly, community policing sees the protection of the community and the individual, primarily, in terms not of establishing rights but of preventing and detecting crime. So, although legislation such as the Police and Criminal Evidence Act 1984 introduced 'safeguards' for suspects, it has proved difficult to integrate into policing and, indeed, into the criminal justice system generally, mechanisms to prevent the abuses inflicted by the police and that system on individuals and communities – not just those seen as suspects, but also those who are the victims of crime (Fitzgerald, 1993; Smith, 1997).

Further reading

Primary materials are more readily accessible for this period, and Harding and Koffman's (1995) book is a convenient collection of materials and commentary on recent developments in sentencing and the penal system. Histories are, unfortunately, even rarer than those for the first half of the twentieth century. Professional historians have left the field almost entirely to criminologists, and from the late 1950s they have poured forth literature, some of which has adopted an historical perspective: King and McDermott (1995) provide an invaluable study of prisons and policy since 1979; the books by Ryan (1983), Norton (1984) and Newburn (1995), and the essays by Bottoms and Stevenson (1992) and Downes and Morgan (1997) as well as the collections edited by Hood (1974b), Reiner and Cross (1991), Saulsbury, Mott and Newburn (1996), and Stockdale and Casale (1992) provide excellent general studies of policy and the politics of law and order; the book by Brake and Hale (1992) is a good critique of Thatcherite criminal justice policy, but also a useful a history of the period (also Rawlings, 1991, 1992b; Easton and Rawlings 1996); and there is a broader and sometimes wonderfully personal account of the whole period by Morris (1989). Rose (1996) is an accessible and intelligent polemic in which he demonstrates how the criminal justice system is not working in that it is neither acquitting the innocent nor convicting the guilty. Reiner (1992) is a valuable starting point for the study of the police. Newburn (1997) reviews developments in juvenile justice and Christoph (1962) discusses efforts to abolish capital punishment, although it was published before that goal was achieved. Corruption within the Metropolitan Police is well charted in a book whose title rather exaggerates the political impact of the scandals, but may accurately indicate the decline in popular confidence in the police (Cox, Shirley and Short 1977). The study of the connections between youth popular culture, crime, race, the media and politics has been the subject of a good deal of work since the early 1970s, but, in spite of their faults, the best books in these areas remain Cohen (1972) and Hall, Cricher, Jefferson, Clark and Roberts (1978).

Notes

1. In essence, the Crown Prosecution Service took over from the police both the power to make the key decision about whether to prosecute and the role of prosecutor in the courts.

2. In the British Crime Surveys people are asked if they have been a victim of crime. This avoids the problems with the official statistics, which consist of crimes recorded by the police and are, therefore, liable to be distorted by victims failing to report, or officers not recording, crime.

3. It might justifiably be said that, while this was indeed a key premise of what might be called theoretical and rhetorical Thatcherism, in practice her government was as interventionist as any before or since.

4. See, for instance, the Ingleby Report commissioned and published by a previous Conservative government: *Report of the Committee on Children and Young Persons,* cmnd 1191, HMSO, London, 1960.

5. For the impact which tactics developed in Northern Ireland had on public order policing in England, Wales and Scotland see Brake and Hale (1992: 58–68).

Conclusion

It is curious that in the last two decades increases in recorded crime, falls in detection rates and a squeeze on funding have been met by what seems at first sight rather like a return to eighteenth-century values: more emphasis on the role of the victim and the community in responding to crime, the expansion of the private security industry, and deterring criminals through severe penalties rather than through detection. Indeed, although over the last three hundred years various projects have been tried and large amounts of money spent on dealing with crime, the statistics would seem to suggest that the effort has been wasted: crime seems always to be rising and the institutions of the criminal justice system seem never up to the task of controlling it. Yet money is still poured in. So, since this continued commitment cannot be explained simply in terms of the ability to control crime, criminal justice policy must fulfil a broader need to establish and support a particular social, political and economic order (Ignatieff, 1978: 120). This conclusion is also suggested by the fact that the tough attitude to crime so beloved of politicians rarely spreads to white collar crime (City frauds and so forth),[1] health and safety at work or the protection of the environment: prosecutions are often difficult to mount and the resources devoted to them inadequate even though judged by the impact of, say, the dumping of pollutants in a river such crimes might seem to be far more devastating than those to which resources are directed. In all of these areas the freedom of the market has been given priority over the goal of crime control.

Anxiety about crime – and, as a result, policy initiatives – often seem to have been symptoms of other problems, such as the final breakdown of feudalism, the rise of capitalism and the Reformation in the sixteenth century; the Civil Wars of the 1640s and the revolution of 1688–9; the radicalism after the French Revolution of 1789; the economic depressions and radicalism of the 1840s and 1880s; the fear of Bolshevism after the Russian Revolution of 1917; the economic decline from the 1960s. Concerns about changes such as these found their expression in a range of social policies, including changes within the criminal justice system. However, while the anxieties may have been palpable enough, they did not lead to simple solutions. So, for example, new thinking about prisons may have been prompted or accelerated by the end of transportation to North America in the 1770s and the concern about what was to be done with convicts, but that did not make prisons in any sense inevitable. Indeed, there was also an increase in the number of people hanged, reforms of the parish police, and, of course, transportation was reinstated. So, while it is tempting – and undoubtedly useful – to focus on one policy initiative – the prisons (Ignatieff, 1978), or the police (Palmer, 1988), or transportation (Hughes, 1988) – it is worth remembering that other, sometimes contradictory policies were being suggested and implemented at the same time.

The history of penal policy has often been seen as the history of reform and as a fairly straightforward struggle between the people who propose change which is regarded, with hindsight, as progressive (the heroes and heroines) and those who oppose it (the villains), with, after many setbacks, the reformers triumphant. This tends to place too much emphasis on the role of individuals. It also detaches change from the context within which it occurred and underestimates the importance of opposition and of negotiation in the formation of policy. On the other hand, the recent habit of attacking those whom past ages have identified as heroes and heroines is equally problematic. It is not difficult to find flaws in individuals such as John Howard, Samuel Romilly, Elizabeth Fry, Mary Carpenter and Alexander Paterson when judged against the standards of the 1990s, and, indeed, in a field like criminal justice it is important continually to redefine the agenda and to challenge the past. But we should not casually dismiss the achievements of such people merely because they no longer match our 'superior' standards: after all, not only does history teach us not to assume superiority over the past (indeed, there is some irony in anyone living in this blood-soaked century criticizing previous generations), but our ability to develop new standards depends on the work done by people in the past. It is also clear that individuals are important in the formation of criminal justice policy. How different might things have been without Howard and the rest? Change might have come anyway, but, perhaps, only later and in a different form.

Nevertheless, closer examination of the emergence of a change of direction in policy generally reveals that it was not simply a battle between reformers and opponents which only one side could win. The dividing lines were not easily drawn. For instance, the rage for prison building which began in the 1770s led to controversy among enthusiasts about the appropriate form of prison discipline – separate or silent? In the twentieth century the liberal progressives (a tag posthumously attached to a loosely-defined group of people which, while admittedly useful for brevity, does imply a degree of unity not always present) roundly condemned Ruggles-Brise as a Du Cane neophyte because they wanted faster and more radical reform than he either supported or thought politically possible. Equally, those seen as opponents of reform often defied such simple categorization in practice by supporting change: Lord Ellenborough's reform of the law on infanticide in a statute which created perhaps ten new capital offences springs to mind; conservatives such as Sydney Smith attacked the new prisons in the early Victorian period as too luxurious, but did not propose a return to the conditions that preceded them.

In a country like England where notions of democracy have been closely connected to traditions of local government, criminal justice policy has also been significantly shaped by the relationship between the local and the central state. Although the early modern criminal justice system was rooted in the local community, central government always regarded its overall control of that system as an important manifestation of its sovereignty, so it controlled the appointment of key officials, such as justices of the peace and judges, and the prerogative of mercy. The political uncertainty that followed the flight of James II in 1688 produced anxiety about social control in general and crime in particular which encouraged central government to increase its involvement in the criminal justice system by enacting a broader criminal code and by funding, or partially funding, rewards and transportation. Later funds were made available for the hulks, the prisons and the police, and this enabled greater central control through the Home Office and through semi-autonomous officials, such as the prison inspectors. Yet these expansionist tendencies were restrained by two principal factors. The first was born out of a constitutional tradition according to which local government was regarded as a protection against the threat to liberty posed by an overpowerful central state, and, therefore, policies which increased the latter's influence were viewed with a large degree of suspicion. However, by the late nineteenth century the idea had emerged that the central state was actually a valuable means of guaranteeing a particular form of liberty by, for instance, its ability to introduce consistency in the police and the prisons and, thereby, protect people and property from crime. The second restraint on central government was the Treasury's reluctance to get drawn into expensive commitments, which meant that during the nineteenth century the Home Office's ability to dictate to local authorities was limited. Instead, government emphasized its role as the purveyor of good practice by, for instance, encouraging local prisons and police forces to come up to minimum standards. At the same time, by the end of the eighteenth century local government had become more efficient and more willing to intervene in the administration of local prisons and police, and this general acceptance of the need for reform and for a degree of consistency in that reform did encourage central government to acquire a larger degree of influence. Nevertheless, local authorities defended their right to control the spending of local ratepayers' money, and, while reform of the local police or the local prison was not something they necessarily opposed, it was often low on the list of spending priorities behind other more prestigious (and, perhaps, more socially and economically valuable) projects, such as the building of a public library or a town hall. The difficulty of unravelling all of this is increased by the realization that within central and local government there were alliances and differences of opinion, such as the clashes between the Home Office and officials like Du Cane and Warren.

Criminal justice policy has also been influenced by those who are meant to be either implementing it or its raw material. Administrators like Crawford, Whitworth Russell, Jebb, Du Cane, Ruggles-Brise and Paterson were increasingly able to affect the direction of policy without the need for legislation. At a lower level, the skill and enthusiasm of police and prison officers and the resources available to them has been important in determining the impact of policy on practice, and also of practice on policy, since a policy which fails to influence practice is likely to be changed. Lawyers, judges and magistrates have been at the forefront of both innovation and opposition, and there is the role played by suspects, offenders and the general public. The shift away from public punishments was, in part, influenced by the spectators: the belief that the condemned were being turned into heroes and heroines was countered by the reduction of the felon to a cipher within the prison in which all were hidden away to be treated and dressed alike; but the hope that the prisoner could be precisely moulded within the prison was dashed in the face of rioting, assaults on staff and recidivism.

All of these nuances in the history of criminal justice policy can be lost in the effort to see who won or in the attempt to locate a key turning point: so, for instance, the location of the 'birth of the modern prison' implies a single model (usually, Pentonville), whereas the study of local prisons and even government-run convict prisons reveals a range of regimes which were often dictated more by finance than by theory (De Lacey, 1986; Foucault, 1977; Garland, 1985; Ignatieff, 1978; Zedner, 1991).

It is possible to identify some long-term trends over the past two centuries. The most obvious are the professionalization and bureaucratization of the criminal justice system, and its apparent disconnection from a base in local, and even popular, participation in the shape of unpaid officials, prosecutors, jurors, witnesses and spectators. In the punishment of serious offenders there was a shift away from public exposure as the gallows, pillory and public whipping were replaced by the prison and transportation. Lawyers began to appear in criminal trials, and, as quasi-scientific methods of proof were developed, so the law of evidence emerged and the role of participants, such as witnesses and jurors, was restricted; then police officers took over the role of prosecutors. By the end of the eighteenth century the focus of those who debated the purpose of the criminal justice system was on its inefficiency in reducing crime. For many the amateurism of the criminal justice system had failed because of its reliance on officials who served, often with reluctance, for a year, or on those, such as many justices of the peace, who did not regard their appointment as requiring them to be active, or on victims who, perhaps, could not afford to spend time detecting and prosecuting offenders. The implication of transportation, imprisonment, the Fieldings' system of crime detection and the new police was that control over key decisions would pass to full-time officials, who would supposedly exercise the discretion they acquired with skill and consistency, and to whom the community would defer. So, Peel, in his speech on the Metropolitan Police Bill in 1829, stressed the need for consistency, expertise and omnipresence, and implicitly criticized the view that the criminal justice system should be sensitive to local conditions and local feelings. It is, of course, true that in practice the justice system depended on victims and witnesses providing information, but by the twentieth century this role had been effectively marginalized by the depiction of crime control as skilled work. Crime statistics in the nineteenth century suggested that this new approach was successful: recorded crime was decreasing and the prison population fell. This encouraged further investment in bureaucracy, and even when the figures were challenged by, for instance, the Gladstone Committee in 1895, this approach was not criticized, indeed the solution was seen as an even more complex bureaucracy. Similarly, in the second half of the twentieth century the response to rising crime statistics has been to argue that resources have never been quite sufficient to achieve the objective of crime control: there are too few police officers, too few prisons, or too little money for research and for the newest bureaucrat, the criminologist. However, by the 1980s it had become clear that the gap in resources between what the bureaucrats wanted and what the Treasury could afford was too wide to bridge. The emphasis was switched back to the general public through schemes which suggested that the community might do more to protect itself and to assist the bureaucrats. But in practice so-called community penalties, like community service orders, have been used as a means, not of involving the public, but of relieving pressure on the prison system, and community policing tends to be seen as a way of improving channels of information to the police not of removing from them the decision about what information is relevant and what should be done with it. The community has never been seen as central to the modern criminal justice system so attempts to involve ordinary people have been unconvincing.

The notion that liberty is defined as protection from crime, rather than protection from an over-powerful central state, had emerged by the early nineteenth century (Gatrell, 1990). Once it was accepted that this protection could best be provided by the police and the prisons, the emphasis on extending the powers of the state (through the police and the prisons) overrode the protection of individual liberty, and this led to the development of 'the crime control industry' (Christie, 1993) – from professional thieftakers working for rewards and contractors paid fees to transport convicts overseas in the eighteenth century to salaried police officers, criminologists and manufacturers of security products in the nineteenth and twentieth centuries. Few seem able or willing to challenge the premise on which this industry is built – namely, that crime can only be under-stood and controlled by skilled professionals: as Nils Christie (1993: 11) has put it, 'The crime control industry is like rabbits in Australia or wild mink in Norway – there are so few natural enemies around.' Those who might contemplate mounting a challenge face marginalization and, if they are politicians, make themselves vulnerable to ridicule from their oppon-ents. The public-sector side of the industry has, it is true, been subject to financial constraints, but it is still huge and fairly well insulated, and the commercial world of crime prevention and private security, with which it enjoys a symbiotic relationship (by, for instance, the employment of ex-police officers as security consultants and the administration of prisons by private firms), has gone on expanding. This industry is driven not by a careful analysis of what problems we as a society are facing and how they might best be tackled, but by its own narrow focus on an artificial category of activities called crime and by its continual demand for growth: problems are problems of crime, not, for instance, of unemployment, so, if crime is rising, the solution is seen as lying in an intensification of existing strategies – more penal institutions, more police, more crimino-logists doing more research. And even when government lays more stress on what the public can do, it does so, typically, in terms which require resort to the crime control industry: locks, alarms, guards.

The history of criminal justice policy in the modern period leads to the profoundly depressing conclusion that the discussion of crime is confused and lacking in an awareness of the broader issues which even as late as the 1940s were of importance. Furthermore, the gap between the promise of protection made by the criminal justice system and its realization has emerged more starkly in the 1980s and 1990s, partly as a result of police officers and the private security industry shouting loudly about the dire consequences of not spending more. People have learnt to fear crime more and to recognize that the criminal justice system is, for whatever reason, unable to do much about that fear. As a result, the encourage-ment to take more interest in crime prevention, which was aimed at getting people to lock up their property and to give the police more information, has also spawned more proactive measures of self-protection and vigilant-ism, such as driving children to school, carrying weapons and attacking paedophiles. Such developments inevitably reduce further the impact of evidence that the criminal justice system actually abuses certain groups within society, such as ethnic minorities (Fitzgerald, 1993; Smith, 1997), and that it ignores notions of individual liberty defined in terms of pro-tection from the state and respect for the individual. The perceived fail-ings of the state to reduce crime leads it to emphasize crime control, and, similarly, fear of crime encourages individuals to improve their own protection without reference to the rights of others: men protect women and parents protect children by restricting their freedom of movement and their ability to make decisions for themselves about their own lives. And, of course, the paradox is that the greatest threat to an individual often comes from those who pose as the protectors of other people's liberty, whether state officials, husbands or parents.

Note

1. The Serious Fraud Office, set up to inquire into the larger white-collar crimes by the Criminal Justice Act 1987, has so far proved rather unsuccessful.

Bibliography

Abel-Smith, B. and Townsend, P. (1965) *The Poor and the Poorest*, London: Bell.

Adams, R. (1992) *Prison Riots in Britain and the USA*, London: St Martin's Press.

Advisory Council on the Penal System (1968) *Report of the Advisory Council on the Penal System on the Regime for Long Term Prisoners in Conditions of Maximum Security*, London: HMSO.

Advisory Council on the Penal System (1970) *Non-custodial and Semi-custodial Penalties*, London: HMSO.

Advisory Council on the Penal System (1974) *Young Adult Offenders*, London: HMSO.

Advisory Council on the Penal System (1978) *Sentence of Imprisonment: A Review of Maximum Penalties*, London: HMSO.

Advisory Council on the Treatment of Offenders (1963) *Preventive Detention*, London: HMSO.

Allen, Dr (1750) *An Account of the Behaviour of Mr James Maclaine*, London.

Allen, R. (1991) 'Out of Jail: the Reduction in the Use of Penal Custody for Male Juveniles, 1981–1988', *Howard Journal*, 30, p. 30.

Amory, H. (1971) 'Henry Fielding and the Criminal Legislation of 1751–2', *Philological Quarterly*, 50: 175–92.

Amussen, S.D. (1985) 'Gender, Family and the Social Order, 1560–1725', in Fletcher, A. and Stevenson, J. (eds) *Order and Disorder in Early Modern England*, Cambridge: Cambridge University Press.

Ancel, M. (1971) *Suspended Sentence*, London: Heinemann.

Andrew, D.T. (1989) *Philanthropy and Police: London Charity in the Eighteenth Century*, Princeton NJ: Princeton University Press.

Anon. (1701) *Hanging Not Punishment Enough*, London.

Anon. (1709) *An Account of the Dying Behaviour of Christopher Slaterford*, London.

Anon. (1722) *The Form of a Petition Submitted to the Consideration and Correction of those Noblemen and Gentlemen who Desire to Subscribe what Sums shall be Necessary for Relieving, Reforming and Employing the Poor*, London.

Anon. (1725) *An Account of Several Work-Houses for Employing and Maintaining the Poor*, London.

Anon. (1732a) *An Account of Several Workhouses for Employing and Maintaining the Poor*, London.

Anon. (1732b) *The Tryals of Jeremy Tooley, William Arch, and John Clauson*, London.

Anon. (1736) *Distilled Spirituous Liquors, the Bane of the Nation*, London.

Anon. (1748) *Memoirs of the Life and Times of Sir Thomas Deveil*, London.

Anon. (1749a) *An Account of the Hospital for the Maintenance and Education of Exposed and Deserted Young Children*, London.

Anon. (1749b) *An Authentick Account of the Life of Paul Wells, Gent.*, London.

Anon. (1750a) *A Complete History of James Maclean, The Gentleman Highwayman*, London.

Anon. (1750b) *M——C L——N's Cabinet Broke Open*, London.

Anon. (1750c) *The Life of Thomas Munn, Alias, The Gentleman Brick-Maker, alias Tom the Smuggler*, London.

Anon. (1751a) *Public Nuisance Considered*, London.

Anon. (1751b) *Serious Thoughts In Regard to the Publick Disorders*, London.

Anon. (1751c) *The Vices of the Cities of London and Westminster*, London.

Anon. (1754) *Proposals to the Legislative, for Preventing the Frequent Executions and Exportations of Convicts*, London.

Anon. (1761) *The Authentic Trial, and Memoirs of Issac Darkin, alias Dumas*, London.

Anon. (1765a) *An Account of John Westcote, Late Porter to the Right Honourable the Earl of Harrington*, London.

Anon. (1765b) *Considerations on Taxes, As they are Supposed to Affect the Price of Labour in our Manufacturies*, London.

Anon. (1770) *Thoughts on Capital Punishments. In a Series of Letters*, London.

Anon. (1774) *A Genuine Account of the Life, Robberies, Trial and Execution, of William Hawke, call'd the Flying Highwayman*, London.

Anon. (1775a) *Mr. Daniel Perreau's Narrative of His Unhappy Case*, London.

Anon. (1775b) *The True and Genuine Lives, and Trials, &c. of the Two Unfortunate Brothers, Robert and Daniel Perreau*, London.

Anon. (1781a) *The Life of Capt. John Donellan*, London.

Anon. (1781b) *The Life of Patrick Madan*, London.

Anon. (1816) *Cooper's Edition. The Remarkable Trials of Vaughan, Dannelly, Johnson, Brock, Pelham, and Power, for High Treason, and Conspiring to Obtain Blood Money*, London.

Archer, J.E. (1990) *By a Flash and a Scare: Incendiarism, Animal Maiming, and Poaching in East Anglia 1815–1870*, Oxford: Clarendon Press.

Ascoli, D. (1979) *The Queen's Peace: The Origins and Development of the Metropolitan Police 1829–1979*, London: Hamish Hamilton.

Ashworth, A. (1997) 'Sentencing', in Maguire, M., Morgan R. and Reiner R. (eds) *The Oxford Handbook of Criminology*, Oxford: Clarendon Press, 1095–1135.

Bahlman, D.R. (1957) *The Moral Revolution of 1688*, New Haven CT.

Bailey, V. (1987) *Delinquency and Citizenship: Reclaiming the Young Offender 1914–1948*, Oxford: Clarendon Press.

Barrister-at-Law, A. (1860) *The Road Murder*, London.

Bartrip, P.W.J. (1981) 'Public Opinion and Law Enforcement: the Ticket-of-leave Scares in Mid-Victorian Britain', in V. Bailey (ed.) *Policing and Punishment in 19th Century Britain*, London: Croom Helm.

Battestin, M.C. (1989) *Henry Fielding: A Life*, London: Routledge.

Baugh, D.A. (1965) *British Naval Administration in the Age of Walpole*, Princeton NJ.

Baugh, D.A. (ed.) (1977) *Naval Administration 1715–50*, Naval Records Society, volume 120.

Beames, T. (1852) *The Rookeries of London: Past, Present, and Prospective*, London.

Beattie, J.M. (1986) *Crime and the Courts in England 1660–1800*, Oxford: Oxford University Press.

Beccaria, C. (1769) *An Essay on Crimes and Punishments*, London.

Beier, A.L. (1989) 'Poverty and Progress in Early Modern England', in Beier, A.L. Cannadine, D. and Rosenheim, J.M. (eds) *The First Modern Society: Essays in English History in Honour of Lawrence Stone*, Cambridge: Cambridge University Press.

Belchem, J. (1981) 'Republicanism, Popular Constitutionalism and the Radical Platform in Early Nineteenth-Century England', *Social History*, 6, 1–32.

Bell, I.A. (1991) *Literature and Crime in Augustan England*, London: Routledge.

Berg, M. (1994) *The Age of Manufactures, 1700–1820: Industry, Innovation and Work in Britain*, London: Routledge.

Bevell, J. (1765) *An Authentic Narrative of the Methods by which the Robbery Committed in the House of the Right Honourable the Earl of Harrington . . . was Discovered*, London.

Biggs, R. (1981) *Ronnie Biggs: His Own Story*, London: Michael Joseph.

Blackstone, W. (1795) *Commentaries on the Laws of England*, 4 volumes, London.

Blagg, H. and Wilson, C. (1912) *Women and Prisons*, London: The Fabian Society.

Bland, L. (1985) 'In the Name of Protection: the Policing of Women in the First World War', in Smart, C. (ed.) *Women-in-Law*, London: Routledge.

Blom-Cooper, L. (1963) *The A6 Murder Regina v. James Hanratty: The Semblance of Truth*, Harmondsworth: Penguin.

Bochell, D. (1976) *Probation and After-care: Its Development in England and Wales*, Edinburgh: Scottish Academic Press.

Boos, F. (ed.) (1982) 'William Morris's Socialist Diary', *History Workshop Journal*, 13, 1–76.

Booth, A. (1977) 'Food Riots in North-West England, 1790–1801', *Past and Present*, 77, 84–107.

Booth, A. (1983) 'Popular Loyalism and Public Violence in the North-West of England, 1790–1800', *Social History*, 8, 295–313.

Boswell, J. (1931) *Boswell's Life of Johnson*, 2 volumes, London.

Bottoms, A.E. (1974) 'On the Decriminalization of the English Juvenile Courts', in Hood, R. (ed.) *Crime, Criminology and Public Policy: Essays in Honour of Sir Leon Radzinowicz*, London: Heinemann, 319–45.

Bottoms, A.E. (1981) 'The Suspended Sentence in England 1967–78', *British Journal of Criminology*, 21, 1.

Bottoms, A.E. and Stevenson, S. (1992) ' "What Went Wrong?": Criminal Justice Policy in England and Wales, 1945–70', in Downes, D. (ed.) *Unravelling Criminal Justice: Eleven British Studies*, London: Macmillan.

Bourke, S. (1970) *The Springing of George Blake*, London: Cassell.

Bowring, Sir John (1865) *On Remunerative Prison Labour, as an Instrument for Promoting the Reformation and Diminishing the Cost of Offenders*, Exeter.

Boyson, R. (1971) *Down with the Poor: An Analysis of the Failure of the 'Welfare State' and a Plan to End Poverty*, London: Churchill Press.

Braddon, L. (1721) *A Proposal for Relieving, Reforming and Employing All the Poor of Great Britain*, London.

Brake, M. and Hale, C. (1992) *Public Order and Private Lives: The Politics of Law and Order*, London: Routledge.

Branch Johnson, W. (1970) *The English Prison Hulks*, Chichester: Phillimore.

Brewer, J. (1980) 'The Wilkites and the Law, 1763–74: a Study of Radical Notions of Governance', in Brewer, J. and Styles, J. (eds) *An Ungovernable People: the English and Their Law in the Seventeenth and Eighteenth Centuries*, London: Hutchinson.

Brewer, J. (1997) *The Pleasure of the Imagination: English Culture in the Eighteenth Century*, London: Routledge.

Brewer, J. and Styles, J. (eds) (1980) *An Ungovernable People: the English and their Law in the Seventeenth and Eighteenth Centuries*, London: Hutchinson.

Briggs, A. (1963) *Victorian Cities*, London: Oldhams Press.

Brittanicus (1750) *A Letter to the Honourable House of Commons, relating to the Present Situation of Affairs*, London.

Brogden, M. (1982) *The Police: Autonomy and Consent*, London: Academic Press.

Brown, J. (1757) *An Estimate of the Manners and Principles of the Times*, London.

Brundage, A. (1986) 'Ministers, Magistrates and Reformers: the Genesis of the Rural Constabulary Act of 1839', *Parliamentary History*, 5, 55–64.

Burke, E. (1996a) 'Notes for Speech on Capital Punishment (ante 14 May 1777)', in Elofson, W.M. (ed.) *The Writings and Speeches of Edmund Burke Volume III: Party, Parliament and the American War 1774–1780*, Oxford: Clarendon Press.

Burke, E. (1996b) 'Some Thoughts on the Approaching Executions 10 July 1780', in Elofson, W.M. (ed.) *The Writings and Speeches of Edmund Burke Volume III: Party, Parliament and the American War 1774–1780*, Oxford: Clarendon Press.

Burke, P. (1988) *Popular Culture in Early Modern Europe*, Aldershot: Wildwood House.

Burn, R. (1797) *The Justice of the Peace, and Parish Officer*, 4 volumes, London.

Burt, C. (1931) *The Young Delinquent*, London: University of London Press.

Butler of Saffron Walden, The Rt. Hon. Lord (1974) 'The Foundation of the Institute of Criminology in Cambridge', in Hood, R. (ed.) *Crime, Criminology and Public Policy: Essays in Honour of Sir Leon Radzinowicz*, London: Heinemann, 1–10.

Butler, T. (1992) 'Police and the Citizen's Charter', *Policing*, 8, 40–50.

Buxton, T. (1818) *An Inquiry Whether Crime and Misery are Produced or Prevented by Our Present System of Prison Discipline*, London.

Cale, M. (1993) 'Girls and the Perception of Sexual Danger in the Victorian Reformatory System', *History*, 78, 201–17.

Campbell, R. (1984) 'Sentence of Death by Burning for Women', *Journal of Legal History*, 5, 44–59.

Carpenter, M. (1851) *Reformatory Schools For the Children of the Perishing and Dangerous Classes and For Juvenile Offenders*, London.

Carlen, P. (1983) *Women's Imprisonment: A Study in Social Control*, London: Routledge & Kegan Paul.

Cary, J. (n.d.) *A Proposal Offered to the Committee of the Honourable House of Commons*, no place of publication.

Cashmore, E.E. and McLaughlin, E. (1991) *Out of Order? Policing Black People*, London: Routledge.

Castro, J.P. de (1926) *The Gordon Riots*, London.

Cavadino, M. and Dignan, J. (1997) *The Penal System: An Introduction*, London: Sage.

Christie, N. (1993) *Crime Control as Industry: Towards Gulags, Western Style*, London: Routledge.

Christoph, J. (1962) *Capital Punishment and British Politics*, London: George Allen and Unwin.

Citizen, A (1832) *The Bristol Riots, their Causes, Progress, and Consequences*, Bristol.

Civis (1752) *A Method Proposed to Prevent the many Robberies and Villainies Committed in the City of London*, London.

Clark, P. (1988) '"The Mother Gin" Controversy in the Early Eighteenth Century', *Transactions of the Royal Historical Society*, (5th series) 38, 63–84.

Clarke, A. and Taylor, I. (1980) 'Vandals, Pickets and Muggers: Television Coverage of Law and Order in the 1979 Election', *Screen Education*, 38, 99–111.

Clay, Rev. W.L. (1861) *The Prison Chaplain: A Memoir of the Rev. John Clay*, Cambridge.

Cockburn, J. (1985) *Calendar of Assize Records: Home Circuit Indictments. Elizabeth I and James I. Introduction*, London: HMSO.

Cockcroft, W.R. (1974) 'The Liverpool Police Force, 1836–1902', in Bell, S.P. (ed.), *Victorian Lancashire*, Newton Abbot: David & Charles.

Cohen, P. (1979) 'Policing the Working-Class City', in Fitzgerald, M., McLennan, G. and Pawson, J. (eds) *Crime and Society: Readings in History and Theory*, London: Routledge & Kegan Paul, 116–33.

Cohen, S. (1972) *Folk Devils and Moral Panics: The Creation of the Mods and Rockers*, London: MacGibbon & Kee.

Cohen, S. (1974) 'Human warehouses: the Future of Our Prisons', *New Society*, 14 November.

Colley, L. (1992) *Britons: Forging the Nation, 1707–1837*, London: Yale University Press.

Collins, W. (1966) *The Moonstone*, Harmondsworth: Penguin.

Colquhoun, P. (1800) *A Treatise on the Commerce and Police of the River Thames*, London.

Colquhoun, P. (1806) *A Treatise on the Police of the Metropolis*, London.

Committee of Inquiry (1979) *Committee of Inquiry into the United Kingdom Prison Services: Report*, cmnd 7673, London: HMSO.

Committee of Physicians (1823) *Report of the Physicians On the State of the General Penitentiary at Millbank*, Parliamentary Papers, (256), Vol. V.

Committee on Abuse of Social Security Benefits (1973) *Report of the Committee on Abuse of Social Security Benefits*, cmnd 5228, London: HMSO.

Committee on Fielding's Plan (1770) 'Report of the Committee of the House of Commons on Sir John Fielding's Plan for Preventing Burglaries and Robberies', *Parliamentary History*, vol. 16, cols. 929–43.

Committee on the Hulks (1847) *Report and Minutes of Evidence Taken upon an Inquiry into the General Treatment and Condition of the Convicts in the Hulks at Woolwich*, Parliamentary Papers, (831), Vol. XVIII.

Committee on the State of the Police (1817a) *First Report from the Committee on the State of the Police of the Metropolis*, Parliamentary Papers, (233) Vol. VII.

Committee on the State of the Police (1817b) *Second Report from the Committee on the State of the Police of the Metropolis*, Parliamentary Papers, (484), Vol. VII.

Committee on the State of the Police (1818) *Third Report from the Committee on the State of the Police of the Metropolis*, Parliamentary Papers, (423), Vol. VIII.

Committee on Westminster Nightly Watch (1812) 'Report from Committee on Westminster Nightly Watch', in *Select Committee Report on the Nightly Watch and Police of the Metropolis*, Parliamentary Papers, (127), Vol. II.

Conway, S.R. (1985) 'The Recruitment of Criminals into the British Army, 1775–81', *Historical Research*, 58, 40–58.

Cooper, D.D. (1974) *The Lesson of the Scaffold*, London: Allen Lane.

Cooper, R.A. (1981) 'Jeremy Bentham, Elizabeth Fry, and English Prison Reform', *Journal of the History of Ideas*, 42, 675–90.

Coward, B. (1994) *The Stuart Age: England, 1603–1714*, London: Longman.

Cox, B., Shirley, J. and Short, M. (1977) *The Fall of Scotland Yard*, Harmondsworth: Penguin.

Cox, J. (1756) *A Faithful Narrative of the Most Wicked and Inhuman Transactions of that Bloody-Minded Gang of Thief-makers Macdaniel, Berry, Salmon, Eagan*, London.

Coyle, A. (1994) *The Prisons We Deserve*, London: Harper Collins.

Craig, A.G. (1980) 'The Movement for the Reformation of Manners, 1688–1715', PhD thesis, University of Edinburgh.

Crawford, W. (1834) *Report of William Crawford, Esq. on the Penitentiaries of the United States, addressed to His Majesty's Principal Secretary of State for the Home Department*, Parliamentary Papers, (593), Vol. XVI.

Creighton, C. (1965) *A History of Epidemics in Britain*, 2 volumes, London: Frank Cass.

Critchley, T.A. (1978) *A History of Police in England and Wales*, London: Constable.

Cross, R. (1971) *Punishment, Prison and the Public: An Assessment of Penal Reform in Twentieth-Century England by an Armchair Penologist*, London: Stevens.

Cross, W.L. (1918) *The History of Henry Fielding*, 3 volumes, New Haven CT.

Custos (1868) *The Police Force of the Metropolis in 1868*, London.

Dagge, H. (1772) *Considerations on Criminal Law*, London.

Davenant, C. (1695) *An Essay upon Ways and Means of Supplying the War*, London.

Davenant, C. (1699) *An Essay upon the Probable Methods of Making a People Gainers in the Ballance of Trade*, London.

Davey, B.J. (1983) *Lawless and Immoral: Policing a County Town 1838–1847*, Leicester: Leicester University Press.

Davey, B.J. (1994) *Rural Crime in the Eighteenth Century: North Lincolnshire 1740–80*, Hull: University of Hull Press.

Davies, M. (1969) *Probationers In Their Social Environment*, London: HMSO.

Davies, S.J. (1985) 'Classes and Police in Manchester 1829–1880', in Kidd, A.J. and Roberts, K.W. (eds) *City, Class and Culture: Studies of Social Policy and Cultural Production in Victorian Manchester*, Manchester: Manchester University Press.

Davis, J. (1980) 'The London Garotting Panic of 1862: A Moral Panic and the Creation of a Criminal Class in Mid-Victorian England', in Gatrell, V.A.C., Lenman, B. and Parker, G. (eds) *Crime and the Law: The Social History of Crime in Western Europe since 1500*, London: Europa.

Davis, J. (1989) 'From "Rookeries" to "Communities": Race, Poverty and Policing in London, 1850–1985', *History Workshop Journal* 27, 66–85.

Davitt, M. (1885), *Leaves From a Prison Diary*, New York.

Defoe, D. (1709) *Review* (Edinburgh edition), 7 Apr.

Defoe, D. (1725) *A True and Genuine Account of the Life and Actions of the late Jonathan Wild*, London.

Defoe, D. (1727) *The Complete English Tradesman in Familiar Letters*, 2 volumes, London.

DeLacy, M. (1981) 'Grinding Men Good: Lancashire's Prisons at Mid-Century', in Bailey, V. (ed.) *Policing and Punishment in 19th Century Britain*, London: Croom Helm.

DeLacy, M. (1986) *Prison Reform in Lancashire, 1700–1850*, Chetham Society (3rd series), volume 38.

Departmental Committee (1932) *Report of the Departmental Committee on Persistent Offenders*, cmnd 4090, London: HMSO.

Departmental Committee on Homosexual Offences (1957) *Report of the Departmental Committee on Homosexual Offences and Prostitution*, cmnd 247, London: HMSO.

Departmental Committee on Prisons (1895) *Report from the Departmental Committee on Prisons*, Parliamentary Papers, (7702) Vol. LVI.

Dixon, D. (1980) ' "Class Law": the Street Betting Act of 1906', *International Journal of the Sociology of Law*, 8, 101–28.

Dobash, R.P., Dobash, R.E. and Gutteridge, S. (1986) *The Imprisonment of Women*, Oxford: Basil Blackwell.

Downes, D. and Morgan, R. (1997) 'Dumping the "Hostages to Fortune"? The Politics of Law and Order in Post-War Britain', in Maguire, M., Morgan, R. and Reiner, R. (eds) *The Oxford Handbook of Criminology*, Oxford: Clarendon Press, 87–134.

Du Cane, Sir E.F. (1885) *The Punishment and Prevention of Crime*, London.

Dudden, F.H. (1952) *Henry Fielding: His Life and Works*, 2 volumes, London.

Dunlop, A.B. and McCabe, S. (1965) *Young Men in Detention Centres*, London: Routledge & Kegan Paul.

East, E.H. (1803) *A Treatise of the Pleas of the Crown*, 2 volumes, London.

Easton, S. and Rawlings, P.J. (1996) 'The Citizen's Charter and the Police', in Willett, C. (ed.) *Public Sector Reform and the Citizen's Charter*, London: Blackstone Press.

Eden, W. (1771) *Principles of Penal Law*, London.

Ekrich, A.K. (1987) *Bound for America: The Transportation of British Convicts to the Colonies 1718–1775*, Oxford: Clarendon Press.

Ellis, H. (1890) *The Criminal*, London.

Emsley, C. (1982) 'The Bedfordshire Police, 1840–1856: a Case Study in the Working of the Rural Constabulary Act', *Midland History*, 7, 73–92.

Emsley, C. (1991), *The English Police: A Political and Social History*, London: Longman.

Emsley, C. (1993) ' "Mother, what *did* policemen do when there weren't any motors?" The Law, the Police and the Regulation of Motor Traffic in England 1900–1939', *Historical Journal*, 36, 357–81.

Emsley, C. (1996) *Crime and Society in England 1750–1900*, London: Longman.

Emsley, C. and Knafla, L.A. (ed.) (1996) *Crime History and Histories of Crime: Studies in the Historiography of Crime and Criminal Justice in Modern History*, London: Greenwood Press.

Evans, E.J. (1983) *The Forging of the Modern State: Early Industrial Britain 1783–1870*, London: Longman.

Evans, P. (1980) *Prison Crisis*, London: George Allen and Unwin.

Evans, R. (1982) *The Fabrication of Virtue: English Prison Architecture 1750–1840*, Cambridge: Cambridge University Press.

Faller, L. (1987) *Turned to Account: The Forms and Functions of Criminal Biography in Late Seventeenth and Early Eighteenth-Century England*, Cambridge: Cambridge University Press.

Fielding, H. (1754) *The Journal of a Voyage to Lisbon*, London.

Fielding, H. (1967) 'The Fathers, or the Good-Natured Man', in Henley, W.E. (ed.), *The Complete Works of Henry Fielding*, 16 volumes, no place of publication, volume 12.

Fielding, H. (1988a) 'A Proposal for Making an Effectual Provison for the Poor', in Zirker, M.R. (ed.) *An Enquiry into the Causes of the Late Increase of Robbers*, Oxford: Oxford University Press.

Fielding, H. (1988b) 'Enquiry into the Causes of the Late Increase of Robbers', in Zirker, M.R. (ed.) *An Enquiry into the Causes of the Late Increase of Robbers*, Oxford: Oxford University Press.

Fielding, J. (1755) *A Plan for Preventing Robberies within Twenty Miles of London*, London.

Fielding, J. (1758) *An Account of the Origin and Effects of a Police Set on Foot by His Grace the Duke of Newcastle in the Year 1753, upon a Plan Presented to his Grace by the Late Henry Fielding, Esq*, London.

Fielding, J. (1768) *Extracts from Such of the Penal Laws, as Particularly Relate to the Peace and Good Order of this Metropolis*, London.

Fielding, J. (1769) *Extracts from Such of the Penal Laws, as Particularly Relate to the Peace and Good Order of this Metropolis*, (new edition), London.

Fiering, N.S. (1976) 'Irresistible Compassion: an Aspect of Eighteenth-Century Sympathy and Humanitarianism', *Journal of the History of Ideas*, 37, 195–218.

Finlayson, G. (1994) *Citizen, State and Social Welfare in Britain 1830–1930*, Oxford: Clarendon Press.

Fitzgerald, M. (1977) *Prisoners in Revolt*, Harmondsworth: Penguin.

Fitzgerald, M. (1993) *The Royal Commission on Criminal Justice Research Study No. 20: Ethnic Minorities and the Criminal Justice System*, London: HMSO.

Foord, A.S. (1964) *His Majesty's Opposition 1714–1830*, Oxford: Clarendon Press.

Forsythe, W.J. (1987) *The Reform of Prisoners 1830–1900*, London: Croom Helm.

Forsythe, W.J. (1991) *Penal Discipline, Reformatory Projects and the English Prison Commission 1895–1939*, Exeter: University of Exeter Press.

Forsythe, W.J. (1995) 'The Garland Thesis and the Origins of Modern English Prison Discipline: 1835 to 1939', *The Howard Journal of Criminal Justice*, 34, 259–73.

Foster, D. (1985) 'The East Riding Constabulary in the Nineteenth Century', *Northern History*, 21, 193–211.

Foucault, M. (1977) *Discipline and Punish: the Birth of a Prison*, London: George Allen & Unwin.

Foucault, M. (1980) 'The Eye of Power', in Gordon, C. (ed.) *Power/Knowledge: Selected Interviews and Other Writings 1972–1977, Michel Foucault*, Brighton: Harvester Press.

Fox, L.W. (1934) *The Modern English Prison*, London: Routledge.

Fox, L.W. (1952) *The English Prison and Borstal Systems*, London: Routledge & Kegan Paul.

Fraser, D. (1973) *The Evolution of the British Welfare State*, London: Macmillan.

Freeman, J.C. (ed.) (1978) *Prisons Past and Future*, London: Heinemann.

Garland, D. (1985) *Punishment and Welfare: A History of Penal Strategies*, Aldershot: Gower.

Gatrell, V.A.C. (1980) 'The Decline of Theft and Violence in Victorian and Edwardian England', in Gatrell, V.A.C., Lenman, B. and Parker, G. (eds) *Crime and the Law: The Social History of Crime in Western Europe since 1500*, London: Europa.

Gatrell, V.A.C. (1990) 'Crime, Authority and the Policeman-State, in Thompson, F.M.L. (ed.) *The Cambridge Social History of Britain 1750–1950*, 3 volumes, Cambridge: Cambridge University Press, volume 3.

Gatrell, V.A.C. (1994) *The Hanging Tree: Execution and the English People 1770–1868*, Oxford: Oxford University Press.

Genders, E. and Player, E. (1989) *Race Relations in Prisons*, Oxford: Clarendon Press.

George, M.D. (1966) *London Life in the Eighteenth Century*, Harmondsworth: Peregrine.

Goodman, J. and Pringle, P. (eds) (1974) *The Trial of Ruth Ellis*, Newton Abbot: David & Charles.

Goring, C. (1913) *The English Convict: A Statistical Study*, London.

Greater London Council (1982) *Policing London: The Policing Aspects of Lord Scarman's Report on the Brixton Disorders*, London: GLC.

Green, T.A. (1985) *Verdict According to Conscience: Perspectives on the English Criminal Trial Jury 1200–1800*, Chicago and London: University of Chicago Press.

Green, D.R. (1995) *From Partisans to Paupers: Economic Change and Poverty in London, 1790–1870*, Aldershot: Scolar Press.

Grigg, M. (1965) *The Challenor Case*, Harmondsworth: Penguin.

Gurney, J.J. (1819) *Notes on a Visit made to some of the Prisons in Scotland and the North of England, in Company with Elizabeth Fry*, London.

H., T. (1705) *A Glimpse of Hell; Or a Short Description, of The Common Side of Newgate*, London.

Hadley, E. (1990) 'Natives in a Strange Land: the Philanthropic Discourse of Juvenile Emigration in Nineteenth-Century England', *Victorian Studies*, 33, 411–37.

Hain, P. (1984) *Political Trials in Britain*, London: Allen Lane.

Hale, L. (1961) *Hanged in Error*, Harmondsworth: Penguin.

Hale, L. (1963) *Hanging in the Balance*, London: Jonathan Cape.

Hall, R.E. (1985) *Ask Any Woman: A London Inquiry into Rape and Sexual Assault*, Bristol: Falling Wall Press.

Hall, R.G. (1989) 'Tyranny, Work and Politics: the 1818 Strike Wave in the English Cotton District', *International Review of Social History*, 34, 433–70.

Hall, S., Critcher, C., Jefferson, T., Clark, J. and Roberts, B. (1978) *Policing the Crisis: Mugging, the State and Law and Order*, London: Macmillan.

Hanway, J. (1757a) *Motives for the Establishment of the Marine Society*, London.

Hanway, J. (1757b) *Three Letters on the Subject of the Marine Society*, London.

Hanway, J. (1776) *Solitude in Imprisonment*, London.

Harding, C. (1988) 'The Inevitable End of a Discredited System? The Origins of the Gladstone Committee Report on Prisons 1895', *Historical Journal*, 31, 591–608.

Harding, C., Hines, W., Ireland, R. and Rawlings, P. (1985) *Imprisonment in England and Wales: A Concise History*, Beckenham: Croom Helm.

Harding, C. and Koffman, L. (1995) *Sentencing and the Penal System: Text and Materials*, London: Sweet & Maxwell.

Harding, C. and Wilkins, L. (1988) ' "The Dream of a Benevolent mind": the Late Victorian Response to the Problem of Inebriety', *Criminal Justice History*, 9, 189–207.

Hay, D. (1975) 'Property, Authority and the Criminal Law: Staffordshire 1750–1800', PhD thesis, University of Warwick.

Hay, D. (1977) 'Property, Authority and the Criminal Law', in Hay, D., Linebaugh, P., Rule, J., Thompson, E.P. and Winslow, C. (eds) *Albion's Fatal Tree: Crime and Society in Eighteenth-Century England*, Harmondsworth: Penguin.

Hay, D. (1982) 'War, Dearth and Theft in the Eighteenth Century: the Record of the English Courts', *Past and Present*, 95, 117–60.

Hay, D., Linebaugh, P., Rule, J., Thompson, E.P. and Winslow, C. (eds) (1977) *Albion's Fatal Tree: Crime and Society in Eighteenth-Century England*, Harmondsworth: Penguin.

Hay, J.R. (1975) *The Origins of the Liberal Welfare Reforms 1906–1914*, London: Macmillan.

Hewitt, J. (1779) *A Journal of the Proceedings of J. Hewitt*, London.

Hewitt, J. (1783) *The Proceedings of J. Hewitt, Alderman,* London.

Hibbert, C. (1958) *King Mob: The Story of Lord George Gordon and the Riots of 1780,* London: Longmans, Green & Co.

Hill, C. (1996) *Liberty against the Law: Some Seventeenth-Century Controversies,* London: Allen Lane.

Historical Manuscripts Commission (1920–3) *Manuscripts of the Earl of Egmont, Diary of Viscount Percival afterwards First Earl of Egmont,* 3 volumes, London: HMSO.

Hobhouse, S. and Brockway, A.F. (eds) (1922) *English Prisons Today: Being the Report of the Prison System Enquiry Committee,* London: Longmans, Green & Co.

Hobsbawm, E.J. and Rude, G. (1973) *Captain Swing,* Harmondsworth: Penguin.

Hoffer, P.C. and Hull, N.E.H. (1984) *Murdering Mothers: Infanticide in England and New England 1558–1803,* New York: New York University Press.

Holford, G. (1825a) *A Short Vindication of the General Penitentiary at Millbank,* London.

Holford, G. (1825b) *The Convict's Complaint in 1815, and the Thanks of the Convict in 1825,* London.

Holford, G. (1826) *Statements and Observations Concerning the Hulks,* London.

Holmes, H.T. (1902) *Reform of Reformatories and Industrial Schools,* London: The Fabian Society.

Home Department (1842) *Report to Her Majesty's Principal Secretary of State for the Home Department, from the Poor Law Commissioners, on an Inquiry into the Sanitary Condition of the Labouring Population of Great Britain,* London: HMSO.

Home Office (1950) *Prisons and Borstal Institutions,* cmnd 8256, London: HMSO.

Home Office (1959) *Penal Practice in a Changing Society,* cmnd 645, London: HMSO.

Home Office (1965a) *The Adult Offender,* cmnd 2852, London: HMSO.

Home Office (1965b) *The Child, the Family and the Young Offender,* cmnd 2742, London: HMSO.

Home Office (1969) *People in Prison (England and Wales),* cmnd 4214, London: HMSO.

Home Office (1978) *Committee of Inquiry on the Police,* cmnd 7283, London: HMSO.

Home Office (1988) *Punishment, Custody and the Community,* cmnd 424, London: HMSO.

Home Office (1990) *Crime, Justice and Protecting the Public,* cmnd 965, London: HMSO.

Home Office (1991) *Custody, Care and Justice: the Way Ahead for the Prison Service in England and Wales,* cmnd 1647, London: HMSO.

Home Office (1993a) *Police Reform: A Police Service for the Twenty-First Century,* London: HMSO.

Home Office (1993b) *Inquiry into Police Responsibilities and Rewards,* London: HMSO.

Home Office (1996) *Protecting the Public,* cmnd 3910, London: HMSO.

Hood, R. (1965) *Borstal Re-Assessed,* London: Heinemann.

Hood, R. (1974a) 'Criminology and Penal Change: a Case Study of the Nature and Impact of Some Recent Advice to Governments', in Hood, R. (ed.) *Crime, Criminology and Public Policy: Essays in Honour of Sir Leon Radzinowicz,* London: Heinemann, 375–417.

Hood, R. (ed.) (1974b) *Crime, Criminology and Public Policy: Essays in Honour of Sir Leon Radzinowicz,* London: Heinemann.

Hough, M. and Mayhew, P. (1983) 'The British Crime Survey', *Home Office Research Study,* 76, London: HMSO.

Howard, D.L. (1958) *John Howard: Prison Reformer,* London: Christopher Johnson.

Howard, J. (1777) *The State of the Prisons in England and Wales, with Preliminary Observations, and an Account of Some Foreign Prisons*, Warrington.

Howson, G. (1973) *The Macaroni Parson: A Life of the Unfortunate Dr Dodd*, London: Hutchinson.

Howson, G. (1987) *It Takes a Thief: the Life and Times of Jonathan Wild*, London: Cresset Library.

Hughes, R. (1988) *The Fatal Shore: A History of the Transportation of Convicts to Australia 1787–1868*, London: Pan Books.

Humphries, S. (1981) *Hooligans or Rebels? An Oral History of Working-Class Childhood and Youth 1889–1939*, Oxford: Basil Blackwell.

Ignatieff, M. (1978) *A Just Measure of Pain: The Penitentiary in the Industrial Revolution, 1750–1850*, London: Macmillan.

Ignatieff, M. (1979) 'Police and People: the Birth of Mr Peel's "Blue Locusts"', *New Society*, 30 August, 443–4.

Ignatieff, M. (1983) 'State, Civil Society and Total Institution: a Critique of Recent Social Histories of Punishment', in Sugarman, D. (ed.) *Legality, Ideology and the State*, London: Academic Press.

Inge, E. and Webb, T. (eds) (1781) *A Defence and Substance of the Trial of John Donellan, Esq*, London.

Innes, J. (1980) 'King's Bench Prison in the Later Eighteenth Century: Law, Authority and Order in a London Debtor's Prison', in Brewer, J. and Styles, J. (eds) *An Ungovernable People: the English and their Law in the Seventeenth and Eighteenth Centuries*, London: Hutchinson.

Innes, J. (1983) 'Prisons for the Poor: English Bridewells, 1555–1800', in Snyder, F. and Hay, D. (eds) *Labour, Law and Crime: An Historical Perspective*, Oxford: Clarendon Press, 42–122.

Innes, J. (1990a) 'Parliament and the Shaping of Eighteenth-Century English Social Policy', *Transactions of the Royal Historical Society*, (5th series), 40, 65–92.

Innes, J. (1990b) 'The Reformation of Manners Movement in Later Eighteenth-Century England', in Hellmuth, E. (ed.) (1990) *The Transformation of Political Culture: England and Germany in the Late Eighteenth Century*, Oxford: Oxford University Press.

Innes, J. and Styles, J. (1986) 'The Crime Wave: Recent Writing on Crime and Criminal Justice in Eighteenth-Century England', *Journal of British Studies*, 25, 380–435.

Issacs, T.B. (1979) 'Moral Crime, Moral Reform, and the State in Early Eighteenth-Century England: a Study of Piety and Politics', PhD thesis, University of Rochester.

Jebb, J. (1844) *Report of the Surveyor-General of Prisons on the Construction, Ventilation and Details of Pentonville Prison*, Parliamentary Papers, (594), Vol. XXVIII.

Jefferson, T. and Grimshaw, R. (1984) *Controlling the Constable: Police Accountability in England and Wales*, London: Frederick Muller.

Jenkins, P. (1986) 'From Gallows to Prison? The Execution Rate in Early Modern England', *Criminal Justice History*, 7, 51–71.

Johnson, S. (1969) *The Rambler* (ed. W.J. Bate and A.B. Strauss), 3 volumes, London: Yale University Press.

Johnston, L. (1991) 'Privatisation and the Police Function: From "New Police" to "New Policing"', in Reiner, R. and Cross, M. (eds) *Beyond Law and Order: Criminal Justice Policy and Politics into the 1990s*, London: Macmillan.

Johnston, L. (1992) *The Rebirth of Private Policing*, London: Routledge.

Jones, B.M. (1933) *Henry Fielding: Novelist and Magistrate*, London: George Allen & Unwin.

Jones, C. (1752) *Some Methods Proposed Towards Putting Stop to the Flagrant Crimes of Murder, Robbery, and Perjury*, London.

Jones, D.J.V. (1982) *Crime, Protest, Community and Police in 19th Century Britain*, London: Routledge.

Jones, D.J.V. (1989) *Rebecca's Children: A Study of Rural Society, Crime and Protest*, Oxford: Clarendon Press.

Jones, D.J.V. (1990–1) ' "Where Did it All Go Wrong?": Crime in Swansea, 1938–68', *Welsh History Review*, 15, 240–74.

Jones, G. Steadman (1983) *Languages of Class: Studies in English Working Class History 1832–1982*, Cambridge: Cambridge University Press.

Jones, G. Steadman (1984) *Outcast London: A Study in the Relationship between Classes in Victorian Society*, Harmondsworth: Penguin.

Jones, T., MacLean, B. and Young, J. (1986) *The Islington Crime Survey: Crime, Victimization and Policing in Inner-City London*, Aldershot: Gower.

Jones, T. and Newburn, T. (1997) *Policing after the Act*, London: Policy Studies Institute.

Joshua, H., Wallace, T. and Booth, H. (1983) *To Ride the Storm*, London: Heinemann.

Joyce, P. (1993) 'The Transition from "Old" to "New" Policing in Early 19th Century Manchester', *Police Journal*, April, 197–210.

Kettle, M. and Hodges, L. (1982) *Uprising!*, London: Pan Books.

King, J.E. (1985) ' "We Could Eat the Police!" Popular Violence in the North Lancashire Cotton Strike of 1878', *Victorian Studies* 28, 439–71.

King, P. (1989) 'Prosecution Associations and their Impact in Eighteenth-Century Essex', in Hay, D. and Snyder, F. (eds) *Policing and Prosecution in Britain 1758–1850*, Oxford: Oxford University Press.

King, P. and Noel, J. (1993) 'The Origins of "the Problem of Juvenile Delinquency": the Growth of Juvenile Prosecutions in London in the Late Eighteenth and Early Nineteenth Centuries', *Criminal Justice History*, 14, 17–41.

King, R.D. and Elliott, K.W. (1977) *Albany: Birth of a Prison – End of an Era*, London: Routledge & Kegan Paul.

King, R.D. and McDermott, K. (1995) *The State of Our Prisons*, Oxford: Clarendon Press.

Kinsey, R., Lea, J. and Young, J. (1986) *Losing the Fight against Crime*, Oxford: Basil Blackwell.

Knapp, A. and Baldwin, W. (eds) (1809) *The New Newgate Calendar*, 5 volumes, London.

Labour Party Study Group on Crime and the Penal System (1964) *Crime: A Challenge To Us All*, London.

Lambert, S. (ed.) (1975) *House of Commons Sessional Papers of the Eighteenth Century*, Wilmington: Scholarly Resources.

Landau, N. (1984) *The Justices of the Peace, 1679–1760*, London: University of California Press.

Langbein, J.H. (1974) *Prosecuting Crime in the Renaissance*, Cambridge, MA: Harvard University Press.

Langbein, J.H. (1978) 'Criminal Trial Before the Lawyers', *University of Chicago Law Review*, 45, 263–316.

Langbein, J.H. (1983) 'Shaping the Eighteenth-Century Trial: a View from the Ryder Sources', *University of Chicago Law Review*, 50, 1–136.

Langford, P. (1989) *A Polite and Commercial People: England 1727–1783*, Oxford: Clarendon Press.

Lawson, P. (1986) 'Property Crime and Hard Times in England, 1559–1624', *Law and History Review*, 4, 95–127.

Layton-Henry, Z. (1984) *The Politics of Race in Britain*, London: George Allen & Unwin.

Lea, J. and Young, J. (1984) *What Is To Be Done About Law and Order?*, Harmondsworth: Penguin.

Leslie-Melville, R. (1934) *The Life and Work of Sir John Fielding*, London: Lincoln Williams.

Lettsom, J.C. (1794) *Hints Respecting the Prison of Newgate*, London.

Levine, P. (1994) ' "Walking the Streets in a Way no Decent Woman Should". Women Police in World War One', *Journal of Modern History*, 66, 34–78.

Lewis, W.S. (1960) (ed.) *Horace Walpole's Correspondence with Sir Horace Mann: volume IV*, New Haven CT: Yale University Press.

Linebaugh, P. (1975) 'Tyburn: a Study of Crime and the Labouring Poor in London During the First Half of the Eighteenth Century', PhD. thesis, University of Warwick.

Linebaugh, P. (1977) 'The Tyburn Riot against the Surgeons', in Hay, D., Linebaugh, P., Rule, J., Thompson, E.P. and Winslow, C. (eds) *Albion's Fatal Tree: Crime and Society in Eighteenth-Century England*, Harmondsworth: Penguin.

Linebaugh, P. (1991) *The London Hanged: Crime and Civil Society in the Eighteenth Century*, Harmondsworth: Penguin.

Locke, J. (1993) *Two Treatises of Government* (ed. M. Goldie), London: Everyman.

Lodge, T.S. (1974) 'The Founding of the Home Office Research Unit', in Hood, R. (ed.) *Crime, Criminology and Public Policy: Essays in Honour of Sir Leon Radzinowicz*, London: Heinemann, 11–24.

Loughborough, Lord (1793) *Observations on the State of the English Prisons*, London.

Loveday, B. (1986) 'Central Coordination, Police Authorities and the Miners' Strike', *Political Quarterly*, 57, 60–73.

Lowson, D.M. (1970) *City Lads in Borstal: A Study Based on 100 Lads Discharged to Addresses in Liverpool*, Liverpool: Liverpool University Press.

Lustgarten, L. (1986) *The Governance of the Police*, London: Sweet and Maxwell.

Lytton, Lady Constance (1914) *Prisons and Prisoners*, London.

McClintock, F.H. and Avison, N.H. (1968) *Crime in England and Wales*, London: Heinemann.

McClintock, F.H., Walker, M.A. and Savill, N.C. (1961) *Attendance Centres: An Enquiry by the Cambridge Institute of Criminology on the Use of Section 19 of the Criminal Justice Act, 1948*, London: Macmillan.

McClure, R.K. (1981) *Coram's Children: The London Foundling Hospital in the Eighteenth Century*, New Haven CT and London: Yale University Press.

McConville, S. (1981) *A History of English Prison Administration: Volume I 1750–1877*, London: Routledge.

McConville, S. (1995) *English Local Prisons 1860–1900: Next Only to Death*, London: Routledge.

McGowen, R. (1983) 'The Image of Justice and Reform of the Criminal Law in Early Nineteenth-Century England', *Buffalo Law Review*, 32, 89–125.

McGowen, R. (1986) 'A Powerful Sympathy: Terror, the Prison, and Humanitarian Reform in Early Nineteenth-Century Britain', *Journal of British Studies*, 25, 312–34.

McGowen, R. (1987) 'The Body and Punishment in Eighteenth-Century England', *Journal of Modern History*, 59, 651–79.

McGowen, R. (1988) 'The Image of Justice and Reform of the Criminal Law in Early Nineteenth-Century England', *Buffalo Law Review*, 32, 89–125.

McGowen, R. (1994) 'Civilizing Punishment: the End of the Public Execution in England', *Journal of British Studies*, 33, 257–82.

McGowen, R. (1995) 'The Well-Ordered Prison: England, 1780–1865', in Morris, N. and Rothman, D.J. (eds) *The Oxford History of the Prison: The Practice of Punishment in Western Society*, Oxford: Oxford University Press.

McLaughlin, E. and Murji, K. (1993) 'Controlling the Bill: Restructuring the Police in the 1990s', *Critical Social Policy*, May–June, 95–103.

McLaughlin, E. and Murji, K. (1995) 'The End of Public Policing? Police Reform and "the new manageralism"', in Noaks, L., Maguire, M. and Levi, M. (eds) *Contemporary Issues in Criminology*, Cardiff: University of Wales Press.

McWilliams, W. (1983) 'The Mission to the English Courts 1876–1939', *The Howard Journal of Criminal Justice*, 22, 129–47.

McWilliams, W. (1985) 'The Mission Transformed: Professionalisation of Probation Practice Between the Wars', *The Howard Journal of Criminal Justice*, 24, 257–74.

Madan, M. (1785) *Thoughts on Executive Justice &c.*, London.

Maddox, I. (1751) *The Expediency of Preventive Wisdom*, London.

Maguire, M., Vagg, J. and Morgan, R. (eds) (1985) *Accountability and Prisons: Opening Up a Closed World*, London: Tavistock.

Mainwaring-White, S. (1983) *The Policing Revolution: Police Technology, Democracy and Liberty in Britain*, Brighton: Harvester Press.

Malcolmson, R.W. (1977) 'Infanticide in the Eighteenth Century', in Cockburn, J.S. (ed.) *Crime in England 1550–1800*, London: Methuen.

Malthus, T. (1798) *An Essay on the Principles of Population*, London.

Manchester Committee (1772) *For the More Effectual Security of This Town*, Manchester (British Library).

Mandeville, B. (1725) *An Enquiry into the Causes of the Frequent Executions at Tyburn*, London.

Mandeville, B. (1924) *The Fable of the Bees: or, Private Vices, Publick Benefits*, 2 volumes, Oxford: Oxford University Press.

Mannheim, H. (1940) *Social Aspects of Crime in England between the Wars*, London: George Allen & Unwin.

Mannheim, H. and Wilkins, L.T. (1955) *Prediction Methods in Relation to Borstal Training*, London: HMSO.

Margery, S. (1978) 'The Invention of Juvenile Delinquency in Early Nineteenth-Century England', *Labour History*, 34, 11–27.

Mason Good, J. (1795) *A Dissertation on the Diseases of Prisons and Poor Houses*, London.

Matthew, R. (ed.) (1989) *Privatizing Criminal Justice*, London: Sage Publications.

Matthews, G. (1986) 'The Search for a Cure for Vagrancy in Worcestershire, 1870–1920', *Midland History*, 11, 100–16.

Mayhew, H. (1967) *London Labour and the London Poor*, 4 volumes, London: Frank Cass.

Mayhew, H. and Binny, J. (1968) *Criminal Prisons of London and Scenes of Prison Life*, London: Frank Cass.

Meacham, S. (1987) *Toynbee Hall and Social Reform 1880–1914: The Search for Community*, New Haven and London: Yale University Press.

Mearns, A. (1883) *The Bitter Cry of Outcast London: An Inquiry into the Condition of the Abject Poor*, London.

Merriman, R.D. (1961) *Queen Anne's Navy*, Naval Record Society, volume 103.

Mildmay, Sir W. (1763) *The Police of France*, London.

Miller, W.R. (1975) 'Police Authority in London and New York City, 1830–70', *Journal of Social History*, 8, 81–101.

Morgan, J. (1987) *Conflict and Order: The Police and Labour Disputes in England and Wales, 1900–1939*, Oxford: Oxford University Press.

Morgan, R. (1996) 'Learmont: Dangerously Unbalanced', *The Howard Journal of Criminal Justice*, 35, 346–53.

Morgan, R. (1997) 'Imprisonment: Current Concerns and a Brief History since 1945', in Maguire, M., Morgan, R. and Reiner, R. (eds) *The Oxford Handbook of Criminology*, Oxford: Clarendon Press, 1137–94.

Morris, N. and Rothman, D.J. (eds) (1995) *The Oxford History of the Prison: The Practice of Punishment in Western Society*, Oxford: Oxford University Press.

Morris, T. (1989) *Crime and Criminal Justice since 1945*, Oxford: Basil Blackwell.

Mountbatten of Burma, Earl (1966) *Report of the Inquiry into Prison Escapes and Security*, cmnd. 3175, London: HMSO.

Muskett, P. (1980) 'A Picturesque Little Rebellion? The Suffolk Workhouses in 1765', *Society for the Study of Labour History*, 41, 28–31.

Nadel, J (1993) *Sara Thornton: The Story of a Woman Who Killed*, London: Victor Gollancz.

Nelson, R.R. (1969) *The Home Office, 1782–1801*, Durham NC: Duke University Press.

Newburn, T. (1991) *Permission and Regulation: Law and Morals in Post-War Britain*, London: Routledge.

Newburn, T. (1995) *Crime and Criminal Justice Policy*, London: Longman.

Newburn, T. (1997) 'Youth, Crime, and Justice', in Maguire, M., Morgan, R. and Reiner, R. (eds) *The Oxford Handbook of Criminology*, Oxford: Clarendon Press, 613–60.

Newing, J. (1990) 'Policing: a Crisis in Confidence?', paper delivered to the Crime and Policing Conference, Islington.

Nield, J. (1812) *State of the Prisons in England, Scotland, and Wales*, London.

Northam, G. (1988) *Shooting in the Dark: Riot Police in Britain*, London: Faber and Faber.

Norton, P. (1984) *Law and Order and British Politics*, Aldershot: Gower.

Oliver, I. (1997) *Police, Government and Accountability*, London: Macmillan.

Ollyffe, G. (1731) *An Essay Humbly Offer'd, for an Act of Parliament to Prevent Capital Crimes*, London.

Paley, R. (1989a) ' "An Imperfect, Inadequate and Wretched System"?; Policing London before Peel', *Criminal Justice History*, 10, 95–130.

Paley, R. (1989b) 'Thief-takers in London in the Age of the McDaniel Gang, c. 1745–1754', in Hay, D. and Snyder, F. (eds) *Policing and Prosecution in Britain 1758–1850*, Oxford: Oxford University Press.

Paley, R. (ed.) (1991) *Justice in Eighteenth-Century Hackney: The Justicing Notebook of Henry Norris and the Hackney Petty Sessions Book*, London Record Society, volume 28.

Paley, W. (1833) *The Works of William Paley, D.D. Archdeacon of Carlisle. With a Life of the Author*, London.

Palmer, S.H. (1988) *Police and Protest in England and Ireland 1780–1850*, Cambridge: Cambridge University Press.

Parker, Rev. J. (1783) *A Sermon Preached in St. Margaret's Church, York, On Sunday, Sept. 7, 1783; Occasioned by the Execution of John Ryley, On the 23d of August, 1783*, York.

Parker, W.K. (1981) 'Radnor County Gaol: the Last Decade, 1868–78', *The Transactions of the Radnorshire Society*, 52, 35–46.

Paulson, R. and Lockwood, T. (eds) (1969) *Henry Fielding: The Critical Heritage*, London.

Pearson, G. (1983) *Hooligan: A History of Respectable Fears*, London: Routledge.

Pease, K. (1980) 'The Future of the Community Treatment of Offenders in Britain', in Bottoms, A.E. and Preston, R.H. (eds) *The Coming Penal Crisis: A Criminological and Theological Exploration*, Edinburgh: Scottish Academic Press.

Pellew, J. (1982) *The Home Office 1848–1914: From Clerks to Bureaucrats*, London: Heinemann.

Petrow, S. (1993) 'The Rise of the Detective in London, 1869–1914', *Criminal Justice History*, 14, 92–108.

Petrow, S. (1994) *Policing Morals: The Metropolitan Police and the Home Office, 1870–1914*, Oxford: Clarendon Press.

Pfautz, H.W. (1967) *Charles Booth On the City: Physical Pattern and Social Structure*, Chicago and London: The University of Chicago Press.

Philips, D. (1980) ' "A New Engine of Authority": the Institutionalization of Law Enforcement in England 1780–1830', in Gatrell, V.A.C., Lenman, B. and Parker, G. (eds) *Crime and the Law: The Social History of Crime in Western Europe since 1500*, London: Europa.

Philips, D. (1989) 'Good Men to Associate and Bad Men to Conspire: Associations for the Prosecution of Felons in England 1768–1860', in Hay, D. and Snyder, F. (eds) *Policing and Prosecution in Britain 1758–1850*, Oxford: Oxford University Press.

Philips, D. and Storch, R.D. (1994) 'Whigs and Coppers: the Grey Ministry's National Police Scheme, 1832', *Historical Research*, 67, 75–90.

Philonomos (1751) *The Right Method of Maintaining Security in Person and Property*, London.

Philo-Patria (1751) *A Letter to Henry Fielding, Esq*, London.

Philo-Patriae (1735) *A Full and Genuine Account of the Murder of Mrs. Robinson, by Elton Lewis, On Monday Night, April 21, 1735*, London.

Philopatriae (1756) *Observations on the Buyers or Receivers of Stolen Goods*, London.

Playfair, G. (1971) *The Punitive Obsession: An Unvarnished History of the English Prison System*, London: Victor Gollancz.

Porter, B. (1985) *The Origins of Britain's Political Police*, Warwick Working Papers in Social History, No. 3.

Porter, B. (1987) *The Origins of the Vigilant State: The London Metropolitan Police Special Branch before the First World War*, London: Weidenfeld & Nicolson.

Porter, R. (1990) *English Society in the Eighteenth Century*, Harmondsworth: Penguin.

Portus, G.V. (1912) *Caritas Anglicana or, An Historical Inquiry into those Religious and Philanthropic Societies that flourished in England between the Years 1678 and 1740*, London.

Potter, H. (1993) *Hanging in Judgment: Religion and the Death Penalty in England from the Bloody Code to Abolition*, London: SCM Press.

Potter, R. (1775) *Observations on the Poor Laws, on the Present State of the Poor, and on Houses of Industry*, London.

Power, M.J. (1985) 'London and the Control of the "Crisis" of the 1590s', *History*, 70, 371–85.

Price, C. and Caplan, J. (1977) *The Confait Confessions*, London: Marion Boyars.

Priestley, P. (1985) *Victorian Prison Lives: English Prison Biography 1830–1914*, London: Methuen.

Priestley, P. (1989) *Jail Journeys: The English Prison Experience since 1918*, Modern Prison Writings, London: Routledge.

Pringle, P. (1955) *Hue and Cry: The Birth of the British Police*, London.

Radzinowicz, L. (1948–68) *A History of English Criminal Law and Its Administration since 1750*, 4 volumes, London: Stevens.

Radzinowicz, L. and Hood, R. (1986) *A History of English Criminal Law and Its Administration since 1750: Volume 5*, London: Stevens.

Ramsay, M. (1977) 'John Howard and the Discovery of the Prison', *Howard Journal of Penology & Crime Prevention*, 16 (2), 1–16.

Randall, A.J. (1982) 'The Shearmen and the Wiltshire Outrages of 1802: Trade Unionism and Industrial Violence', *Past and Present*, 7, 283–304.

Randall, A.J. (1985) 'The Gloucestershire Food Riots of 1766', *Midland History*, 10, 72–93.

Randle, M. and Pottle, P. (1989) *The Blake Escape: How We Freed George Blake – And Why*, London: Harrap.

Rawlings, P.J. (1985a) 'Bobbies, Aliens and Subversives: the Relationship Between Community Policing and Coercive Policing', in Baxter, J. and Koffman, L. (eds) *The Police, the Constitution and the Community*, Abingdon: Professional Books.

Rawlings, P.J. (1985b) 'Judges, Politics and Property: the Interpretation of Legislation on Race Relations and Immigration', *Cambrian Law Review*, 16, 98–115.

Rawlings, P.J. (1990) 'Recent Writing on Crime, Criminal Law, Criminal Justice and Punishment in the Early Modern Period', in Hines, W.D. (ed.) *English Legal History: A Bibliography and Guide to the Literature*, London: Garland.

Rawlings, P.J. (1991) 'Creeping Privatisation? The Police, the Conservative Government and Policing in the Late 1980s', in Reiner, R. and Cross, M. (eds) *Beyond Law and Order: Criminal Justice Policy and Politics into the 1990s*, London: Macmillan.

Rawlings, P.J. (1992a) *Drunks, Whores and Idle Apprentices: Criminal Biographies of the Eighteenth Century*, London: Routledge.

Rawlings, P.J. (1992b) 'Who needs a Royal Commission?', *Policing*, 8, 15–25.

Rawlings, P.J. (1993) 'The Bloody Code Reconsidered: Criminal Law in the Eighteenth Century', Paper Delivered at British Criminology Conference, Cardiff.

Rawlings, P.J. (1995) 'The Idea of Policing: a History', *Policing and Society*, 5, 129–49.

Reaney, B. (1970) *The Class Struggle in 19th Century Oxfordshire: The Social and Communal Background to the Otmoor Disturbances of 1830 to 1835*, History Workshop Pamphlets, No. 3.

Reiner, R. (1991) *Chief Constables: Bobbies, Bosses, or Bureaucrats?*, Oxford: Oxford University Press.

Reiner, R. (1992) *The Politics of the Police*, Hemel Hempstead: Wheatsheaf.

Reiner, R. and Cross, M. (eds) (1991), *Beyond Law and Order: Criminal Justice Policy and Politics into the 1990s*, London: Macmillan.

Renold, P. (ed.) (1987) *Banbury Gaol Records*, The Banbury Historical Society, volume 21.

Richter, D.C. (1981) *Riotous Victorians*, London: Ohio University Press.

Roberts, D. (1969) *Victorian Origins of the British Welfare State,* no place of publication: Archon Books.

Robinson, L.W. (1862) *Female Life in Prison,* London.

Rogers, N. (1990) 'Crowd and People in the Gordon Riots', in Hellmuth, E. (ed.) *The Transformation of Political Culture: England and Germany in the Late Eighteenth Century,* Oxford: Oxford University Press.

Rogers, P. (1979) *Henry Fielding: A Biography,* London: Elek.

Romilly, S. (1786) *Observations on a Late Publication, intitled, Thoughts on Executive Justice,* London.

Rook, C. (1979) *The Hooligan Nights: Being the Life and Opinions of a Young and Impertinent Criminal Recounted by Himself and Set Forth by Clarence Rook,* Oxford: Oxford University Press.

Rose, D. (1996) *In the Name of the Law: The Collapse of Criminal Justice,* London: Jonathan Cape.

Rowntree, B.S. and Lavers, G.R. (1951) *Poverty and the Welfare State: A Third Social Survey of York Dealing Only with Economic Questions,* London: Longmans, Green & Co.

Royal Commission (1839) *First Report of the Commissioners Appointed to Inquire as to the Best Means of Establishing an Efficient Constabulary Force in the Counties of England and Wales,* Parliamentary Papers, (169) Vol. XIX.

Royal Commission (1863) *Report of the Commissioners Appointed to Inquire into the Operation of the Acts (16 & 17 Vict. c. 99 and 20 & 21 Vict. c. 3) Relating to Transportation and Penal Servitude,* Parliamentary Papers, (3190), Vol. XXI.

Royal Commission (1878–9) *Report of the Commissioners Appointed to Inquire into the Working of the Penal Servitude Acts,* Parliamentary Papers [c. 2368] xxxvii–viii.

Royal Commission (1884–5) *First Report of Her Majesty's Commissioners for Inquiring into the Housing of the Working Classes,* Parliamentary Papers [c. 4402] Vol. XXX.

Royal Commission (1909) *Report of the Royal Commission on the Poor Laws and Relief of Distress,* cmnd 4499, London: HMSO.

Royal Commission (1929) *Report of the Royal Commission on Police Powers and Procedure,* cmnd 3297, London: HMSO.

Royal Commission (1960) *Royal Commission on the Police: Interim Report,* cmnd 1222, London: HMSO.

Royal Commission (1962) *Royal Commission on the Police: Final Report,* cmnd 1728, London: HMSO.

Royal Commission (1981) *Royal Commission on Criminal Procedure: Report,* cmnd 8092, London: HMSO.

Royal Commission (1993) *Royal Commission on Criminal Justice: Report,* cmnd 2263, London: HMSO.

Ruck, S.K. (ed.) (1951) *Paterson on Prisons: Being the Collected Papers of Sir Alexander Paterson MC, MA,* London: Frederick Muller.

Rude, G. (1964) *The Crowd in History: A Study of Popular Disturbances in France and England 1730–1848,* New York.

Rude, G. (1974) *Paris and London in the Eighteenth Century; Studies in Popular Protest,* London: Fontana.

Ruggles-Brise, E. (1921) *The English Prison System,* London: Macmillan.

Rule, J. (1992) *Albion's People: English Society, 1714–1815,* London: Longman.

Rumbelow, D. (1971) *I Spy Blue: The Police and Crime in the City of London from Elizabeth I to Victoria,* London: Macmillan.

Rumbelow, D. (1988) *The Houndsditch Murders and the Siege of Sydney Street,* London: W.H. Allen.

Ryan, M. (1983) *The Politics of Penal Reform*, London: Longman.

Ryan, M. and Ward, T. (1989) *Privatization and the Penal System: The American Experience and the Debate in Britain*, Milton Keynes: Open University.

Samaha, J. (1974) *Law and Order in Historical Perspective: The Case of Elizabethan Essex*, London: Academic Press.

Samuel, R. (1981) *East End Underworld: Chapters from the Life of Arthur Harding*, London: Routledge & Kegan Paul.

Saulsbury, W., Mott, J. and Newburn, T. (1996) *Themes in Contemporary Policing*, London: Independent Committee of Inquiry into the Role and Responsibilities of the Police.

Saunders, A. and Young, R. (1994) *Criminal Justice*, London: Butterworths.

Saunders, J. (1986) 'Warwickshire Magistrates and Prison Reform, 1840–75', *Midland History*, 11, 79–99.

Scarman, Sir Leslie (1975) *The Red Lion Square Disorders of 15 June 1974*, London: HMSO.

Scarman, Lord (1981) *The Brixton Disorders 10–12 April 1981: Report of an Inquiry by the Rt. Hon. the Lord Scarman, OBE*, cmnd 8427, London: HMSO.

Scraton, P., Sim, J. and Skidmore, P. (1991) *Prisons under Protest*, Milton Keynes: Open University Press.

Select Committee on Cold Bath Fields (1833) *Report from Select Committee on Cold Bath Fields Meeting*, Parliamentary Papers, (718), Vol. XIII.

Select Committee on Gaols (1863) *Report from the Select Committee of the House of Lords, on the Present State of Discipline in Gaols and Houses of Correction*, Parliamentary Papers, (499), Vol. IX.

Select Committee on Prisons (1822) *Report from the Select Committee appointed to Consider the Law Relating to Prisons, &c.*, Parliamentary Papers, (300), Vol. IV.

Select Committee on the Criminal Law (1819) *Report from the Select Committee on the Criminal Law*, (585), Vol. VIII.

Select Committee on the Nightly Watch (1812) *Select Committee Report on the Nightly Watch and Police of the Metropolis*, Parliamentary Papers, (127), Vol. II.

Select Committee on the Petition of Frederick Young (1833) *Report from the Select Committee on the Petition of Frederick Young and Others (Police)*, Parliamentary Papers, (627) Vol. XIII.

Select Committee on the Police (1822) *Report from the Select Committee on the Police of the Metropolis*, Parliamentary Papers, 1822 (440) Vol. IV.

Select Committee on the Police (1828) *Report from the Select Committee on the Police of the Metropolis*, Parliamentary Papers, 1828 (533) Vol. VII.

Select Committee on the Police (1834) *Report from the Select Committee on the Police of the Metropolis*, Parliamentary Papers, (600) Vol. XVI.

Select Committee on Transportation (1837–8) *Report from the Select Committee on Transportation*, Parliamentary Papers, (669) Vol. XXII.

Semple, J. (1993) *Bentham's Prison: A Study of the Panopticon Penitentiary*, Oxford: Clarendon Press.

Shapiro, B.J. (1983) *Probability and Certainty in Seventeenth-Century England: A Study of the Relationships between Natural Science, Religion, History, Law, and Literature*, Princeton NJ: Princeton University Press.

Sharpe, J.A. (1982) *Crime in Seventeenth-Century England: A County Study*, Cambridge: Cambridge University Press.

Sharpe, J.A. (1984) *Crime in Early Modern England 1550–1750*, London: Longman.

Shaw, A.G.L. (1966) *Convicts and the Colonies: A Study of Penal Transportation from Great Britain and Ireland to Australia and Other Parts of the British Empire*, London: Faber.

Shebbear, J. (1776) *An Essay on the Origin, Progress and Establishment of National Society*, London.

Sheehan, W.J. (1975) 'The London Prison System, 1666–1795', PhD thesis, University of Maryland.

Sheehan, W.J. (1977) 'Finding Solace in Eighteenth-Century Newgate', in Cockburn, J.S. (ed.) *Crime in England 1550–1800*, London: Methuen.

Shelton, W.J. (1973) *English Hunger and Industrial Disorders: A Study of Social Conflict during the First Decade of George III's Reign*, London: Macmillan.

Shoemaker, R.B. (1991) *Prosecution and Punishment: Petty Crime and the Law in London and Rural Middlesex, c. 1660–1725*, Cambridge: Cambridge University Press.

Short, T. (1750) *New Observations, Natural, Moral, Civil on Town and Country Bills of Mortality*, London.

Sim, J. (1982) 'Scarman: the Police Counter-Attack', *Socialist Register*, pp. 57–77.

Sindall, R. (1983) 'Middle-Class Crime in Nineteenth-Century England', *Criminal Justice History*, 4, 23–40.

Sindall, R. (1990) *Street Violence in the Nineteenth Century: Media Panic or Real Danger?*, Leicester: Leicester University Press.

Slack, P. (1988) *Poverty and Piety in Tudor and Stuart England*, London: Longman.

Slyboots, Saynought (1726) *The Tavern Scuffle; or, The Club in an Uproar*, London.

Smith, D. (ed.) (1979) *Life-Sentence Prisoners*, London: HMSO.

Smith, D. (1990) 'Juvenile Delinquency in Britain in the First World War', *Criminal Justice History*, 11, 119–45.

Smith, D. (1997) 'Ethnic Origins, Crime, and Criminal Justice in England and Wales', in Tonry, M. (ed.) *Ethnicity, Crime, and Immigration: Comparative and Cross-National Perspectives*, Chicago IL: The University of Chicago Press.

Smith, D. and Gray, J. (1983) *Police and People in London*, 4 volumes, London: Policy Studies Institute.

Smith, Dr W. (1778) *Mild Punishments Sound Policy: or Observations on the Laws relative to Debtors and Felons*, London.

Smithies, E. (1982) *Crime in Wartime: A Social History of Crime in World War II*, London: George Allen and Unwin.

Sparks, R. (1971) 'The Use of the Suspended Sentence', *Criminal Law Review*, June, pp. 384–401.

Spencer, S. (1985) *Police Accountability During the Miners' Strike*, London: Cobden Trust.

Spierenberg, P. (1991) *The Prison Experience: Disciplinary Institutions and Their Inmates in Early Modern Europe*, London: Rutgers University Press.

Stanko, E.A. (1990) *Everyday Violence: How Women and Men Experience Sexual and Physical Danger*, London: Pandora.

Steedman, C. (1984) *Policing the Victorian Community: The Formation of English Provincial Police Forces, 1856–80*, London: Routledge & Kegan Paul.

Stern, V. (1993) *Bricks of Shame: Britain's Prisons*, London: Penguin.

Stockdale, E. (1976) 'The Rise of Joshua Jebb, 1837–1850', *British Journal of Criminology*, 16, 164–70.

Stockdale, E. and Casale, S. (eds) (1992) *Criminal Justice under Stress*, London: Blackstone Press.

Storch, R.D. (1975) 'The Plague of Blue Locusts: Police Reform and Popular Resistance in Northern England, 1840–57', *International Review of Social History*, 20, 61–90.

Storch, R.D. (1976) 'The Policeman as Domestic Missionary: Urban Discipline and Popular Culture in Northern England 1850–80', *Journal of Social History*, 9, 481–509.

Storch, R.D. (1989) 'Policing in Rural Southern England Before the Police: Opinion and Practice, 1830–1856', in Hay, D. and Snyder, F. (eds) *Policing and Prosecution in Britain 1758–1850*, Oxford: Oxford University Press.

Straw, J. (1997) Interview on Radio Four's *Today* programme, 30 Oct.

Styles, J. (1980) ' "Our Traitorous Moneymakers": the Yorkshire Coiners and the Law, 1760–83', in Brewer, J. and Styles, J. (eds) *An Ungovernable People: the English and their Law in the Seventeenth and Eighteenth Centuries*, London: Hutchinson, 172–249.

Styles, J. (1983a) 'Embezzlement, Industry and the Law in England, 1500–1800', in Berg, M., Hudson, P. and Sonenscher, M. (eds) *Manufacture in Town and Country before the Factory*, Cambridge: Cambridge University Press.

Styles, J. (1983b) 'Sir John Fielding and the Problem of Crime Investigation in Eighteenth-Century England', *Transactions of the Royal Historical Society*, (5th series), 33, 127–49.

Styles, J. (1989) 'Print and Policing: Crime Advertising in Eighteenth-Century Provincial England', in Hay, D. and Snyder, F. (eds) *Policing and Prosecution in Britain 1758–1850*, Oxford: Oxford University Press.

Sugden, P. (1995) *The Complete History of Jack the Ripper*, New York: Carroll & Graf.

Swift, R. (1988) 'Urban Policing in Early Victorian England, 1835–56: a Reappraisal', *History* 73, 211–37.

Taylor, I. (1987) 'Law and Order, Moral Order: the Changing Rhetoric of the Thatcher Government', *Socialist Register*, 297–331.

Taylor, M. and Pease, K. (1989) 'Private Prisons and Penal Purpose', in Matthews, R. (ed.) *Privatizing Criminal Justice*, London: Sage Publications, 178–94.

Taylor, R.S. (1960–1) 'The Habitual Criminal: Observations on Some of the Characteristics of Men Sentenced to Preventive Detention', *British Journal of Criminology*, 1, 21–36.

Thane, P. (1996) *Foundations of the Welfare State*, London: Longman.

Thirsk, J. (ed.) (1967) *The Agrarian History of England and Wales*, London: Cambridge University Press.

Thomas, K. (1978) *Religion and the Decline of Magic: Studies in Popular Beliefs in Sixteenth- and Seventeenth-Century England*, Harmondsworth: Peregrine Books.

Thompson, E.P. (1968) *The Making of the English Working Class*, Harmondsworth: Pelican.

Thompson, E.P. (1977) *Whigs and Hunters: The Origin of the Black Act*, Harmondsworth: Penguin.

Thompson, E.P. (1993) *Customs in Common*, Harmondsworth: Penguin.

Thompson, E.P. and Yeo, E. (eds) (1973) *The Unknown Mayhew: Selections from the Morning Chronicle 1849–50*, Harmondsworth: Pelican.

Thompson, F.M.L. (ed.) (1990) *The Cambridge Social History of Britain 1750–1950*, 3 volumes, Cambridge: Cambridge University Press.

Thomson, B. (1925) *The Criminal*, London.

Thornton, D., Curran, L., Grayson, D. and Holloway, V. (1984) *Tougher Regimes in Detention Centres: Report of an Evaluation by the Young Offender Psychology Unit*, London: HMSO.

Thurmond Smith, P. (1985) *Policing Victorian London: Political Policing, Public Order, and the London Metropolitan Police*, Westport: Greenwood Press.

Thurston, G. (1967) *The Clerkenwell Riot: The Killing of Constable Culley*, London: George Allen & Unwin.

Thwaites, W. (1991) 'The Corn Market and Economic Change: Oxford in the Eighteenth Century', *Midland History*, 16, 103–25.

Tobias, J.J. (1979) *Crime and the Police in England 1700–1900*, Dublin: Gill & Macmillan.

Tomlinson, M.H. (1981) 'Penal Servitude 1846–1865: a System in Evolution', in Bailey, V. (ed.) *Policing and Punishment in 19th Century Britain*, London: Croom Helm.

Torrington, F.W. (ed) (1972–8) *House of Lords Sessional Papers*, 58 volumes, Dobbs Ferry, New York: Oceana.

Underdown, D. (1987) *Revel, Riot and Rebellion: Popular Politics and Culture in England 1603–1660*, Oxford: Oxford University Press.

Underdown, D. (1996) *Freeborn People: Politics and the Nation in Seventeenth-Century England*, Oxford: Oxford University Press.

Unofficial Committee of Enquiry (1980) *Southall 23 April 1979*, London: NCCL.

Vass, A. (1990) *Alternatives to Prison*, London: Sage Publications.

Wake, K. (1801) *The Case of Kid Wake. Being a Narrative of His Suffering, During Five Years Confinement!!! In Gloucester Penitentiary House for Hooting, Hissing, and Calling out No War! As His Majesty was Passing in State to the House of Peers, on the 29th December, 1795*, London.

Walker, T. (1728) *The Quaker's Opera*, London.

Walkowitz, J.R. (1992) *City of Dreadful Delight: Narratives of Sexual Danger in Late-Victorian London*, London: Virago.

Ward, T. and Benn, M. (1987) 'Were the Police Ever Innocent?', *New Society*, 80(1277), 19 June: 14–17.

Watkins, J. (1815) *The Important Results of an Elaborate Investigation into the Mysterious Case of Elizabeth Fenning*, London.

Webb, S. and B. (1922) *English Prisons under Local Government*, (special subscription edition), no place of publication.

Weinberger, B. (1991) *Keeping the Peace: Policing Strikes in Britain*, Oxford: Oxford University Press.

Weinberger, B. (1993) 'Policing Juveniles: Delinquency in Late Nineteenth and Early Twentieth Century Manchester', *Criminal Justice History*, 14, 43–55.

Weiner, M.J. (1990) *Reconstructing the Criminal: Culture, Law, and Policy in England, 1830–1914*, Cambridge: Cambridge University Press.

Wells, R. (1988) *Wretched Faces: Famine in Wartime England, 1793–1803*, Gloucester: Alan Sutton.

West, D.J. (1963) *The Habitual Prisoner*, London: Macmillan.

Whitfield, D. (1991) 'John Howard: a Biographical Note', in Whitfield, D. (ed.) *The State of the Prisons – 200 Years On*, London: Routledge.

Whiting, J.R.S. (1975) *Prison Reform in Gloucestershire 1776–1820*, London: Phillimore.

Wildeblood, P. (1955) *Against the Law*, London: Weidenfeld and Nicolson.

Williams, K. (1981) *From Pauperism to Poverty*, London: Routledge & Kegan Paul.

Williams, P. (1979) *The Tudor Regime*, Oxford: Clarendon Press.

Wilson, R. (1722) *A Full and Impartial Account of all the Robberies Committed by John Hawkins*, London.

Wilson, Rev. W. (1739) *A Full and Genuine Account . . . of the Four Malefactors that were Executed on Friday the 6th Day of this Instant April 1739*, London.

Wilson, Rev. W. (1743) *A Genuine Account of the Behaviour, Confessions, and Dying Words, of the Malefactors viz. James Day, Ann Hazzard, James Harris, Richard Keble, James Hunt, and Thomas Collins*, London.

Wilson, Rev. W. (1749) *The Solemn Declaration of Richard Coleman*, London.

Windlesham, Lord (1996) *Responses to Crime: Volume 3*, Oxford: Oxford University Press.

Winslow, C. (1977) 'Sussex Smugglers', in Hay, D., Linebaugh, P., Rule, J., Thompson, E.P. and Winslow C. (eds) *Albion's Fatal Tree: Crime and Society in Eighteenth-Century England*, Harmondsworth: Penguin.

Wise, E. (1751) *The Remarkable Tryal of Thomas Chandler, Late of Clifford's Inn, London, Gent.*, London.

Woodward, J. (1697) *Sodom's Vices Destructive to Other Cities and States*, London.

Woodward, J. (1702) *A Sermon Preach'd at the Parish-Church of St. James's, Westminster, on the 21st of May, 1702. At the Funeral of Mr. John Cooper, a Constable*, London.

Woolf, Rt. Hon. Lord Justice and Tumim, His Hon. Judge S. (1991) *Prison Disturbances April 1990: Report of an Inquiry*, cmnd 1456, London: HMSO.

Young, F. (ed.) (1923) *Trial of Frederick Bywaters and Edith Thompson*, Edinburgh and London: William Hodge.

Young, G.M. (1934) 'Portrait of an Age', in Young, G.M. (ed.) *Early Victorian England 1830–1865*, 2 volumes, London: Oxford University Press.

Zedner, L. (1991) *Women, Crime, and Custody in Victorian England*, Oxford: Clarendon Press.

Zirker, M.R. (1966) *Fielding's Social Pamphlets. A Study of An Enquiry into the Causes of the Late Increase of Robbers and A Proposal for Making an Effectual Provision for the Poor*, London: University of California.

Zirker, M.R. (1988) 'Introduction', in Zirker, M.R. (ed.) *An Enquiry into the Causes of the Late Increase of Robbers*, Oxford: Oxford University Press.

Other sources

Reports of debates of Parliament in the eighteenth century were taken from *Parliamentary History*, supplemented by the official diaries of the proceedings of both Houses in the *Commons Journal* and the *Lords Journal*. The shift to full reporting of debates came in the nineteenth century in *Commons Debates* and *Lords Debates*.

Periodicals

Annual Register
British Magazine
Covent Garden Journal
Daily Gazetteer
Daily Journal
Daily Post
Daily Universal Register
General Advertiser
Gentleman's Magazine
The Guardian
The Independent
Independent on Sunday

Lloyd's Evening Post
London Evening Post
London Magazine
Monthly Review
The Observer
Old Bailey Sessions Paper
Ordinary of Newgate's Account
Original Weekly Journal
Penny London Post
Police
Police Review
Public Advertiser
The Sunday Times
The Times
Westminster Journal
Whitehall Evening Post

Collections and manuscripts

Finally, reference is made in the text to the following collections of broadsheets, newspaper cuttings and manuscripts:

British Library Broadsheets, Collection of broadsheets (shelved at 1889.d.3).
BM (British Museum), Add. Mss 27,991, fo. 49b.
NLW (National Library of Wales), letter from Harriet Frankland, Harpton Court C/230, 7 Jun. [1780].
NLW (National Library of Wales), Radnorshire QS/OB Quarter Sessions, Order Books.
Purland, T. collection of newspaper cuttings, British Library.

Index